READINGS IN MORAL THEOLOGY NO. 2:
THE DISTINCTIVENESS OF CHRISTIAN ETHICS

READINGS IN MORAL THEOLOGY

No. 2:

The Distinctiveness of Christian Ethics

Edited by
Charles E. Curran
and
Richard A. McCormick, S.J.

PAULIST PRESS
New York/Ramsey

ACKNOWLEDGEMENTS

The articles reprinted in *Readings in Moral Theology No. 2: The Distinctiveness of Christian Ethics* first appeared in the following publications and are reprinted by permission: Joseph Fuchs, "Is There a Specifically Christian Morality?" first appeared in German in *Stimmen der Zeit* 185 (1970), pp. 99–112, under the title "Gibt es eine spezifisch christliche Moral?"; Dionigi Tettamanzi, "Is There a Christian Ethics?" first appeared in Italian in *Scuola Cattolica* 99 (1971), pp. 163–193 under the title "Esiste un' ethica christiana?"; Charles Curran, "Is There a Catholic and/or Christian Ethic?", *Proceedings of the Catholic Theological Society of America* 29 (1974), pp. 125–154; James J. Walter, "Christian Ethics: Distinctive and Specific," *American Ecclesiastical Review* 169 (September 1975), pp. 470–489; Norbert Rigali, "Christ and Morality" from *Concilium* 110 *Moral Formation and Christianity* (1978), by Stichting Concilium and the Seabury Press. John Macquarrie, "Rethinking Natural Law," *Three Issues in Ethics* (1978), New York: Harper and Row, pp. 82–110; James Gustafson, "Can Ethics Be Christian?" from *Can Ethics be Christian?* (1975), Chicago: University of Chicago Press, pp. 169–179; Richard A. McCormick, "Does Religious Faith Add to Ethical Perception?" from *Personal Values and Public Policy* (1979), New York: Paulist Press, pp. 155–173; Joseph Ratzinger, "Magisterium of the Church, Faith, Morality," from *Problems of the Church Today*, pp. 74–83, Publications Office, U.S. Catholic Conference (this document in its entirety may be purchased from: Publications Office, U.S.C.C., 1312 Massachusetts Ave., N.W., Washington, D.C. 20005); Hans Urs von Balthasar, "Nine Theses in Christian Ethics," first appeared in *Prinzipien christlicher Moral*, pp. 67–93 under the German title "Neun Sätze zur christlichen Ethik"; Bruno Schüller, "The Debate on the Specific Character of a Christian Ethics: Some Remarks," first appeared in German in *Theologie und Philosophie* 51 (1976), pp. 321–343, under the title "Zur Discussion über das Proprium einer christlichen Ethik"; Ph. Delhaye, "Questioning the Specificity of Christian Morality," first appeared in *Revue Theologique de Louvain* 4 (1973), pp. 308–339, under the French title "La mise en cause de la spécificité de la morale chrétienne" with the agreement of *Revue Theologique de Louvain* (La Neuve); Enrico Chiavacci, "The Grounding for the Moral Norm in Contemporary Theological Reflection," first appeared in Italian in *Revista de teologia morale* 37 (1978), pp. 9–38, under the title "La fondazione della norma morale nella riflessione teologica contemporanea."

Contents

v

Foreword

This is the second volume in an ongoing series of readings in moral theology and Christian ethics. This volume centers on a very important issue in contemporary debate—is there a specifically Christian morality or ethic? The selection of essays for this type of book is always difficult, but four criteria have guided our choices: (1) a significant contribution to the debate, (2) presentation of all sides in the debate, (3) ecumenical and international representation, (4) exchange and discussion between and among the different articles.

Although this debate has attracted widespread interest in many countries, there are some interesting lacunae. The discussion has taken place primarily in Roman Catholic circles rather than in Protestant literature, but the very nature of the Roman Catholic theological tradition explains the interest from this Catholic perspective. Traditionally Catholic moral theology has shown its catholicity by its insistence on reason and the natural law, by emphasizing the goodness and importance of the human and by recognizing God's universal salvific will which offers all persons the saving gift of God's love. In the last two decades renewal in moral theology has attempted to provide a scriptural basis for the discipline and to overcome the dichotomies between supernature and nature, between faith and daily life. In this context the question of a specifically Christian ethic became very significant. Unfortunately, even within Catholicism the discussion has not been as universal as it could be, for there are no appropriate considerations from the perspective of countries in which the so-called Christian culture does not predominate and from third and fourth world countries. In the future such perspectives would be most helpful for the discipline of moral theology.

There are few questions in moral theology as fundamental as the issue of a specifically Christian ethic. In practice it raises the question of the relationship between Christian ethics and non-Christian ethics or philosophical ethics. In theory, the response to this question says much about the methodological approach used in moral theology and the whole structure of the discipline. In the course of the debate both terminological and substantive questions arise. What is the difference between ethics and morality? What is the exact meaning of such terms as specific, distinctive, and exclusive when used to describe Christian ethics in its relationship to other ethics? Although terminological differences influence the discussion, the substantive questions remain primary. The foremost issue concerns Christology, but intimately connected with Christology are the areas of anthropology and soteriology.

The purpose of this series is to make available to a wider audience important articles on fundamental questions in moral theology. Although both of us have taken positions on the question under discussion, our aim is not to advocate our positions but to stimulate discussion. We hope that this volume will contribute to the refinement of the continuing debate on the question of a specifically Christian ethic and to the development of the discipline of moral theology.

Charles E. Curran
Richard A. McCormick, S.J.

Is There a Specifically Christian Morality?[1]

Joseph Fuchs, S.J.

Was it Paul VI's intention to offer a specifically Catholic or Christian solution to the problem of birth control in his encyclical HUMANAE VITAE? A significant number of oral and written positions on this question—both before and after the encyclical's publication—seem to answer in the affirmative. Such a view implies that there is a Catholic or Christian morality which is valid only for Catholics or other Christians and which differs from another, a non-Christian, morality. Is such a view legitimate? If we read Paul VI's encyclical carefully it will become clear that the Pope in no way intended to provide a specifically Christian solution for a universal human problem. It was precisely this that enabled him to address himself also to non-Christians, in order to put before them a "humane" solution of a universal human problem. In the same way his predecessor, John XXIII, had addressed himself in his encyclical *Pacem in Terris* to all men and women of good will, thereby implying that his statements about human dignity and human rights are not specifically Christian, but universally human.

Many questions of Christian morality concern not merely Christian, but universally human problems; consequently, Christians and non-Christians can discuss them together. Norms are not distinctly Christian simply because they are proclaimed officially within the church. Rather, we might put it as follows: To the extent to which they proclaim truth they are universally human and therefore also Christian, hence, not distinctly Christian. When, however, a statement does not truly address genuine humaneness, the norms it sets

3

forth are not authentically human, hence also not Christian, let alone specifically Christian ethical norms.

If, on the other hand, we take as our starting point not the above mentioned encyclical, but the Sermon on the Mount or Jesus' words about carrying the cross, we will presumably tend to think—at least at first—that we have here a morality which contradicts all human morality and which is therefore—insofar as it is a morality proclaimed by Jesus and Christianity—*specifically* Christian.

Our subject, "Is there a specifically Christian morality?" cannot have as its purpose a comparison between a lofty morality of good Christians and a less lofty one of bad non-Christians. Rather, our concern is to discover whether Christian morality is basically different from, or even in contradiction to, *in content*, a morality concerned with the dignity of men and women everywhere.

1. No doubt many Christians formulate this question for themselves as follows: Human beings as human beings are capable of discovering moral values and norms; the Christian is sustained, in addition, by the revelation of higher ethical values and norms, which either surpass the values and norms of a genuinely human morality or, at least partially, challenge it. Is such a view correct?

Others may state the question differently: Christians consult scripture, the tradition and teaching authority of the church about the norms and values of Christian morality. Insofar as they derive them from Christian sources they will consider such a morality as "specifically Christian." Such a solution, however, proves too simple. For the concrete directives of scripture are relatively few and must each be carefully studied in its context and meaning. Neither Christian tradition nor the church's teaching authority provides us with a closed and readily applicable morality in themselves. We must keep in mind, moreover, that the Christians of the first centuries did not yet possess such directives from the Christian tradition and teaching authority; nonetheless they sought to live a "Christian" morality. Finally, much of what we find in scripture, in Christian tradition and the church's teaching authority is universally human morality. The question therefore remains: What is distinctly Christian in Christian morality?[2]

Perhaps we shall discover in the pages that follow a better approach to the solution of our question. Christian morality is morality of men and women who believe in Christ. This does not simply mean believing that Christ is the one the scriptures say him to be and whom the Christian community proclaims. To believe means to set our ultimate hopes for life and our expectation of salvation on Christ—more yet: to give him our entire love and capacity for dedication. Whoever thus loves and believes, that is, all those who follow Christ with their entire heart and soul, will ask what form a life of such an imitation of Christ, a life of such faith and love, should take. They will ask how such faith and love, how such an imitation of the Lord, can manifest and express themselves in external deeds and in the secret depths of the heart.

It is already clear that we must distinguish two elements of Christian morality. They are basically different from each other, yet belong together, and constitute Christian morality in their togetherness and interpenetration. On the one hand there is the particular *categorical* conduct, in which categorical values, virtues and norms are realized—values, virtues and norms of different categories, such as justice, faithfulness, and purity. On the other hand there are *transcendental* attitudes and norms, which inform various ethical categories and go beyond them, virtues such as faith, love, allowing oneself to be redeemed, living as a sacramental person, following Christ, etc. Such transcendental attitudes and norms refer to and involve, obviously, not only one's conduct in a specifically human sphere—such as justice, faithfulness, purity—but the human person in his or her entirety. It is the whole human person, as person, who gives herself or himself in faith and love, in imitation of Christ, in surrender to Christ who died and rose again.

Scripture speaks unambiguously and frequently about transcedent and Christian attitudes, making quite clear that they are *specifically Christian attitudes.* Scripture speaks more rarely about the particular, categorical approaches to the various spheres of life (social attitudes, family and conjugal morality, etc.), and is less clear about their meaning and application to various historical periods. The question now arises: Are there *distinctly Christian categorical ways of conduct,* or are genuinely human attitudes and life styles in the various spheres of life not also those of Christians?

2. However we answer this question, one thing should by now be clear: The specific and *decisively Christian* aspect of Christian mo-

rality is not to be sought first of all in the particularity of categorical values, virtues and norms of various human activities. Rather, it resides in the believer's fundamental Christian decision to accept God's love in Christ and respond to it as one who believes and loves, as one who assumes the responsibility for life in this world in imitation of Christ, that is, as one who has died with Christ and is risen with him in faith and sacrament, thus becoming a new creation. If, in what follows, we refer to this Christian decision and fundamental attitude as *"Christian intentionality,"* our reason for this will soon become evident.

This "Christian intentionality" should of course not be mistaken for a pious mood or peak religious experience. Let us keep two things in mind. First, "Christian intentionality" refers to a full, personal decision that is made—not, however, once and for all, or as an occasionally repeated past act, but as full, personal, enduring decision, a being-decided in each particular situation; hence the permanent, present, and not past act of decision. Secondly, "Christian intentionality" refers to its actual presence in the particular attitude and conduct in the various spheres of life in concrete situations, its living and conscious presence in the daily shaping of life and the world, so that this daily life in its manifold particularity—regardless of whether this conduct in everyday life is specifically Christian or simply human—represents at the same time and in its depths the living, conscious and free actualization of the decisiveness of "Christian intentionality."

How are we to understand this conscious presence and actuality of "Christian intentionality" in the categorical variety of daily life? Let us not forget that morality always has a twofold aspect: On the one hand it makes concrete a particular moral value, such as justice, kindness, faithfulness; on the other, man actualizes or realizes himself as person, ultimately in the light of the Absolute in the living of certain specific values. Whoever practices justice, does not turn away the poor, educates children, by so doing realizes not only all this, but also himself. For in and precisely through his concrete deeds he himself enters as person into a specific relationship with the Absolute, that is, with God. We must keep in mind, however, that there is a considerable difference in the various types of consciousness of both these aspects of moral conduct. For we tend to reflect more or less thematically and explicitly on the particular-categorical aspect of our lives. The self-realization of the person as person before the Absolute, on the contrary, tends to escape thematic reflection; indeed, it cannot properly be accessible in the center of the "I" to a *full* thematic reflection. Nonetheless, we are conscious of this self-realization as person before the Absolute, as flowing from the concept of self-realization as an act of freedom. Just as the realization of a particular attitude, insofar as it is particular, tends to take place in a thematic-reflexive consciousness, so too our self-realization before the Absolute takes place in awareness, but largely without thematic reflection. This non-thematic, unreflexive consciousness must not be considered as a lower degree of awareness, but is at bottom deeper and richer than the thematic-reflexive consciousness. The aspect of self-realization of the person before the Absolute constitutes objectively the more essential and decisive element of the moral act, in contrast to the aspect of the particular-categorical doing of justice, of one's duty to the family, etc. The self-realization of the human person before the Absolute God thus takes place *through* and manifests itself in the realization of particular individual acts.

We spoke of the realization of the self as person before the Absolute, and said that this Absolute is in the last analysis God. The Christian, however, does not simply know the Absolute or God, but knows him as Father, who is our life and salvation in Jesus Christ. And as believer in the full sense of the word he does not only *know* God as Father of Jesus Christ, but *lives*—as person—in the decision for him. He makes this decisiveness at times, and insofar as possible, part of the express reflection of his consciousness; but not ordinarily, not in the everyday shaping of life and the world. And yet the believer is aware, in unthematic, unreflexive consciousness, of his salvation, of his self-realization as person before Jesus Christ and the Father: he carries out his self-realization as "Christian intentionality." This intentionality is, therefore, present, alive, and conscious in the Christian's daily moral life, as Christian realization of the self, as the deepest and most challenging element of morality, which addresses the whole person, and not only the individual deed. "Christian intentionality" as actual decision for Christ and the Father of Jesus Christ, consciously active in daily moral conduct, is to be seen as the most important and decisive element of Christian morality.

3. "Christian intentionality" is an element which, while pervading and completing the particular-categorical conduct, does not determine its content. The question therefore remains, whether the categorical content of the morality of Christians—their concrete moral conduct—is distinctly Christian, different from the morality of the human person as such, different not only from a morality which is infected by error or malice, but different also from the purest and noblest, most deeply human morality. This is a fundamental question, independent from the question of when, where, and how Christians and non-Christians discover their morality in authenticity and truth.

Our answer to the question about the *Christian nature of a categorical morality* of Christians, that is, of their concrete conduct, is basically as follows: If we abstract from the decisive and essential element of Christian morality, of "Christian intentionality" as transcendent aspect, Christian morality in its categorical orientation and materiality is basically and substantially a "Humanum," that is, a morality of genuine being-human. This means that truthfulness, uprightness and faithfulness are not specifically Christian, but generally human values in what they materially say, and that we have reservations about lying and adultery not because we are Christian, but simply because we are human. This does not, however, negate that there is in Christian morality also a specifically Christian element; rather, it affirms it. Our reflection about the genuinely human and genuinely Christian dimensions of Christian morality derives basically from the fact that believers must translate their livnig faith, that is, their "Christian intentionality," into concrete living and manifest it in their lives. This is the reality of *the human person,* but the human person in the manner and situation in which she experiences and knows herself as believing. We must therefore speak in turn of the "Humanum" and the "Christianum" of Christian morality, of its norms and values.

The "Humanum" of Christian Morality

1. Since the 1920's and 1930's a strong tendency has been present in Catholic moral theology to move from the predominantly hu-

man study (or, the natural-law study) of Christian ethics of a past era to the "Christianum" of Christian ethics. This movement has led at times to a one-sided Christianization, along with a leveling off of the "Humanum" of Christian morality. Not only was the "Christian intentionality" that pervades all morality discovered, but it was also believed that a purely Christian valuation of the categorical morality of concrete living must be opposed to a "human" valuation; the Sermon on the Mount was perceived in opposition to the "Humanum."

More recently moral theology, under the impact of secular, even of secularistic tendencies in theological and moral thought, sees itself challenged to take a new look at the "Humanum" in Christian morality. The existentially believing Christian discovers, in the search for a life style which can express his faith, his "Christian intentionality," that it is the human person who believes existentially, that therefore this belief must be lived and expressed by the human person, in the genuine realization of being-human, of the "Humanum." Thus Christians are directed, as Christians, to understand their being-human and the corresponding "Humanum" of a genuinely human morality. We should add that this does not exclude the possibility that, in the attempt to arrive at the understanding of self and of "human" morality, Christians may find help in the sources of revelation, help not only for a distinctly Christian morality, but for a genuinely human understanding of the person and of human morality.

2. What is the nature of this "Humanum" of the Christian's genuinely human morality? Many will perhaps think of it as a purely immanent human reality, separate from or even in contrast to a transcendent morality, one which teaches men and women of flesh to do the will of a transcendent God. Such a distinction is based on a misunderstanding of the nature of "human" morality, but also on a misconception of the nature of God. God is perceived far too anthropomorphically if we think of him as Someone who exists somehow somewhere, and with whom one must *also,* in addition to (other) people, reckon decisively. Instead, it is precisely God's otherness that establishes his immanence as sustaining personal ground in everything and everyone, while he himself is not part of or within this contingent world. We must, therefore, not perceive man and his world either—pantheistically or mythically—as "divine," or as a world of

humans on whom a detached, external God *also* imposes a moral law—his "will." God's creation is not man (or humanity) with his world *plus* God's will for man (that is, a moral order), but quite simply, humanity and its world. If we wish to speak of God's will, this is nothing else than the divine desire that man might exist and live. This implies, however, that he live as man, that he discover himself and his world as well as their latent possibilities, that he understand them, that he shape and realize himself as genuinely human, as bodily-spiritual being.

It is, therefore, up to man to discover what kind of life is proper to him as one who is responsible to the Absolute and oriented toward his fellow human beings, responsible for human-worldly reality—so that his whole life may do justice to the nature and personal dignity of being-human. By so acting he does God's will. It is the will of God that man himself construct the "blueprint" of genuinely human conduct, that he take into his own hands the reality of man and his world, in order to lead it to its highest human potential, and turn himself and humanity toward a lofty, truly human history and future. If beyond this we speak of God's will and his commandments in the plural, we imply only that either revelation makes "fallen" man, who is so selfish and so easily errs, conscious of a number of necessary ways of expressing the genuine "Humanum"—which he could find also by himself—or that we ourselves, in society and church, believe we have found some essential values of the genuine "Humanum" and formulate them accordingly.

3. We may ask whether these thoughts are in agreement with the ethics of Jesus, of the apostle Paul, and of Christian tradition. *Jesus* does indeed say that we must not be "of this world" (John 15:19; 17:16); but let us not forget that "world" here does not refer to that which is truly human, but to that which is selfish and inhuman, that is, the world of sin. Christ demands the morality of a true and pure being-human.

The same is true of the apostle of the gentiles, *Paul.* He does not speak in his letters of a morality of Christians in contrast to a morality of genuine humanness. The difference between Christians and non-Christians on which he does indeed insist is the difference between the true morality of the pneumatic Christian and that of the egotistical sinner. According to Paul, the same material norm of moral living, a truly human norm, applies objectively to Christians and non-Christians, Jews and gentiles (cf. Rom. 2:1f, 6–11). That is why he warns Christians to live honorably, because non-Christians too, Jews and gentiles, can discern what is honorable and dishonorable, moral and immoral. He insists on this because dishonorable conduct on the part of Christians would bring dishonor upon Christianity (Rom. 12:17; I Cor. 10:32; I Thess. 4:12) in the eyes of Jews and gentiles—precisely because they too can recognize human morality (it is written "in the heart" of all). Paul thus presumes that the moral conduct of Christians is identical, in its material content, with the moral conduct of non-Christians. In light of the teaching of Christ and his apostle it is therefore also part of the *tradition* of Christian theology that Christ has not added new moral laws to the "moral codex" of genuine being-human (cf. Thomas Aqinas, Sum. Th. I–II 108, 2).

It follows from this that Christians and non-Christians face the same moral questions, and that both must seek their solution in genuinely human reflection and according to the same norms; e.g., whether adultery and premarital intercourse are morally right or can be so, whether the wealthy nations of the world must help the poor nations and to what extent, whether birth control is justified and should be provided, and what types of birth control are worthy of the dignity of the human person. Such questions are questions for all of humanity. If, therefore, our church and other human communities do not always reach the same conclusions, this is not due to the fact that there exists a different morality for Christians from that for non-Christians.

4. Let us become more concrete. The question arises whether certain moral laws are not specifically Christian after all. Has it not often been said that justice is indeed a universally human commandment, but love of neighbor distinctly Christian, and that the latter is true especially of certain forms of love of neighbor, such as the caring for the terminally ill, and above all love of one's enemies? One could interpret this view of the Christian essence of love of neighbor in the sense that without Christ's revelation it is not possible to comprehend its demands; to this we might respond in a variety of ways, but they do not concern us here directly. The same is true of the question whether these demands can be fulfilled without the inner

grace that comes from Christ. What concerns us here is the following question: Are these demands valid only for Christians, or are they demands of all true being-human? We reply that, on the basis of *"humanitas,"* neither Christians nor non-Christians may foster hatred in themselves and in others, not even hatred of their enemies; they are called upon to love, with all the consequences for daily life.

But does not the *Sermon on the Mount* (Matt. 5–7), which is often rightly praised as the charismatic summation of Christian morality, proclaim a morality that is far above any "human" morality? We cannot here enter into a discussion of the many different interpretations of the Sermon on the Mount. The true meaning of its individual demands must be drawn not from the literal text, but from interpreting hyperbolic ways of speaking; then they will be understood not as legal obligations, but rather as daring "ethical models." In this perspective it becomes clear that the Sermon on the Mount is not at all directed against a genuine human morality but, on the contrary, against the profoundly inhuman conduct of the creature who is mired in egoism, that is, of "fallen" man. This sermon rejects man insofar as he is selfish and sinful, but not insofar as he is human in the best and truest sense of the term. The grace of the Kingdom of God which Christ brings is able to overcome selfishness in human beings. Insofar as we renounce our egoism in grace, we will understand the demands of the Sermon of the Mount—which are the demands of love—not as negating our being-human, but as its purest expression. The newness that Christ brings is not really a new (material) morality, but the new creature of grace and of the Kingdom of God, the man of divinely self-giving love.

This may give us an insight into the belief that *the cross of Christ* as Christian challenge reduces to naught all merely human morality, standing in radical opposition to it. Let us first of all point out that non-Christians, and atheists, also have a certain understanding of renunciation, self-denial and the cross. For they too experience their egoism as "fallen" men and are able to understand that in this situation renunciation and self-denial, hence the cross, may be part of authentic being-human. They know that without such renunciation neither the harmonious shaping of one's own self which true being-human demands, nor the just and kind treatment of one's fellow human beings, are possible. It becomes clear right away that the view of the radical opposition between the Christian cross and human morality should not be accepted without further qualification. For while it is true that the cross of Christ is our salvation, this is so not primarily because it is denial of life, destruction and sacrifice, but rather because it is totally giving love, a love that does indeed lead to the cross, since it takes up its abode in the world of selfish "fallen" human beings. That self-denying love which translates itself into caring for the terminally ill or the needy, or into forgiving one's enemies, will also be cross or experienced as cross, insofar as the egotistic tendency of "fallen" man is still alive. Precisely, however, the insight into the inhumanness of egoism and into the humanness of love can help us understand that the overcoming of egoism in the concrete, and hence the cross, represent for "fallen" man a basic requirement of authentic being-human. However, only the Christian teaching of the redemption of "fallen man," ultimately the form of the crucified and risen God-man, enables us to fathom the full depth and riches of the Christian doctrine of the cross. This doctrine enables us to understand more deeply especially the meaning of the cross in the sense of free renunciation (such as freely chosen poverty) in the world "of the fall" (and of redemption.)[3]

5. We encounter one last obstacle to the fine Christian thesis that Christian conduct is substantially truly human conduct. The problem is frequently formulated as follows: A humane morality is necessarily an "essential" morality, that is, it is static, impersonal. For man in his nature is a given, to be understood as much; human morality, therefore, calls for the realization of this nature. Christian morality, on the other hand, is an existential, dynamic, personal morality; for in the Christian order of salvation man is not fulfillment of his own self, but total openness to the call of the God of our salvation that is given in divine freedom and arbitrariness.

This fascinating concept again needs further precision. First, the relationship to God and hence also the radical openness and availability toward him belong to the "Humanum," to human nature. Were it not so we would have no categories with which to understand Christian revelation about man's dynamic and personal openness. Secondly, Christians do indeed know themselves to be open vis à vis the always possible and never fully predictable call of grace of the God of our salvation. This does not cancel out the truth, however, that the call to salvation is directed to man, hence is always also a "human" call, pointing toward a morality of man—and not in the opposite direction. The "Christian-ness" of radical openness vis à vis God's salvific call may therefore also be explained as follows. First: The clear and explicit awareness of man's true relationship, as man, to God cannot be achieved easily by him—the "man of the fall"—without Christian revelation; Christian anthropology provides an excellent help for man's deeper knowledge about himself. Secondly: Only in faith in the God who reveals himself do we experience that God's personal call to us is indeed a call to salvation.

The "Christianum" of Christian Morality

1. If we have shown that "Christian intentionality," namely living Christian faith, exists and manifests itself in a concrete categorical way of life which is basically and substantially human, we must not at any cost lose sight of the distinctly Christian element in the concrete categorical conduct of Christians. The study of the "Humanum" of (categorical) Christian morality must be followed by a study of its "Christianum." It goes without saying that "Christian intentionality" must live and express itself in the total reality of the concrete being-human, that is, of its "Humanum" as well as its "Christianum." This should not make us afraid that the "Christianum" might come to contradict the genuine "Humanum" (and not only the "Inhumanum"), and displace it. For the existence of the "Humanum" as "Humanum Christianum" should enable us to discover that the "Humanum" is of its very nature open and relative to Christian existence.

The realities that constitute the "Christianum" of the "Humanum Christianum" are realities such as the person of Christ, the Spirit at work in us, the Christian community, the hierarchical church, the sacraments, Christian anthropology. Our relationship to these realities, which we recognize and accept in faith, is part of our very being. Therefore it must be taken into account and also become concrete in our lives; otherwise we would fail to live our truth as believers. We should not forget, however, that this relationship to the

"Christian realities" is also the relationship of "man," hence a *human* relationship.

2. We should try to understand how the distinctly Christian realities can determine our concrete (categorical) conduct over and above the "Humanum." The meaning of the "Christianum" for our concrete living is to be found in its *motivating power.* Christian motivation provides human conduct with a deeper and richer meaning, which is subjectively part of the action itself. The examples of such Christian motivation may be taken from the letters of Paul. When Paul exhorts Christians to do and speak the truth, he does not base himself on the "Inhumanum" of lying—this is presupposed—but on the negation of their shared existence in the one mystical Body of Christ that is the church (Eph. 4:25). When he warns the Christians of Corinth against prostitution, he presupposes the "Inhumanum" of such conduct, explicitly reminding his readers that their bodies belong to Christ, are holy as temples of the Holy Spirit, and that the body's goal is to be glorified with the risen Lord (I Cor. 6:12–20). We do not deny that Christian motivation at all times animates much of the human conduct of Christians, such as: almsgiving at one time, concern for social justice at another, then the readiness to work for a just distribution of goods and for economic aid to the developing nations. Moreover, Christian motivation has undoubtedly not only given a richer meaning to the human conduct of Christians, but also, as is expressed in Paul's warning, has frequently *caused* and inspired a truly human life.

This brings us to a second meaning which the "Christianum" has for the Christian's concrete (categorical) conduct. It not only motivates human conduct more deeply and inspires it, but it will also determine the ways of our conduct *in their content.* Whoever lives truly in faith within the community of believers and the hierarchically led church will not remain, in their way of life, outside the influence of the ethos of the community and church; their ethos will fundamentally be an ethos of the "Humanum Christianum." The believer who is familiar with the person of Christ and his work and with the basic elements of a Christian anthropology—with the man of "the fall," of redemptive grace, and of an eschatological destiny—will acquire a specific and concretely effective understanding of the meaning of renunciation and the cross. The believer alone will understand the meaning of Christian virginity (which should be distinguished from the single life), and may even be able to live it in response to a charsmatic calling. What we said earlier about the Christian's radical openness vis à vis God's continuing call to salvation can also be understood and realized in its concrete Christian form only on the basis of a Christian anthropology accepted in faith. The traditional doctrine of sensitivity to personal guidance through the Spirit of God in us, and the teaching of a Christian existential morality—such as that developed thematically by Karl Rahner—perceive man simultaneously in his "Humanum" and in his existence in the Holy Spirit; both together determine the concrete (categorical) conduct of Christians in the plenitude of their personhood.

Third and last, let us not forget that man's religious and cultic relationship to God is also moral conduct. It goes without saying that this conduct is largely determined, in its Christian concretization, by the Christian's "Christianum."

Christian and Humanistic Morality

In speaking of the Christianness of Christian morality, we should not simply ask to what extent Christian morality is distinctly Christian, and to what extent it is universally "human," or humane. Rather, we must also ask how Christian morality relates to the morality of non-Christians. We shall speak only of the "humanists." And, since there are many types of humanists, let us take those who live purely immanently to this world, although they sincerely seek to pursue a lofty "human" ethos.

1. In our attempt to analyze Christian morality we distinguished first two different aspects: the transcendental dimension of "Christian intentionality," which is distinctly Christian and permeates any particular conscious conduct of Christian life, even if it does so ordinarily without thematic reflection; and the categorical dimension, to which corresponds the concrete moral conduct of particular objects, values, virtues and norms. We noted, however, that the Christian's "Christianum" may also influence his particular (categorical) conduct, especially through Christian motivation—which may awaken not only philanthropy, but Christian love of neighbor—and lead to a religious and cultic life.

While the humanist as non-believer does not have access to the "Christianum" and hence to its influence on particular categorical conduct, the access to the "Humanum" and its ethos is open to him. With regard to the moral determination of our concrete conduct, then, Christian and humanist stand basically on the same plane. Both must seek to understand the phenomenon of man, in order to discover, on the basis of the criteria of an ethical epistemology, what is conduct worthy of human dignity in a given case; but also, which ways of acting are generally to be called moral or immoral. Whether Christians and humanists have to date already sufficiently worked out such an epistemology and such criteria is another matter. The numerous discussions of moral questions among Christians as well as humanists show clearly that all of us, Christians and humanists, are still en route to recognizing moral truth more accurately and in a truer relationship to the given historical situation. We are not likely to reach the goal in the near future.

If Christians and non-Christians do indeed agree on many questions of a humane morality, it remains also true that on many other questions there is no agreement. Let us not forget, however, that lack of concensus exists not only between Christians and humanists, but also between Catholic and non-Catholic Christians, and, to some extent, even between Catholic and Catholic. This should not surprise us. For moral questions are not resolved through logical and clear deductions from the concrete being-human. Rather, moral "solutions" are an "insight" and "understanding" capable of corresponding to the concrete conduct of being-human in each specific situation. Therefore it is not possible to "prove" such "solutions" in the strict sense of the word; we can only explain and describe them, make them intelligible. While it may happen that our partner in dialogue may arrive at the same insight and understanding, agreement is an ideal that is hardly ever attained.

It is true that Christians receive help, in their quest for a human morality, from the context of revelation and its handing down in the Christian and ecclesial community. We are aware today, however, that in the course of time non-Christian influences have become part of Christian moral teaching, some of which do not even represent a genuinely human morality (we need only recall certain questions relating to the body and sexuality). Christians should always be concerned to eliminate such influences. Occasionally humanists may be of help in this endeavor, because they are less burdened by the weight of tradition.

The most difficult aspect of dialogue about morality between Christians and humanists will be the question concerning the religious implications of a purely human morality. For while it is clear that the Absolute of moral living can ultimately be interpreted validly only religiously, that is, in relation to a personal God, this cannot be convincingly proved and demonstrated. What is essential here, perhaps, is that in the course of dialogue the absolute character of the human, moral value be understood as deeply and completely as possible. The humanist partner in dialogue may perhaps never arrive at an explicitly religious interpretation of the moral Absolute; but it could happen that God will be experienced and affirmed by both partners more intensively and in greater fullness at that deeper level of unthematic consciousness mentioned above.

2. The humanist, then, can be dialogue partner in the realm of the categorical *humane* morality of Christian ethics, even though— as long as he remains world-immanent humanist—he has no access to understanding the "Christianum" of categorical Christian morality. This leaves open an important question concerning, not the possible dialogue, but our full understanding of the humanist's morality. What role does what we have called "Christian intentionality" play for him? It goes without saying that he is not aware of it in the realm of reflexive, thematic consciousness. Did we not say, however, that this "Christian intentionality" also for the Christian remains essentially in the realm of unreflexive, unthematic consciousness? May we not assume that in this realm of consciousness the Absolute is present ultimately as the living God, though not thematically and conceptually? May we not, then, also assume that in this same realm the offer of salvation and the salvific call which must be addressed to all persons for their salvation are experienced?

If this is so, we would have to assume that also the humanist, in his deepest nature, responds at this same level to the gift of grace and to the salvific call, and that his response animates and permeates his categorical moral conduct. It does not matter here whether or not we call the transcendent intentionality of moral conduct "Christian" or not. Beyond doubt it signifies true acceptance of that salvific call which comes to us in Christ from the Father of our salvation.

Notes

1. This article was originally a conference to University students given at Zurich in December 1968 and subsequently published in *Stimmen der Zeit* in 1970. Fuchs has continued to address this problem in subsequent articles. For his comment on some articles in the Italian literature, see "Esiste una morale non-cristiana?" *Rassegna di teologia* 14 (1973, 361–373). For his comments on the discussion as it took place in Germany, see "Autonome Moral und Glaubensethik," in *Ethik im Kontext des Glaubens: Probleme-Grundsätze-Methoden,* ed. D. Mieth and F. Compagnoni (Universitätsverlag, Freiburg Schweiz—Verlag Herder, Freiburg-Wien, 1978).

2. As we have already said, we are concerned with the *content* of an authentically Christian morality. This must be kept in mind because a morality which is called "Christian" or which is proclaimed in the Christian community is not necessarily infallible in every aspect nor above correction. The question concerning the "Christian" or "human" *content* of Christian morality must be distinguished from another question: How do we, in the Christian community, come to an awareness of this content, at least insofar as it is purely "human" and not simultaneously contained in the scriptural revelation? Neither individual Christians nor the church authorities come to the knowledge of moral truth through some sort of private revelation. It may indeed happen that the context of Christian revelation may guide individual believers and the community in a direction where certain aspects of human morality become more clear. For this reason, and thanks to the constant assistance of the Holy Spirit—who does not, let us remember, guarantee the truth of each specific question—the Christian community and the church in its official interpretation is a "place" in which the presence of a genuine awareness of "human" morality may be somehow presumed. We can therefore say of this ethical awareness of the Christian community, insofar as it does not stem from scriptural revelation, that

1. the content of this morality is "human," not distinctly Christian,
2. the moral consciousness of the community is derived from a "human" understanding,
3. in the attempt to understand "human" morality the believer will have to take into account the moral consciousness of the Christian community according to the theological validity of the community's understanding.

3. Let us not forget, however, that the cross of selfless engagement in this world is no less Christian cross than the cross of free renunciation. Both forms of carrying the cross correspond to a calling; both are legitimate and meaningful in the midst of "fallen-redeemed" humanity. See also what follows below.

Is There a
Christian Ethics?

Dionigi Tettamanzi

Among the problems which nowadays hold particular interest for moral theology is the problem of the *proprium* or specificity of Christian ethics with respect to a purely human ethics.[1]

As a first approach to the problem we may describe it in the following elementary but no less true and profound manner: Does Christian ethics, namely, the revealed ethics taught by Jesus Christ and proposed by the church, differ from merely human ethics which refer to man's existence and dignity? If the response is affirmative, is it possible eventually to specify the difference between the two ethics, thus succeeding in uncovering the element or the complex of elements which characterize Christian ethics as "Christian" and thereby constitute its proper, specific, and original aspect?

No one is unaware of the fundamental importance of the problem which is being discussed again today. Its solution contributes to the possibility of *critically grounding moral theology.* Indeed, it is well known that every science or discipline is called to give an exact definition of its proper physiognomy or "identity," that is, its proper nature and its proper tasks, either in its own sphere or in the dialogue with the other sciences. The same must be said also of moral theology, inasmuch as it is a true and proper science of the Christian moral life, of the ethical experience of the Christian. Thus, this science too has always been, and is still today, obliged to specify its proper countenance via the search for and the definition of its object—not only the purely generic one (ethical experience) but also and above all the specific one ("Christian" ethical experience).

To this first consideration, the perennially important one of defining the object of moral theology, are added other considerations connected with the historico-cultural context of the contemporary world both ecclesial and civil.

We believe that it is most necessary to start with the description—even a summary one—of such a context. The responses given by moral theologians to the problem of the specificity of Christian ethics will better reveal, in this arrangement, their full meaning. At the end, we will give a critical analysis of the responses encountered and propose a solution which may be more satisfying both in method and in content.

Accordingly, the order we intend to follow is: (1) the problem in the present historico-cultural context, (2) the principal responses given to the problem, and (3) an attempt at a critical analysis and a solution.

I

THE PROBLEM IN THE PRESENT HISTORICO-CULTURAL CONTEXT

The problem of the specificity of Christian ethics is certainly not one which has arisen for the first time in our day. It has constantly accompanied the life and the faith-reflection of the church and Christians, though with notable diversity of perspective, sensibility, and urgency. In a general way, we can affirm that the problem arises with particular acuteness whenever Christianity and Christian ethics encounter a new cultural situation. By way of example we can recall the moral teaching of the apostolic Fathers and the apologists, obliged to highlight the newness of Christian ethics with respect to the moral ideal of the pagan world.[2]

Today the problem is proposed anew and is very relevant, either as the natural result of the profound changes in the contemporary world reaching even into the field of thought and moral practice, or as the requirement for the proper contribution of Christianity toward the solution of the new moral problems of contemporary human beings.

It is manifestly impossible to be complete and to attempt a deep analytical study, nor is this required by the nature and scope of our inquiry. We will therefore restrict ourself to a description of those diverse and complex orientations—both theoretical and practical—which may be termed the causes or the historical matrices which have once again raised the problem of what unmistakably characterizes Christian ethics. These orientations can be broken down to three: the process of secularization, the theological problematics, and the position of the church.

The Process of Secularization

The present secularizing process has inevitably influenced and profoundly modified the sector of ethics, as the Council recognizes in the Constitution *Gaudium et spes* (nos. 4 and 7). Some aspects of secularization can be retained as valid and positive if they remain within the proper limits based on the demand of the autonomy of the human person.[3]

This emphasis on man's autonomy has repercussions on the manner of understanding, willing, and experiencing morality. Contemporary man is particularly attentive and sensitive to the values of the person, and seeks to discover and understand these values through his own reason and experience. Contrariwise, he is less interested in, or suspicious of, or even opposed to definitive responses of an authoritative or religious character, such as those which stem from the magisterial and pastoral interventions of the Church. As is true with respect to other values, so also with respect to ethical value, the man of a secularized age wants to withdraw himself from the guardianship of religion and, with the help of his own reason and experience, resolve the moral problems of his intramundane existence and his activity in history.

The general orientation just described is accentuated in a characteristic fashion for all those moral problems which concern the socio-economic and socio-political order in the present historical situation. In the face of the challenge hurled at man by enormous problems, such as war and revolution, poverty and hunger, various social injustices of world-wide proportions, and overpopulation—in the face of these what meaning can reference to the Gospel and the church possess when neither of the latter seems to harbor the proper and specific elements for a solution? Even non-believers are confronted with the same problems and they commit themselves to finding a solution with a zeal in no way inferior to that of believers. Hence, it is not perhaps an ingenuous and arrogant pretense when Christians approach non-believers with a "Christian" ethics, that is, with "possibilities" which are different (at least on the doctrinal plane) from those available to nonbelievers?

In the social economico-political field the legitimacy of a Christian ethics attempting to solve the problems mentioned above is contested by those who are convinced that the eschatological conception of man and of his historical activity, affirmed by Christianity, necessarily leads to an alienation from earthly tasks, to a flight from the world and to a disengagement from the construction of a terrestrial human civilization.[4]

From a more typically doctrinal perspective and in close connection with the phenomenon of secularization, mention must be made of the so-called radical theology or the theology of the death of God. With respect to ethics, the message of such a theology can be synthesized, briefly but accurately, in the message of a human philanthropy: to be a Christian signifies simply to be like Jesus, a man for others, that is, a man committed to love, respect, tolerance, justice, honesty, and so on.[5] But if in a secularized theology, Christian ethics and human philanthropy are so similar as to coincide, we must ask ourselves if we can still legitimately speak of an "originality" of Christian ethics. Moreover, if this originality were to be salvaged by the affirmation of a relationship existing between Jesus Christ and life-in-the-world, there would still remain the problem of specifying the nature and meaning of this very relationship.[6]

Thus, in a context of secularization and under the impetus of the death-of-God theology we see raised once again the problem of the existence of a specifically Christian ethics.

The Theological Problematics

The problem of the *proprium* of Christian ethics, even though it is precise and determinate, is connected in more or less explicit fashion with other problems currently discussed in theology. Here too we will restrict ourselves to very brief remarks, for our primary purpose is to sketch the general theological framework which gives rise to the question of a specifically Christian ethics.

Among the theological problematics which have influenced the theme of the specificity of Christian ethics we must mention, first of all, the general problematic of the relationship between nature and grace, the natural and the supernatural, according to the different perspectives of an incarnationalist or an eschatological understanding of the relationships of world-church, progress-history of salvation, earthly reality—spiritual life, etc.[7]

Of more direct and immediate interest are the recent reflections on situation ethics, on the natural law as regards its content and its historicity and the magisterial competence of the church toward it, on the interpretation of the ethical norms of scripture, and on the relations between faith and ethics.

Situation ethics has stimulated Catholic theologians to study the moral-religious value of the situation, understood as a personal call of God in a unique and unrepeatable situation—social and individual. The believer, consequently deduces or should deduce ethical imperatives not exclusively from the pages of the gospel and the interventions of the church, but also from the concrete situation in which he finds himself. Therefore, there exists a concrete normative source of moral life which accompanies Christians and non-Christians, to the extent that both share the same situation.

In the line of situation ethics we must include the present emphasis on the "signs of the times" as a *locus theologicus,* of God's will concerning the ethical behavior of the individual person.[8] But what is the specific and original contribution of Christian faith in the understanding of, and of Christian ethics in the involvement in, events and experiences in comparison to a purely rational understanding or involvement? Do Christians and non-Christians have identical or diverse interpretative and operative possibilities?

Added to these are the *recent discussions on natural law,* whether in reference to its content and its historicity or in reference to the competence of the church's Magisterium in this field.[9] The encyclical *Humanae vitae* has clearly recognized that the moral principles set forth in it concerning the regulation of births can be discovered and comprehended in the light of reason which reflects on man's existence, just as it has newly confirmed the church's competence concerning the natural law. In so doing, Paul VI did not exclude but called for theological reflection, which cannot escape the following question: Does the Magisterium of the church perhaps have a cognitive source different from reason for solving the problems of the natural law in general and in particular for solving those problems which are not contained in Revelation?

Even at this stage, as can be seen, we encounter the problem of the *proprium* of Christian ethics, at least for the content of the natural law. In this latter area, do Christians and non-Christians have the same possibilities for understanding and interpretation, and are they called to live the same moral values? Does a Christian ethics, for example, concerning the regulation of births or some other social economico-political problem, possess something properly or specifically "Christian"? something regarding the "motivation" or something regarding the very "content"?

Even the effort which has been in process for the last few decades to give a biblical soul to moral theology has in its course encountered the problem of a specifically Christian ethics. *The study of scripture* has shown with increasing clarity how many ethical norms cannot be called typically "Christian," because they are the simple assumption of ethical norms of the natural law or of the positive law proper to the historico-cultural setting to which the sacred books necessarily refer.

We are not interested here in knowing directly the results reached by biblical studies in their hermeneutical work on the moral commandments of the Old and the New Testaments, a labor which is still almost entirely to be done;[10] it is important for us only to point out what follows. If the problem of the specificity of Christian ethics must be confronted and resolved "theologically," that is, starting from the word of God (written and lived in the church under the guidance of the Magisterium), the biblical study to establish what are the commandments, or better, the values, manifestly "Christian" and what are not (as also which ones are absolute and which ones relative to a determinate historico-cultural context) must obviously occupy the first place.

In a more explicit fashion the problem of the *proprium* of Christian ethics necessarily arises when theology discusses the *relations between faith and ethics,* between the will of God and moral obligation between supernatural salvation and practical conduct, between the "verticalism" of the relationship with God and the "horizontalism" of brotherly love.[11] Once again, our intent does not lie in analytically following the diverse responses given in such discussions; it lies rather in pointing out the ultimate significance of the studies dedicated to these problems. We believe it is this: these studies seek to make precise the relation between Christian faith and Christian practice, to determine the proper nature of the meeting-point between the salvific message of revelation and the moral action of man. In this sense, the studies mentioned end up by confronting, in the ultimate analysis, the problem of the proper nature of Christian ethics, whose solution is precisely the key to the question concerning the originality of Christian ethics.

Under the impetus of the recent and present theological orientations noted, some authors during the last few years have directly and explicitly raised the problem of the *proprium* of Christian ethics.

The Position of the Church

Our problem has received added stimulus in being brought anew to the attention of theologians and Christians even by the position adopted by the church both in its magisterial pronouncements and in its more pastoral attitudes.

The most significant fact is that the Popes, starting with Leo XIII, have had recourse with particular frequency to the natural law for the moral solutions they give to a multiplicity of social economico-political problems: the so-called "social encyclicals" represent a massive testimony to this fact. In this way, the Popes presuppose or even recognize that every man "of good will" is on the way toward seeking and finding the solution of these moral problems with his own reason-experience, that is, starting from the proper needs of the human person considered in himself and in his relations with others. But in this context the question can be newly posed: Does Christian ethics have something proper or specific at least for the socio-economic and socio-political problems if not for all problems?

A second significant fact is the renewed conception and resolution of the problem of the relations between the church and the world. *Gaudium et spes* acknowledges the help received by the church from the contemporary world, which possesses its own legitimate autonomy as well as authentic values and norms. On the other hand, the church continues to assert that it has a message of its own to offer to the world.[12] In this way, the renewed conception of the church-world relationship poses once again, in a certain sense more radically, the problem of what characterizes the message of the church to the world as "Christian" and thereby distinguishes it from a purely human, cultural patrimony. And situated within this general question is the more specific one concerning the originality of Christian ethics.

Finally, we believe that the ecumenical thrust of the conciliar and postconciliar period must also be singled out. As is well known, Vatican II called for an extensive cooperation between the diverse churches even in the resolution of economic and social problems. Such cooperation presupposes both the possibility and the fact of the agreement of Christians—and in a certain sense of all men no matter to what religion they belong—concerning some moral values and norms. On the other hand, a correct ecumenical dialogue does not suppress some divergences in the ethical interpretation of the gospel and of the church. Rather, such differences serve to raise again in a more precise form the question of discovering those moral values and norms which are to be considered as unmistakably Christian, and not merely historical interpretations of the phenomena and exigencies of the natural law. In this ecumenical framework, the very lively problematic among Protestants concerning the relationship between *lex et Evangelium* and concerning the natural law is not entirely forgotten.

We believe that this is the historico-cultural context (described in broad terms) which once again sets before moral theologians the problem of the *proprium* of the Christian ethics. We will now consider the principal responses to it.

II
The Principal Responses Given to the Problem

We are limited to mentioning only studies which deal with our problem in a direct and explicit fashion, leaving aside works which contain only hints or allusions or even kindred themes. A reading of these articles reveals, besides points of agreement, notable differences in method and content. For this reason we believe it is more useful to examine—if only in synthetic fashion—the thought of individual authors.[13]

The XXVIII Week of French Catholic Intellectuals (March 2-8, 1966)

The basic merit of this week is that of having posed the problem in an explicit manner. In the words of R. Remond: "Some will dispute the existence of a natural morality, while others will tend to doubt that there is a Christian morality distinct from the morality common to all men. The two terms of the relationship enunciated (human morality, Christian morality) are thus placed in discussion and subjected to a radical critique. But the question that brings us together for a common study is even more fundamental. It regards the very existence of morality. Is there reasonable possibility for establishing an ethical reflection? Does the definition of morality have a meaning and a justification? This is the real thrust of the debate which commences tonight."[14]

The problem was addressed by some thirty discussants, not all of whom were Christian. We are interested in the papers given in the session on "Morals, Metaphysics, and Religion," and in particular that of Jean Lacroix, professor of philosophy at Lyons and a collaborator on *Le Monde,* and of Jean-Jacques Latour of the Catholic Institute of Paris.

Jean Lacroix is clear and explicit in his position: "To state it clearly from the outset, my conclusion will be that there is only one morality, a human morality, but that Christianity confers on it a kind of interior dimension—which I would like to define as a second sense—which neither modifies nor adds anything to it" (p. 124). And after an interesting analysis of human morality in its dynamic or constructive aspect (morality "consists in the building up of a universe of persons"), Lacroix denies to Christian morality its own content, maintaining that Christianity has a "repercussion" in the moral existence of the believer: "There is no properly Christian morality, but only morality, Christianity, and the manner in which Christianity has a repercussion on morality" (p. 135).

The phenomenon of repercussion is explained by the author in the light of Christian existence immersed in the climate of the fall and the redemption. Morality asks itself the question: "What must I do?" pertaining to duty, while religion asks itself: "What may I hope?" pertaining to grace. More specifically: "The moral universe is that of dualism and of dissociation; the religious universe is that of rediscovered unity and of reconciliation.... In an all-embracing word, the Christian is the person who lives a unity and reconciliation in the very midst of stress and dualism. To be a Christian is to live the unity of freedom and grace to its limit and in a mysterious fashion. Christianity teaches the virtuous man that the apparently inaccessible ideal to which he aspires can be reached and that he is given grace at every moment to pursue it without weakness or discouragement" (pp. 137, 138).

Lacroix concludes: "Human morality is not modified in any way. It retains its difficulties and its hopes. It is only open and, to use Ricoeur's term, challenged. It remains the same, and even receives a new vertical dimension. Christianity does not transform but merely situates morality. Thus, for the Christian, morality becomes a moment of hope. Christianity situates it in the history of salvation, that is, in a history where all is already lost or saved . . . " (p. 139). In the end, it is the relation to Jesus Christ dead and risen that specifies Christianity and has repercussions on morality: "If the expression Christian morality has any meaning, it can only be that of morality lived in the presence of Christ, under the gaze of Christ. It is, in effect, the experience of a look, a voice, a gesture, an attitude: such as when we begin to act morally simply because we are acting under the gaze of a loved one" (p. 140).

A more theological perspective marked the paper of Jean-Jacques Latour. For him, the ethical project of Christians is characterized by the event, ever actual, of Jesus Christ dead and risen. Starting from this event and using the words of K. Barth, he affirms the simultaneity and in fact the identity of law and grace, commandment and love, precisely because "Jesus Christ is at the same time the problem that God poses to me, as call and as demand, as well as the response that he gives me, as precept and as judgment" (p. 152).

Pursuing the line proposed by Ricoeur, Christian originality is to be seen in the unique relationship which it establishes between desire and precept, between love and law: "If in ethics we shift our attention to the desire for existence as the principle of morality, we arrive at this: the religious kernel of ethics resides not in a reinforcement of obligation and of an accusatory demand but in a "kerygma," a message of salvation announced to human desire, a desire for which obligation is a secondary function. . . . A Christian ethics would thus be a morality which explicitates the vital consequences of the impact of the testimony of Jesus Christ on the meaning of human desire, and the law which disciplines it, taking its starting point from the gospel and from the history it inaugurates, the history of salvation. A human morality would probably reach practical conclusions at least partly analogical, but starting from man's desire" (p. 157).

Christian ethics responds to this question: "What does Christ want of me, when in the event of faith he claims my freedom for the service of love, imposing on me this love not only as the internal object of my human desire but also as an immediate law?" (p. 158). Christian morality lies in the gospel considered as interior law of grace and hence of freedom: "The true gospel is never proposed solely from without. The foundation of the gospel as law is a strengthening on the part of the Holy Spirit of the cradle of freedom. The true gospel is the interior gospel, the freedom of the Spirit of God communicated to a free conscience. This is the true and profound principle of Christian ethics: a reinforcement of freedom under the form of exigency, summons, and spiritual presence—a presence whose name will be theological charity. . . . The gospel announces to me this freedom of love to be carried out under the form of law . . . " (pp. 158–159).

F. Böckle: Love as the Central Point of the Christian Ethos

In the search for the *proprium* of Christian ethics, F. Böckle, the moral theologian from the University of Bonn, proceeds in a twofold manner. First, he identifies whatever is unmistakably Christian in Christianity and then he examines the consequences which follow for Christian ethics.[15]

Böckle answers the question: What differentiates Christianity?

with the reply: Only Jesus Christ! The element specifying Christianity is the salvific event with which God has revealed and communicated—in Jesus Christ—his love. Such an event establishes the eternal and almost infinite value of the human person in a positive way. Uniquely starting from God and from Christ, from their love, man has dignity and can attain forgetfulness of self which constitutes love of neighbor. The first proposition of a Christian ethics is therefore a proposition of theological anthropology: the value and the dignity of each man insofar as loved-saved by God in Christ. Such a faith in divine love—rather than a pure law or a simple ethical principle—can thus be called the *novum* of ethics.

This proper and specific element of Christianity gives rise to some consequences for Christian ethics. The first, according to Böckle, consists in the absolute and radical exclusion of every form of human auto-salvation. Salvation, both individual and collective, is the fruit of grace. Man's actions are eschatologically already saved. He must accept this fact, declining to seek the ultimate explanation of the world and of concrete existence in any scientific or social system.

The second consequence is that the central point of every material exigency of a Christian *ethos* is love. Revelation itself is very clear in proposing love of God and neighbor as "law of the law." The primitive church bears witness as to how the Christian must take inspiration from this law in his moral activity. The apostles applied and concretized the commandment of love in the particular situations of the various ecclesial communities. We must note, however, that the moral norm is love rather than the concretizations of love in the apostolic epoch, even though the moral indications of the apostles are to be understood as paradigms or privileged examples insofar as being the word of God they enable us to grasp the genuine meaning of the moral message of Jesus Christ.

The third consequence regards primarily the application of the commandment of love. Since an appropriate application entails a knowledge and an interpretation of the historical (and as such mutable) reality and the existential projects of man, the moralist can give only "indications" to man, who will decide in a personal and responsible manner in his concrete situation.

The *proprium* of the Christian *ethos* is therefore the radical demand for love, which can be understood only by looking at the example of Christ. Sacrificing himself in love to God for his brothers, he reconciles humanity with God and reveals—communicates to men that force capable of transforming the world and restoring it to order.

Finally, warns Böckle, we must not forget how this *proprium* of the Christian *ethos* can be found even outside the Christian sphere, as a reflection of Christian salvation over all creation.

A. Jousten: A Religious Moral and a Moral of Charity

Starting from a few statements of a type of "secular ethics" (J.A.T. Robinson and P. van Buren), A. Jousten asks himself what is the role of the evangelical kerygma, and in particular of the person of Christ, in the field of morality.[16]

A fundamental datum, which we cannot bypass in attempting a response to the question, is the revealed teaching about the intimate connection between faith and moral life, between the salvific event worked by God in Christ and the conduct of men who are saved. We think of the Old Testament and the morality of the covenant: ethical norms are an expression of the salvation centered on the covenant. We think of the New Testament and the moral message of Christ and the apostles: it evidences the connection between "salvific indicative" and "moral imperative" (cfr. Mk 1:15; Eph 4:22–24). In fact, according to the study of G. Strecker, the gospel of Matthew presents rather an "imperative indicative," because the gift of salvation is present in the moral demand of Jesus.

With respect to the specific theme of Christian ethics, Jousten finds the proper elements in the twofold fact that it is a religious morality and a morality of charity.

Before everything else, Christian morality is essentially a religious morality. It is situated in fact in the religious message of Christ who, proclaiming the coming of the kingdom, reveals the original meaning of the will of God, namely, of scripture as an ethical norm, and places all who want to heed it face to face with the fundamental decision. Christian morality thus possesses a vertical dimension: it is a response not to a simple human call but to the ever-actual summons of Christ. "In appearance the morality which the Christian practices is not something other than human morality, the laws or norms which he observes are not different or must not necessarily be diverse from the natural laws. But for the Christian, moral life is not solely a response to his human vocation; it wants to be at the same time, in the same moment, a response to the ever-actual summons of Christ. Moral life thus becomes the expression of faith in Christ" (p. 427). Now Christian faith is an interpretation of life in the name of Christ's resurrection and its eschatological consequences, so that he who believes in Christ is of necessity confronted by and in conflict with a world which is not necessarily oriented toward God: "The believer's morality is Christian to the extent that the living Christ is present in it, to the extent that it expects salvation from him alone. Herein lies its uniqueness and its specificity" (p. 428).

The second element proper to Christian morality resides in the commandment of love, which constitutes its content. This is a clearly revealed datum and it is in this sense that we must understand the "fulfillment" of the Law on the part of Christ. He reduces the written Law to the will of God, centers it on the commandment of love, and fulfills it by means of its perfect realization (W. Trilling).

At this point we meet again some observations already encountered in Böckle's article: love-agape is not an ethical norm in the technical sense of the word, but an operative principle of the concrete context of Christian faith. The concrete indications of the apostles, to be interpreted as typical "schemas for moral action" (J. Blank), as well as the ethical models formulated by moralists do not dispense the acting subject in the situation from personally deciding about the exigencies of love: "This summons (of love) and above all the response are unique and personal; hence we speak willingly of 'morality *in* the situation.' Only the person challenged *can* and *must* understand what concrete act, in the final analysis, love demands from him; moral theory can only orient him in this personal decision" (p. 436). Even the natural law becomes a mode for expressing and actuating love; the specificity of the content of Christian morality in relation to natural morality lies in "a deepening and a radicalizing of the natural law": "no man has ever experienced to the same extent as Jesus the demands of morality and hence of love" (p. 437).

Finally, let us indicate the conclusion which seems of particular interest: "Human morality or Christian morality? At the end of this study . . . we believe only one conclusion can be drawn: we must not posit a dilemma, since far from excluding each other the two elements condition each other reciprocally. It is legitimate and just to speak of *Christian* morality, because of the original contribution given by the person of Christ. But at the same time this morality is *fully human* because it is Christian; Christ has in fact revealed the 'integral meaning' of human activity, and God's plan assumes and elevates—without altering or dissolving—everything human, including natural moral norms. Far from being able to juxtapose or oppose human morality and Christian morality, we must say that Christian morality encompasses human or natural morality" (p. 440).

The author brings his reflections to a close by thus specifying the place of Christ in Christian morality: Christ is not a simple model or ideal of life, but he is the external and internal norm of Christian morality; the Christian, in fact, lives in unity of life with Christ, participating in this way in his charity: "Therefore, reference to, Christ is of utmost importance: we must do good not solely *like* Christ but also *because* Christ wills it and *with* him" (p. 441).

J.-M. Aubert: The Thought of St. Thomas and Faith

The specificity of Christian ethics was the theme of the Congress of French language professors of morality (Dreux, September 19–22, 1969). Among the papers of particular importance, we may single out two, one historical and the other a theological reflection, given respectively by J.-M. Aubert and R. Simon.

According to J.-M. Aubert, even if the Angelic Doctor never dealt *ex professo* in our terms with the problem of the *proprium* of Christian ethics, he can still offer us elements or tips toward resolving it with his teaching on the relationship between (moral) human virtues and (theological) Christian virtues, and between the new law or law of Christ and the natural or human law.[17]

As far as the first problem is concerned, the position of St. Thomas is well known: it lies in the simultaneous safeguarding of the originality or "density" of the natural or the human (in the face of a certain Augustinian pessimism and a certain ascetical development) and of the supremacy of the theological order. The moral virtue-theological virtue relationship finds felicitous explanation both in the teaching on the infused moral virtues and in the teaching on the role of charity as the form of all the virtues (*caritas forma virtutum*). In this framework the human virtues are not only the means of reaching God but also and above all "the ways of charity."

Thomist thought is also of interest on a second point: the relationship between the new law or law of grace and the natural law or simply human law. The new law has charity as its content and presupposes someone to transform, hence a human life, which already has its moral content and to which a new sense is given. The law of Christ does not of itself add any particular prescription. Revelation itself documents how Christ and the apostles in their moral message presupposed and refined a natural-human law, previously known to their hearers. Thus the question arises: Where lies the newness of the Christian commandment of love? Is it a newness with regard to the natural law?

The newness is to be understood in a historico-biblical sense, or in reference to fallen or "carnal" human nature. But if human nature is understood in the metaphysical sense, there is no fundamental opposition, because the natural law already comprises the precept of love of God and neighbor. As a spiritual creature, man has as his goal to tend toward God, to love him and to love others as "images of God." But we must also say that Christian love, in relation to natural love, entails a radical newness both in the *manner* and in the *dynamism* of realization. Christian love raises man above his possibilities as a creature and introduces him into the intimacy of the divine life.

In the light of the teaching of St. Thomas briefly sketched, J.-M. Aubert attempts to resolve the problem of the specificity of Christian ethics, distinguishing the diverse "causes" (material, final, efficient, and formal) of Christian moral activity. With respect to the *material cause,* there is only one morality, common to activity informed by faith and to simply human activity; it follows that the *proprium* of Christian ethics is not to be sought in the material content. The *final cause* is given by charity which, as the *forma virtutum,* informs the whole moral life; every moral act is posited to attain by itself a trans-cedent and immanent term—God loved as Father and loved in his children by all men. The *efficient cause* lies in grace as the participa-tion in the divine love; it is still charity, understood as the principle of moral activity in conjunction with the human will. In particular, the dynamism of grace assumes for the moral act the strength and ef-ficacy to reach the goal of participation in the Kingdom of God as well as *rectitude* in the face of the possible deviations of sin. Finally, the *formal cause,* or the element which "specifies" Christian moral-ity as Christian, is faith. Since there is only one goal for man, a su-pernatural one, we must hold that existentially (on the historical plane) there can be only one morality both for Christians and for non-Christians, whose norm is principally reason.

The conclusion follows that there is "a material identification" between the Christian moral exigency and the exigency perceptible by reason. But such an identification does not suppress the "formal distinction" which consists in the mode and the intentionality to live and put into practice the common moral prescriptions. More precise-ly, faith—as the formal cause of moral activity—"does not change the matter of moral prescriptions but gathers together in the Chris-tian all this activity. ... And how? Simply by making explicit the significance of the presence of charity in the moral act posited by it" (p. 72).

Thus the believer who knows that his moral activity has a tran-scendent and extramundane finality is alerted to the danger of abso-lutizing the earthly finality. Without alienating him from human values, this admonition can lead him, in certain sectors and by means of certain vocations, to modify his scale of values (renunciation, practice of the evangelical counsels, and prophetic activity).

R. Simon: The Constructive and Critical Function of Christian Ethics

The problem of the specificity of Christian ethics is approached by the French Salesian, R. Simon, from two complementary points: the creation-salvation relationship and the natural moral law-law of grace relationship.[18]

The creation-salvation relationship, according to the "unitary" design of God in Jesus Christ (Col 1:16), leads to the assertion of the assumption in Christ, the incarnate Word, of everything that is human; by becoming incarnate the Word assumes the human condition, even in its ethical dimension. This consideration is then developed by Simon within the anthropological perspective of contemporary theology and within the perspective of the existence of a Christian morality.

According to the first perspective, we must affirm that every spiritual activity has a "transcendental" perspective, insofar as it entails—beyond the limited object which it takes into account—an orientation "toward being in all its fullness" (God). This is reflected in ethics. Man is called, along a path which is situated within the very depths of being, to take a position for God or against God (transcendental option), even if this taking of a position can be accompanied by the ignorance of or indeed the explicit denial of God in the categorical sphere. The significance of what has been said is that man in his very metaphysical structure (that is, in his very reality as a creature) is concretely (that is, through his situation as a creature called *de facto* to salvation in Christ) led to make a decision in answer to the summons from the Absolute, from God.

We can thus pose the question whether a "Christian" morality exists. Simon responds with *sic et non*: "*No*, because in a certain sense faith leaves human morality to itself and refers it to its essence; faith does not substitute itself for morality in order to take away from the latter what it must do and what is within its competence. . . . *Yes*, there is a Christian morality, in the sense that the impact of faith or, to use J. Lacroix's term, the repercussion of faith, on human morality makes the latter change meaning, integrating it into the economy of salvation, which is the primary and fundamental reality, and which situates man with regard to the summons which comes to him from God in Jesus Christ" (p. 81). Consequently, we can understand why "the function of Christian morality is less that of adding to human morality than that of *revealing* human morality to itself while at the same time *manifesting* it in its divine dimension as grace of God" (p. 82).

Simon undertakes a second theological approach to make precise the proper nature of Christian ethics, namely, by considering the relationship between *lex naturae* and *lex gratiae*. Closely following the reflections of B. Schüller,[19] he asserts that the natural law is the necessary mediation for the analogical understanding of the law of grace, that the newness of the *lex gratiae* resides not so much in the content of its precepts as in the fact of the intervention of God in the life of man—and to such an extent that, on the plane of moral conduct, the precepts of the *lex naturae* become at the same time precepts of the *lex gratiae*. Thus in the link between law of nature and law of grace we find the link between order of creation and order of redemption. Jesus Christ also lives the moral imperative which he draws from his human existence, but by divinizing it, that is, by conferring on it a dimension which pertains to God: "The Christian's existence and activity are no different from the existence and activity of man, those which he shares with other men. Only—and this difference is critical—this *human* existence and this *human* activity become through grace the activity of the *Christian* who exists in Christ and through Christ, and they are open to the absolute future, which is assured through the hope of faith" (p. 87).

We can gather from the preceding the threefold function of Christian ethics (and of faith). It has a *constructive function*: faith reveals not only the precepts which pertain to revealed "data" but also those of the *lex naturae*; in addition, faith enters into the field of praxis, bringing to light the eschatological dimension of morality. A second function is the *critical function* or that of contestation of the world and its sin. The death of Christ functions as the manifestation of the impossibility of any alliance between God and the world's idols. This is a dialectic of yes and no, of rupture and of *engagement*, which no secularization or any desacralization will be able to change without suppressing the cross of the Lord" (p. 95). Lastly, the author describes the *major Christian attitudes*, as found in evangelical poverty, evangelical obedience, and heterosexual love. These attitudes show that the influence of revelation on Christian existence and activity affects less "the plane of exemplarity and imitation than the plane of the structuralization of the Christian's existence. It is a question of structuring the existence and conscience of the Christian with the resources and energies of faith. It is the Christian man, indwelt by the Spirit of the Father and the Son, who is placed before the problems of man and who must—in the light and power of this Spirit and in submission to the binding needs of rational analysis—

give human and Christian responses to the changeable situations of the contemporary world" (p. 103).

J. Fuchs: Christian Intentionality

The response of J. Fuchs, the noted moralist from the Gregorianum University in Rome, starts from a distinction within Christian moral activity.[20] There is first of all the transcendental aspect, according to which man-the-Christian gives himself totally to God who calls him in Jesus Christ (fundamental option-intention); and there is also the particular-categorical aspect, through which man-the-Christian expresses and lives the total disposition of self in determinate individual actions, in which values, virtues, and categorical norms find application. In the light of this distinction Fuchs affirms that "the authentically and decisively Christian element of Christian morality is not sought in the first place in the particularities of values, virtues, and categorical norms typical of the diverse spheres of life. Rather it is found in the fundamental Christian decision of the believer to accept and respond to the love of God in Christ. . . . The 'Christian intentionality,' understood as the actual decision for Christ and the Father of Jesus Christ, consciously present in the moral behavior of each day, is considered as the most important and characteristic element of Christian morality" (pp. 16–17, 19).

Since the "Christian intentionality" permeates and perfects the particular behavior of man-the-Christian but does not determine its content, "the problem remains open as to whether the categorical content of the morality of the Christian—that is, his concrete moral action—is unmistakably Christian and therefore different from the morality of man as such" (p. 20). Formulated in this way, the problem is resolved by Fuchs by rediscovering in categorical Christian morality both a *humanum* and a *Christianum.* The "decisively human," comes before all: "Christian morality, seen in its particularity and categorical materiality, is fundamentally and substantially a *humanum,* hence a morality of authentic humanity" (p. 20). The proof is found again in Paul's teaching (cf. Rom 2:1ff; 12:1; 1 Cor 10:32; 1 Thes 4:12) and in that of St. Thomas, for whom Christ has not added any new moral commandment to the "moral code" of true and genuine humanity (cf. *Summa Theologica* I–II, 102, 2). The author confirms this *humanum* in opposition to those who find "unmistakably Christian moral commandments" in love of neighbor and especially of enemies, in the demands of the Sermon on the Mount, in the requirement of the cross, in the total openness to the call of God the Savior. According to Fuchs, in all these cases, it is a question of human requirements although grace aids their comprehension and actuation.

On the other hand, in the categorical behavior of the Christian there is also a *Christianum*, such as the person of Christ, the Holy Spirit working in us, the Christian community, the hierarchical Church, the sacraments, and Christian anthropology: "Our relation to these realities which we recognize and accept with our faith forms part of our existence. Precisely for this reason, this relationship of ours to these realities must be co-present and co-realized in our actions; otherwise we would not live what we are as men of faith" (p. 29). But how do these Christian realities orient our concrete behavior beyond the *humanum*? Fuchs speaks of a twofold influence: (1) as a motivational force insofar as Christian motivations infuse a meaning which is more profound and richer (as Paul teaches concerning veracity and charity: Eph 4:15; 1 Cor 6:12–20) and which calls forth authentically human actions; (2) and as content, both through man's religious-cultural relationship with God and through the understanding and living out of renunciation and the cross, of the choice of virginity, and of obedience to the personal guidance of the Spirit in us.

Finally, concerning the Christian morality for non-Christians, Fuchs follows the well-known Rahnerian thesis of "anonymous Christianity" and affirms the possibility of a "Christian intentionality" for the atheist-humanist. Indeed, such an intentionality can be unrecognized or even denied on the level of a reflexive-thematic awareness but it can be embraced and lived on the level of a non-reflexive and non-thematic awareness.

Charles E. Curran:
Ethics of "Human Experience"

The specificity of "social" Christian ethics is a particular aspect of our problem which has received the attention among others[21] of

Charles E. Curran.[22] The *proprium* of Christian ethics cannot be discovered on the basis of history (which—according to Curran—does not bear witness to a specific contribution to the content of social moral) or of experience (since it is not possible to observe for a long time the very substance of the natural law without the aid of grace, even though the individual is not aware of the presence of grace).

The problem has been traditionally discussed in terms of the natural law but with the limitation of frequently considering the natural not only as distinct from, but also as set off against, the supernatural (as autonomous or only extrinsically connected areas). Lutheran theology has adopted the same general approach, formulating the well-known theory of the two kingdoms (which corresponds to the distinction between creation and redemption, and between law and gospel). The approaches of the natural law and of the Lutheran theory of the two kingdoms seem to lead to the negation of a specifically Christian ethics, at least for social structures and for institutions. And if the Barthian school (K. Barth, R. Niebuhr, D. Bonhoeffer, P. Lehmann) has reacted to the absolute dichotomy between God's left hand and his right hand, between creation and redemption, and between law and gospel by emphasizing Christ's central position in the moral life (the Word of God is at one and the same time gospel and law!), it has by its "Christological monism" led to the exclusion of the role of reason and every human experience as a way of access for Christian reflection on the moral problem.

Accordingly, Curran disagrees with these approaches and resolves the problem of the specificity of Christian ethics by denying a dichotomy between Christian ethics and human ethics, for a twofold reason. Considering the subjective pole of human reality, namely, the person, he refutes the general or at least current opinion which would affirm the existence of a specific difference between Christians and non-Christians. The reason adopted by Curran is the truth of the universal salvific will of God whether explained according to traditional Catholic theology or according to the Rahnerian theory of "anonymous" or "implicit" Christians. Then, considering the objective pole of Christian existence, namely, the world, Curran reaches the same conclusion. The world is not, in fact, totally disfigured by sin and governed by God's left hand, and it is not the sphere of the "natural" absolutely distinct from the "super-natural"; but it is entirely permeated by the redemption of Christ and related to the future eschatological existence. Hence, we must affirm the relation between creation and redemption, in the sense that redemption brings creation to its ultimate completion. Thus, the *Christian* is not opposed to the *human*, neither is it totally separated from it, but the Christian brings the human to perfection (cf. *Gaudium et spes,* nos. 22 and 38).

In conclusion, a specifically Christian ethics does not exist: "It is evident that the recognition of Jesus as Lord touches at least the consciousness of the individual and his thematic reflection on consciousness; but Christians and explicit non-Christians can arrive at the same moral conclusions; they can share in the same moral actions, the same dispositions, the same goals and results. . . . It is in this precise sense that I deny the existence of a specifically Christian ethics: namely, that non-Christians can reach the same moral conclusions and value the same dispositions, the same goals and actions as Christians. . . . To deny the existence of a specifically Christian ethics signifies simply that others who have never adhered to Jesus Christ or have not even heard speak of him, not only can arrive at the same moral decisions in particular areas but are even capable of having the same dispositions and the same attitudes, such as hope, freedom, and love for others even to the sacrifice of self" (pp. 54–55).

For this reason, Curran, following *Gaudium et spes* no. 46, prefers to speak of "human experience," thus avoiding the traditional dichotomy between the gospel and reason or evangelical law and natural law. Human experience in the actual world comprises elements which belong to the order of the incarnation, of the redemption, and of resurrection destiny, as well as elements of the order of creation and of sin. The author concludes his study with a reference to the eschatological dimension of morality: "What is truly human includes the notion of redemption and of resurrection destiny, but there is still the danger of forgetting the transcendent and eschatological dimension of this authentic human morality. . . . In today's conditions, moral theology and the Christian churches must underline the eschatological perspective of Christian morality. A proper eschatological perspective acts as a negative critique on every institution or structure existing in society. . . . The eschatological element of Christian morality recalls the importance of the virtue of hope" (p. 57).

The above-mentioned voices are those we have deemed the most significant to have discussed the problem of the *proprium* of Christian ethics. The reviews (which in spite of their brevity we believe to be faithful) of the thought of the authors should bring to light the points of agreement or of affinity as well as the points of divergence, the different methods followed, the various perspectives of consideration, and the points needing further clarification. In an attempt to give a comprehensive reconstruction of the discussions, we could say that they affirm a link between ethics and Christianity as history of salvation in Christ, so that Christian ethics results in being an aspect or moment of the *historia salutis* in Christ. In the further search for the significance of Christ's salvation on man and on his moral activity, the authors treated manifest more or less profound divergences, which are sometimes related with the different concerns which guide them. Some concentrate on establishing the *ultimate inspiring principles* of Christian moral activity (faith, charity, hope); others dwell rather on the *material content* of activity (commandment of love of God and neighbor); still others consider the diverse levels of *personal profundity* which gives rise to the moral obligation (distinction between the transcendental aspect and particular-categorical aspect); and lastly others recall the *characteristic consequences* of Christianity on ethics (unity between love and commandment, relation between *lex naturae* and *lex gratiae,* critical function of faith, the understanding and living out of particular ethical values like virginity, acceptance of the cross, etc.).

We will now attempt to make a critical evaluation of the thought summarized above and set forth some guidelines for a solution to the problem of the *proprium* of Christian ethics.

III
ATTEMPT AT A CRITICAL ANALYSIS AND A SOLUTION

The first impression which can be drawn from a reading of the thoughts of the authors mentioned is that of a missing or insufficient concern to define the precise content of the terms confronted: Christian ethics and human ethics; indeed, we can notice a certain generality or even diversity of significance precisely about the terms under discussion. The relationship between the two ethics and the search for the specificity of Christian ethics are not even minimally possible without first making an accurate distinction among the various concepts of human and Christian ethics, and among the various levels on which the comparison takes place. Hence, the necessity for a conceptual clarification.

Conceptual Clarification

In an initial approach to the theme of the *proprium* of Christian ethics we believe we can define the two ethics as follows.

1. *Christian ethics* is the ethics revealed by God to mankind in Jesus Christ and proposed as such by the church. With respect to this ethics the adjective "Christian"—taken in an all-inclusive sense—could serve to designate in detail three somewhat distinct aspects. We can term as "Christian" the ethics which refers to the example and the teaching of Jesus Christ, or the ethics which refers to the entire revelation of God to mankind, or lastly the ethics proposed to men by the church of Jesus Christ. We are here speaking of Christian ethics in this all-inclusive sense.

2. *Human ethics* is the ethics of man and his personal dignity. But the description is still too generic. In the interests of making it even more precise we believe that we must point out three fundamental contents or meanings of human ethics. It can signify:

—a "natural" morality in the strict sense of the term, that is, a morality proper to man insofar as he is—in whole or in part—purely natural, i.e., not introduced into the supernatural order;

—a human morality put together according to an atheistic anthropological conception, that is, of man as completely immanent and autonomous and not open to God;

—*a morality founded on man's very existence as man* (prescinding from the fact that his existence as "man" finds realization only in a supernatural order and hence solely as a "new man" in Jesus Christ) *and knowable in its exigencies by human reason* (even here prescinding from the fact that this is aided by supernatural grace).

Only the third of the above meanings is acceptable. The first is not acceptable because of the existence of a unique historical order, the supernatural; and the second is not acceptable because man can be defined only as ontologically related to God. We will therefore make the third meaning more precise. For us, human ethics is the one which describes the exigencies (or tasks) which human reason can discover (and, at least in part, does in fact discover) as proper to man, rather as so proper and ineradicable that he not only possesses them in the supernatural order—the sole existent historical order— but also would possess them in a hypothetical natural order (otherwise, he would cease to be man). In this acceptance of the term "human ethics" we prescind from (but do not deny) the fact that the existence of "man" finds "historical" actuation only in the supernatural order and hence in the sole perspective of the "new man" in Jesus Christ. We also prescind from (but do not deny) the fact that human reason which reflects on man's existence and its ethical exigencies function in a supernatural order where—especially in the religious-moral sphere—it is under the influence of actual grace. Here we consider man's reason in its "natural" capacity to know the true and the good.

The observations just made demonstrate that *human nature, to which human ethics refers, can be considered according to a twofold perspective: metaphysical and historical.* The first considers those elements of man which are "absolute," that is, those without which man would no longer be man, and consequently those which must be present in every historical period of realization *(natura ut sic);* the second considers those elements of man which are "contingent," in the sense of existential or historical, that is, in reference to the unique existing historical order, which is a supernatural one *(natura ut hic).* Fuchs justly remarks: "If nature is opposed to the supernatural it is undoubtedly an abstraction but it is a true abstraction based on man as he really and actually is. It follows that it is *realized in him in a true and altogether proper sense.* It is a necessary consequence that the supernatural is also an abstraction from the total reality of man and must be unhesitatingly and necessarily affirmed to be accidental to nature. . . . As distinct from the supernatural, nature is but a part of that total reality which is man and which we know exclusively from Revelation. This is the only source from which it is possible to know that in the complete human being there is a 'supernature' and that 'nature' is open to receiving it. . . ."[23]

Now how does one discussing the relationship between Christian ethics and human ethics understand human nature? The response concerning the *proprium* of Christian ethics, or more radically concerning the very existence of a Christian ethics (and the question, from another point of view, could also read thus: Does a human ethics exist?), varies depending on the different understandings of human nature.

Furthermore, human ethics and Christian ethics can be considered according to *different aspects or levels:* their ontological foundation (the existence of man and the existence of the Christian), their objective content (the exigencies which objectively stem from human and Christian existence), their noetic foundation (reason as such and reason enlightened by faith as acceptance of the word of God), and their subjective actuation (morality is understood not as the proposal of the moral ideal but as its incarnation in concrete moral existence). When we discuss the human ethics-Christian ethics relationship we can refer to any of the different aspects mentioned. As far as we are concerned, the comparison is not to be instituted on the level of subjective actuation comparing the actual moral life of Christians and the moral life of non-Christians. Nor is it to be instituted, at least primarily, on the level of cognitive foundation, but in reference to the content and hence ultimately on the ontological level. It is well known that, while the non-Christian attains the moral values and norms which inspire and guide his existence from his reason and his life experience, the Christian attains these values and these norms also from "sources" which are qualified as typically Christian—scripture, tradition, and the magisterium of the church. On the level of the subjective aspect, therefore, the Christian is inspired by "faith" as the interpretative-directive criterion of his proper moral conduct, while the non-Christian is inspired exclusively by reason (even if historically he is under the influence of grace). Now the simple reference to the Christian sources of knowledge and faith is not always and necessarily sufficient to indicate the proper and specific content of Christian ethics. In reality, scripture, tradition, and magisterium do not always present only typically Christian ethical contents; they also present values and norms of a purely human morality. The same may be said of the faith of the Christian; his every moral action must be inspired by faith, but this does not qualify the action as an unmistakably Christian action in its content.

Since the objective content refers ultimately to the ontological foundation, it is understandable that the comparison between human ethics and Christian ethics reveals itself as secondary and derived, that is, it refers to a more radical, primary, and fundamental comparison—the one between the human person and the Christian person. In fact, moral activity is the expression or actuation of one's existence, and the moral regulation of activity is the normative indication for the human person and for the Christian person of the objective structure of their being.

The observation just made provides us with an immediate understanding both of the essential context within which to discuss the problem of the *proprium* of Christian ethics and of its multiple possible formulations. Our problem is one aspect of the general problem of the specificity of Christianity, and consequently it could be formulated according to different emphases, especially the following: What is the relationship existing between creation and redemption? between the natural law and the law of grace? between the world and the church? between human progress and the Reign of God? It is a question of different formulations which go back to the fundamental problem of the relationship between the natural and the supernatural.

Methodological Criteria

The problem of the *proprium* of Christian ethics can be studied in other ways. It can be studied by the method of listening and dialogue, in the sense of listening to non-Christians giving the specific contents which they recognize or do not recognize in Christianity in general and in its ethics in particular. This is a method which we have not seen followed very much.[24] An explanation can perhaps be found in the fact that the present formulation of our problem has found the stimulus for critical reflection in so many men of the age of secularization, who refuse to recognize in Christian ethics a content and a power for the construction of a human world "diverse from" or even "superior to" the content and the power of an ethics of true humanity. But it is also true that there are not lacking, even today, non-Christians who respect and also admire Christianity and its moral theory and practice; aware that Christian ethics always has "its" word to say and "its" power to offer for the solution of common human problems.

However, it is evident that such a method for discovering the *proprium* of Christian ethics cannot be considered adequate. The results which might be reached would have to be submitted to a critical interpretation, which for believers can be made in the most profound manner possible by starting from the word of God. This is the typically theological method to which we intend to refer.

This is not the place to recall the essential structure of the theological method, which is involved in a criticoscientific interpretation of the word of God. But we consider it useful to recall how the word of God, to which theology refers to find the response to the problem of a specifically Christian ethics, is the word of God which reveals itself and communicates itself in its source which is at both one and three: the word of God as written in the Bible (sacred scripture); as heard-interpreted-lived in the experience of the faith of the entire ecclesial community throughout the centuries (tradition) and as taught under the authentic guidance of pastors (magisterium).[25]

This observation, more than obvious in itself, is also suggested by two lacunae which we seem to have encountered in some of the authors considered. The appeal to the written word of God to resolve the question of the specific content of Christian ethics has never been sufficient, and for many reasons. We intend to point first of all to the complex and difficult hermeneutical problem of the ethical norms of the Bible: we are still waiting for its results, which will be of great importance for the definition of the *proprium* of revealed ethics. Moreover, it seems to us that we must suggest to Bible scholars an investigation concerning the manifold "newness" of which the inspired authors often speak, when they discourse about the new man, the new life, the new covenant, the new law, and the new spirit. Of course, the primary interest concerns the "content" of this new Christian reality; but it would also be helpful to do a more accurate study of the frequent characterization of "newness" attributed to the ethical content of the word of God.

We feel it is fair to point out a second lacuna: the reference to the word of God coincides for more than one author with the reference merely to "scripture." This occurs, for example, when one treats the theme of the relationship between the commandment of love and its historical realizations. The word of God is involved also in these historical realizations, if not as the "written" word of God (but this is still to be made precise both along general lines and along specific themes), then as the word of God present and operative in the "time of the church."

In this sense, the problem of the *proprium* of Christian ethics would demand to be approached especially from an historical point of view, both with respect to scripture (we think of the significant words of Jesus Christ: "Do not think that I have come to abolish the Law and the Prophets; I have come not to abolish but to fulfill"—Mt 5:17) and with respect to tradition and to the teaching of the magisterium. This last point does not seem to have been considered by our authors. It constitutes a whole work to be undertaken before arriving at a systematic response.

Our Response

We will first recall the essential aspects of Christian ethics: "The question which the Christian must ask himself is not primarily that of how the Christian is different ('In comparison with the non-Christian what more do I possess? What does the fact of being Christian add to me?') but that of *Christian identity*?"[26] We are not here concerned so much with a complete and documented discussion which by its nature tends to involve the entirety of Christian ethics but with the indication of a series of themes and their possible developments. Only in a second phase will it be possible to institute a comparison of Christian ethics with human ethics, and the response should not be difficult in the light of the conceptual clarification previously made.

1. *The Morality of the Covenant.* It seems to us that the fundamental and ultimately decisive aspect of Christian ethics is the covenant between God and men. Christian ethics derives from and leads to the historical fact of the covenant, as one of its fundamental expressions and exigencies.

This signifies, first of all, that ethics has a point of departure, a well-defined and determinate *historical fact* which challenges the life experience of all men and of each person in particular. Such a fact is both complex and unitary: complex, because it is given by the whole

history of salvation in its different phases of manifestation and actuation, "from the time of Adam, from Abel, the just one, to the last of
the elect" (*Lumen gentium,* no. 2); unitary, because Jesus Christ, the
covenant made person, constitutes the "synthesis" and the "center"
of the *historia salutis,* which is all summed up in him and centered on
him, converges in him and derives from him (*Gaudium et spes,* no.
45). More precisely, therefore, the historical fact is Jesus Christ, the
incarnate Son of God dead and risen. In him the covenant between
God and men reaches its completion and the "mystery of reconciliation" becomes especially operative (2 Cor 5:17–21).

If ethics starts from the historical fact of the covenant of God in
Jesus Christ with men, one of its fundamental aspects is rendered immediately clear. Christian ethics cannot be reduced to the theoretical
discovery and practical realization of an abstract idea, a personal value, or a simple law; it is transformed into an *interpersonal relationship,* a true and proper encounter and dialogue between persons.
Biblical morality does not start from "nature" and from "rational reflection" on nature and its ethical exigencies, but from the "history"
of salvation and from "faith" as the acceptance of such a history of
salvation. This certainly does not signify the denial of "nature" and
of "rational reflection" on nature but such values must be integrated
into those of the history of salvation and of faith.

The historical fact of the covenant expresses and actuates a *relationship of salvific love* between God and men in Jesus Christ. In him,
dead and risen, there is revealed and communicated the *agape* of the
Father for the favored Son and for all men, as well as the *agape* of
the Son and of mankind in him for the Father. It follows that Christian ethics, by its connection with the salvific covenant, is essentially
a special kind of religious dialogue. Indeed, this finds its most expressive category not so much in "law" as in "vocation," as Vatican II
has recalled.[27] The term "vocation" intends to emphasize the dialogic
character of ethics. Not only does this refute an ethics which would
consist in self perfection, through which man would cultivate his values and actuate his exigencies without reference to the God who
challenges him, but it also underlines the characteristic trait of moral
dialogue. It is a question of a dialogue in which the two parties are
not "on a par," not only because it is God who takes the initiative in
calling man, whence the latter cannot but "respond," but also and

above all because it is the very call of God which grounds both the possibility and the obligation of human response. Man "can" and "must" respond to God, precisely because he is challenged by him with a call which is not addressed to man already constituted but which is constitutive of man himself ("hearer of the word").

The ethical dialogue, insofar as it derives from the covenant presents itself as a dialogue of salvation: it is a call to salvation and a response to salvation. In this sense, Christian ethics possesses an intrinsic religious dimension. And since salvation, signified and produced by the covenant, is the exclusive fruit of God's gratuitous love in Jesus Christ (Dt 7:7–9), the ethics which is connected with it cannot fail to reject every claim of human self-sufficiency.

2. *God's Salvation and Ethics.* Revelation is explicit and constant in relating the historical fact of the gratuitous salvation of the God of the covenant and the ethical obligation of the man saved. The Old Testament never wearies of presenting the *magnalia Dei* as the title which empowers and obliges Israel to moral action: "The active presence of Yahweh in the history of Israel is in fact the foundation of Hebrew morality."[28] The New Testament situates itself in a line of continuity and newness with regard to this point. It continues to affirm that ethical behavior is a response to the salvific intervention of God, but with the newness that this response must henceforth be given in Christ and to Christ, since he is the full revelation and perfect actuation of the salvific intervention of God in the world. This truth is proclaimed by Christ himself: "The time has come and the Reign of God is imminent: repent and believe in the good news" (Mk 1:15), and it is taken up by the apostles: by Paul for whom the Christian's moral existence is grounded on the *einai en Christò* of baptism (Rom 6:3–5), and by John, who records how the believer's new ontological situation—of being born of God and consequently of being a child of God in Jesus Christ—is the foundation of the moral life: "He who says that he is in him must also walk as he has walked" (1 Jn 2:6).

This leads to the deduction that *the specific elements of Christian ethics are to be sought precisely within the salvific work of Jesus Christ as the foundation of that ethics.* Now supernatural salvation presents itself—in accord with the clear indication of scripture later taken over by all of Christian tradition although with a diversity of emphases—as "liberation" from sin and Satan, and as "communication" of the divine life to men. In this way, the salvation of Jesus Christ touches man profoundly in his whole being, and therefore even in his ethical obligation, not only liberating him from the limits owing to sin but also opening him out to new horizons, those connected with the new supernatural goal set before him.

The salvation of Jesus Christ is, before all else, liberation from sin. It follows that in the consideration of ethics we cannot neglect this primary aspect of the historical situation of man, of all and everyone: the situation in sin. And sin impairs moral effort, manifesting and actuating a twofold impediment. Sin as "darkness" (Jn 8:12) and as "falsehood" (1 Jn 1:6; 2:4; 4:20) "obscures" the normative content of moral value, and as a form of slavery to Satan it "weakens" the motivating power of moral value.

Christian ethics, as the fruit and demand of the liberating salvation of Jesus Christ, is aware of and proclaims to all the incapacity or at least the inadequacy of the sinful historical man to know and to actuate moral value in a perfect way. Certainly, we cannot reduce the whole content of Christ's salvation to liberation from sin, Satan, flesh, death, and slavery. But it is still an essential aspect of salvation and this must be termed the first "repercussion" of the covenant on Christian ethics. A fully historical consideration of the problem of the *proprium* of Christian ethics is never exhausted, in the recollection that the sole existing order for all men is that of supernatural elevation; even when this is primary as we will see, it must also stress in adequate fashion the condition of sinners proper to all. When we speak of human ethics, in which would also enter into play the values of love of neighbor and especially of enemies, the requirements of the Sermon on the Mount, and the openness of self to the cross, we are referring to the exigencies of an "ideal" mankind, so that in the comparison between human ethics and Christian ethics we must distinguish the relationship to human nature in its ideal state or perfection and to human nature in its historical state.

Salvation in Jesus Christ is the communication of the divine life; it is the elevation of man to the supernatural order of participation in the intimate life of knowledge and love of the Father, the Son, and the Holy Spirit. Precisely because the single goal historically given to men is not a "natural" goal, but a "supernatural" one, we must affirm that even within the hypothesis of a condition bereft of sin man would have been inevitably incapable—by his own moral effort—of reaching the goal held out to him. We thus grasp the full implication of salvation in relation to ethics; ethics can be itself, namely, the regulation of man in reaching his goal, only by starting from salvation. Henceforth the only way given to men for salvation is Jesus Christ, and he is also the only way for the moral life: "I am the way and the truth and the life; no one comes to the Father except through me" (Jn 14:6). *The ultimate meaning of ethics thus becomes a following and an imitation of Jesus Christ.* He fulfills in a perfect way the Father's will and he serves him especially in the sacrifice of himself out of love for God and his brothers; by realizing perfectly the Father's will, Jesus Christ "fulfills" the law (Mt 5:17).[29] Precisely herein lies the newness of Christian ethics; the obedience of Christ to the Father, the obedient and loving docility of the Servant of Yahweh, through grace becomes henceforth "model" and "source" of the believer's obedience to the will of God. The believer's ethical response to the salvific plan of God is a "visibilization" and a "reactualization" of the obedience of Christ: only "in" Christ, "with" Christ, and "through" Christ. A filial response to the Father becomes blissfully possible and the response of every believer to God becomes urgently obligatory.

3. *The Dialectic Between Law and Liberty.* A characteristic trait of Christian ethics, as the result of salvation in Christ, is the original resolution of the law-liberty dialectic. Tradition, from Paul to St. Thomas, has insisted on this in a particular way: law and liberty are resolved in grace, or better, grace is the new law for the believer (Rom 8:2) and it is also the source of liberty (Gal 5:1; 2 Cor 3:17).

Grace is liberty: grace "gives" liberty and at the same time it "demands" liberation. Not only is liberty the "goal" of the *lex gratiae,* but it also constitutes the latter's content. This must be said with reference above all to the so-called fundamental and transcendental liberty, as the *"anima"* of particular-categorical liberty.

Grace is law: the Spirit of Christ "illumines the eyes of our heart" (Eph 1:17, 18; Heb 6:4) and guides us to the actuation of the will of God (1 Cor 2:10ff).

What has been said is fully validated in reference to the historical situation of sin, in which the relationship between liberty and law is constantly under the sign of a dialectic and a conflict, difficult, if not impossible, to resolve. To the man "divided" existentially between liberty and law, grace is offered as "reconciliation," as "unity." Nor is it a question merely of a rediscovered unity, but also of a most singular deepening of the two very realities at issue. The believer's liberty, in fact, lies in the more radical "service" of God and neighbor (1 Cor 7:22); and the law succeeds in binding man's responsibility with the force which alone can derive from love.

4. *Charity, Faith, Christian Intentionality.* In identifying the *proprium* of Christian ethics the authors speak of the commandment of love (Böckle, Jousten), faith (Aubert, Simon), and "Christian intentionality" (Fuchs). In regard to these we offer the following observations.

The *love* in question is evidently the *agape* which derives from God and which the Spirit of Christ pours out into our hearts. It is, therefore, a "supernatural" love, proper to the "children of God." In addition, if we speak of "commandment" of love or of this as "law" of the Christian, the terms "commandment" and "law" must be referred to love only in an analogical sense, in contrast with the use of the same terms in relation to other moral values. Personally, we suggest speaking of charity as "fundamental law" or the transcendental aspect of Christian ethical existence, which, precisely because it is fundamental and transcendental, is expressed and actuated in the different laws or individual precepts. In this sense, charity is not reducible to a precept, a value, a particular moral value to be equated—even in a primary position—to other precepts, values, or categories. Charity lies "above" (without thereby lying "outside") every other particular law; moreover, charity is "mediated" by the other particular laws (and this indicates not only "the relation" existing between charity and the other values, but also the "type" of relation). In addition, we believe that the problem of charity as the *proprium* of Christian ethics can be faced and resolved by following the indications which Christian tradition has offered in dealing with the relation between the *lex gratiae* and precepts. The latter, even detailed and minute, constitute the formulation of the "objective" exigencies of grace, just as the various precepts of the natural law express the exigencies of man as such. It is thus a question not of "identifying" the *lex gratiae* with precepts, and not even of "separating and contrasting" them, while giving an intrinsic and objective connection between them.

Others regard the "formal" element of Christian ethics as given by *faith*—which "does not change the matter of the moral prescriptions but affects in the Christian his whole moral activity . . . and how? By simply making explicit the meaning of the presence of charity in the act wrought with it";[30] in addition, it frees the Christian's moral activity from the temptation to absolutize earthly finalities ("critical" function) and enriches it with an understanding and realization of particular values, such as the cross, poverty, virginity, and docility to the Spirit ("constructive" function).

We believe it is necessary to specify better the concept of faith as the formal cause of Christian moral activity. Is faith limited to "revealing" to its possessor "the presence of charity in the moral act" or the "ultimate meaning" of the real? Or does it transform the believer, "creating" in him a newness of being and action, that is, by imparting supernatural salvation which, on the one hand, frees moral activity from the limitations of sin and on the other broadens it by rendering it suitable for new acts and actions, which alone can bring man to his supernatural goal? Let us say that faith is not only "revelation" but also "salvation."

Furthermore, we have the impression that the terms "charity" and "faith" are used without the concern to distinguish the various meanings: sometimes they refer to the "content," and other times to the "inspiration" of moral activity; a few times they are taken up in a "categorical" sense and other times in a "transcendental" sense. In this last case, charity and faith tend to replace one another, as Fuchs seems to suggest by speaking of Christian intentionality.

Concerning *Christian intentionality,* envisioned by Fuchs as the primary element of the *proprium* of Christian ethics, we deem it indispensable to underline strongly the "interdependence" between the transcendental aspect and the particular-categorical one, not only with respect to the "motivation" but also with respect to "content."

This is required by a twofold consideration. The first is provided by the connection between being and action, insofar as action reveals and actuates being. The "newness" which characterizes a Christian as a "new creature in Christ" must be seen in the "newness" of activity. In addition, recall the connection between motivation and the material content of the concrete action. The study of the material content of the moral activity, of Christian and non-Christian, is undoubtedly legitimate and obligatory: it is the discovery of the so-called "matter" or "object." But the "morality," as is known, is to be derived in the concrete from the convergence of all the "sources of morality," and among these the purpose or end of the person who acts has an essential and determinative function. The problem of the *proprium* of Christian ethics, resolved by many theologians in the sense of a *proprium* on the intentional rather than the content level, runs the risk of considering abstractly the moral activity of the person, of stopping at the act in its material content to affirm the "material" identification of the moral activity of the Christian and the non-Christian. We must not forget that the asserted difference of "motivation" does not touch the activity in its total morality in a merely superficial or marginal fashion, but determines a "newness" of value or moral meaning. This seems even more decisive if we accept faith (charity, Christian intentionality) in its function not only as "revealing" but also as "transforming" the believer in his existence and hence in his concrete activity.

Conclusion

Our response to the problem of the *proprium* of Christian ethics must be manifest in what has preceded. It lies in the *grace of Jesus Christ* as the *lex nova* of the believer. If by "human ethics" we refer to the objective norm valid for man considered only metaphysically, we can speak of diversity of Christian ethics. If, however, by "human ethics" we refer to the objective norm valid for the historically existing man, we must affirm that this is realized in Christian ethics and hence coincides with it: grace assumes and perfects every authentic value of mankind. In this sense, man cannot be good *in a true sense* unless he is also good *in a Christian sense.*[31] On the other hand, we must not forget that grace becomes present and operative also where there is not yet an explicit faith in Jesus Christ and in his grace, no matter how we wish to explain such a presence and work of grace (universal salvific will, actual grace through the observance of the natural law, or "anonymous Christianity"). Let us add that believers are taught by their faith about God's plan to lead all men to salvation and hence to live the new life of the risen Christ, but with the requirement to believers to become "missionaries" of salvation to their brothers. Thus, believers are called, by their words and even more by the testimony of their own moral life, to reveal to everyone that newness or the ultimate meaning of the ethics which Jesus Christ proposes in grace to every man who has come into the world.

Notes

1. We are using indifferently the terms "Christian ethics" and "Christian morality." In any case, we refer to a "theological" ethics. Cf. J. Rief, "Moraltheologie oder christliche Ethik? Ein Literaturbericht" in *Theol. Prakt. Quartalschrift* 116 (1968), pp. 59–80.

2. See G. Borgeault, "La spécifité de la morale Chrétienne selon les Pères des deux premiers siècles" in *Science et esprit* 23 (1971), pp. 137–152.

3. We point out the study of J. Ramos Regidor, "Secolarizzazione, desacralizzazione e cristianesimo" in *Rivista Liturgica* 56 (1969), pp. 473–565. With reference to morality we refer to C. Van Ouwerkerk, "Secularism and Christian Ethics" in *Concilium 25: Understanding the Signs of the Times* (New York: Paulist Press, 1967), pp. 97–139.

4. Cf. *Gaudium et spes,* nos. 20 and 21. As a response to the objection noted we may refer to the twofold development of a "theology of hope" and a "political theology."

5. "Jesus is the 'man for others,' the one in whom love has completely taken over, the one who is utterly open to, and united with, the ground of his being. And this 'life for others, in the participation in the Being of God,' *is* transcendence. . . . Christ was utterly and completely 'the man for others,' because he *was* love, he was 'one with the Father,' because 'God is love.' But for this reason he was exclusively man, the son of man" (J. A. T. Robinson, *Honest to God,* Philadelphia: The Westminster Press, 1963) pp. 76–77. On this theme, cr. C. Van Ouwerkerk, *art. cit.,* which summarizes the moral thought of J. Robinson, D. Bonhoeffer, P. van Buren, W. Hamilton, T. Altizer, and H. Cox.

6. "One thing that always strikes and surprises me in even the most liberal discussions on the possibility of a Christian ethic is the fact that people seem able to reject God, but not the figure of Christ, no matter how he is interpreted. . . . In any case secular ethics has compelled traditional Christian morality to face up to the question of what it really means by union with Christ as the fundamental norm of Christian life, and what it means when it says that grace is a *lex indita*" (C. Van Ouwerkerk, *art. cit.,* pp. 133, 135–136).

7. See G. Colombo, "Escatologismo ed incarnazionismo: le due posizioni" in *La Scuola Cattolica* 87 (1959), pp. 344–376, 401–424.

8. Cf. *Gaudium et spes,* no. 11. It is interesting to note how K. Rahner

used the terms of "existential formal ethics" to interpret the pastoral constitution in the collective work *La Chiesa nel mondo contemporane* (Brescia, 1967²), pp. 19–60. Concerning the "signs of the times," see M.-D. Chenu, "I segni dei tempi," *ibid.*, pp. 85–102; M. van Caster, "Signs of the Times and Christian Tasks" in *Lumen Vitae* 21 (1966), pp. 324–366.

9. See the works of J. David, *Nuovi aspetti della dottrina ecclesiastica sul matrimonio* (Rome, 1967); *idem., Il diritto naturale: problemi e chiaramenti* (Rome, 1968); F. Böckle, *Dibattito sul diritto naturale* (Brescia, 1970).

10. We recall the study of the Danish theologian K. Loestrup, *Die ethische Forderung* (Tübingen, 1959); the works of T. W. Adorno, *Eingriffe, Neuen kritische Modelle* (Frankfurt a. M., 1963); *Idem., Negative Dialektik* (Frankfurt a. M., 1966); J. Blank, "Does the New Testament Provide Principles for Modern Moral Theology?" in *Concilium 25: Understanding the Signs of the Times* (New York: Paulist Press, 1967), pp. 9–22; W. Kerber, "Hermeneutik in der Moraltheologie" in *Theologie und Philosophie* 44 (1969), pp. 42–66.

11. Of interest are some studies of C. Van Ouwerkerk, W. H. van der Marck, J. Ratzinger, K. Rahner, and B. Willems which are summarized under the question "How to reconcile ethics with faith" by Th. Beemer, "The Interpretation of Moral Theology" in *Concilium 45: Dilemmas of Tomorrow's World* (New York: Paulist Press, 1969), pp. 127–148.

12. Among the latest interventions we might recall the letter *Octogesima adveniens* of Paul VI to M. Cardinal Roy (May 14, 1971).

13. For a discussion of some of these works, see F. Compagnoni, "Esiste una morale propriamente cristiana?" in *Rivista di Teologia Morale,* 1970, no. 8, pp. 101–126; R. A. McCormick, "Specificity of Christian Morality" in "Notes on Moral Theology" in *Theological Studies* 32 (1971), pp. 71–78; D. Tettamanzi, "Etica e Cristianesimo" in *Rivista del Clero Italiano* 52 (1971), pp. 196–207.

14. *Morale humaine, morale chrétienne* (Récherches et débats, no. 55: Brussels, 1966; Italian translation: Rome, 1968). We quote from the Italian edition, pp. 7–8. Concerning the Week, see the critique of J. M. Aubert, "La Morale chrétienne est-elle à la mesure de l'homme?" in *Etudes* (1966), pp. 529–545.

15. F. Böckle, "Was ist das Proprium einer christlichen Ethik?" in *Zeitscr, für Evang. Ethik* (1967), pp. 148–159. The author has also proposed his position in a lecture given at Gazzarda at the Convention of Moralists of North Italy (1969): cf. *La legge naturale* (Bologna, 1970), pp. 213–217.

16. A. Jousten, "Morale humaine ou morale chrétienne" in *La Foi et le Temps* (Namur, 1968), pp. 419–441.

17. J. M. Aubert, "La spécificité de la morale chrétienne selon saint Thomas" in *Le Supplément,* 1970, no. 92, pp. 55–73.

18. R. Simon, "Spécificité de l'éthique chrétienne" in *Le Supplément,* 1970, no. 92, pp. 74–104. See an account by the same author in the article "Nouvelles orientations de la morale chrétienne" in *Supplément de la Vie Spirituelle,* 1968, no. 87, pp. 491–494.

19. B. Schüller, "La théologie morale peut-elle se passer du droit natur-elle?" in *Nouvelle Revue Théologique* 88 (1966), pp. 449–475.

20. J. Fuchs, "Gibt es eine spezifisch christliche Moral?" in *Stimmen der Zeit* 185 (1970), pp. 99–112. This article has appeared in Italian in J. Fuchs, *Esiste una morale cristiana?* (Brescia, 1970), pp. 13–44. In the various articles which make up this book, the author returns again to the problem, in particular dealing with moral theology and theological life (pp. 141–160). See also J. Fuchs. *Human Values and Christian Morality* (Dublin, 1970).

21. A. Manaranche, *Y a-t-il une éthique sociale chrétienne?* (Paris, 1969).

22. Charles E. Curran, "Y a-t-il une éthique sociale spécifiquement chrétienne?" in *Le Supplément,* 1971, no. 96, pp. 39–58. The original is in Curran, *Catholic Moral Theology in Dialogue* (Notre Dame, 1972), pp. 1–23.

23. J. Fuchs, *Natural Law: A Theological Investigation* (New York: Sheed and Ward, 1965), p. 45.

24. In this respect, we can reread the intervention of the different participants, not all Christian, at the XXVIII Week of French Catholic Intellectuals (March 2–8, 1966), in the work already cited.

25. Cf. *Dei verbum,* no. 10.

26. R. Simon, "Spécificité de l'éthique chrétienne" in *Le Supplément,* 1970, no. 92, p. 103.

27. *Optatam totius,* no. 16. See the lengthy comment of J. Fuchs, *Teologia e vita morale alla luce del Vaticano II* (Brescia, 1968).

28. F. Festorazzi, "La Sacra Scrittura anima del rinnovamento della teologia morale" in *La Scuola Cattolica* 94 (1960), pp. 9–115.

29. We depend in particular on C. Larcher, *L'attualità cristiana dell'Antico Testamento secondo il Nuovo Testamento* (Rome, 1968), pp. 253–363. See also B. Corsani, "La posizione di Gesu di fronte alla legge secondo il vangelo di Matteo e l'interpretazione di Matteo 5, 17–20" in *Ricerche Bibliche e Religiose,* 1968, pp. 193–230.

30. J.-M. Aubert, *art. cit.,* p. 72.

31. This is the sense in which E. Hamel concludes one of his studies: "Moralitas christiana, ut sit plenissima christiana, debet esse plene humana, quod non erit, nisi sinat se a mundo hodierno illuminari. Moralitas humana, ut sit plenissima humana, debet esse christiana, quod non erit, nisi sinat se a luce Evangelii illuminari" ["Christian morality, in order to be most fully Christian, must be fully human; and it will not be such unless it allows itself to be illumined by the contemporary world. Human morality, in order to be most fully human, must be Christian; and it will not be such unless it allows itself to be illumined by the light of the Gospel"] "Lux evangelii in constitutione 'Gaudium et spes' ": *Periodica* 60, 1971, p. 120).

Is There a Catholic and/or Christian Ethic?

Charles E. Curran

In one sense the title of this paper has been a perennial question. Catholic and/or Christian ethics have constantly needed to reflect on their own identity *vis-à-vis* other types of ethics whether they are religious ethics or philosophical ethics. However, this questioning has become even more acute in the last few years. Our own age in many ways can be characterized as a time of crisis and radical questioning which has taken place in theology on the most ultimate of issues, namely, the God issue. It should not surprise us that the same type of questions arise about the identity of Christian and/or Catholic ethics in relationship to other ethics.

I
THE CONTEXTS

To situate the discussion it will be helpful to indicate the major contexts within which the questioning about the identity of Christian and/or Catholic ethics has arisen in the last few years. The first context that gives rise to the question of the identity of Christian and/or Catholic ethics is the dialogue between Christians and non-Christians in the modern world. All men of good will, to use a phrase employed by Pope John XXIII in addressing his encyclical letter *Pacem in terris* to these people as well as to the bishops and members of the Roman Catholic Church,[1] seem to share many of the same ethical values as Christians. In actual experience Christians have worked side by side with non-Christians for the same social causes and ethical concerns. Many Catholics and Christians have personally experienced with non-believers the common ethical concerns which unite them and frequently feel more in harmony with the ethical concerns of non-Catholics and non-Christians.

Such a practical experience has been mirrored in the more theoretical realm through dialogue with atheists and with Marxists. These two types of dialogue and discussion characterized much of Roman Catholic theology in the 1960's. The Pastoral Constitution on the Church in the Modern World devotes a large section to the phenomenon of atheism and, generally speaking, recognizes some positive values in this phenomenon.[2] "While rejecting atheism, root and branch, the Church sincerely professes that all men, believers and unbelievers alike, are to work for the rightful betterment of this world in which we alike live. Such an ideal cannot be realized, however, apart from sincere and prudent dialogue" (n. 21).

In a parallel way with Marxism, while the Roman Catholic Church continues to reject the basic tenets of Marxism, there has been a growing recognition of the agreement on many issues confronting society and also in some countries a growing practical alliance between Marxists and some Christians and Roman Catholics.[3] In this same connection, the phenomenon of a theology of the secular and secularization has also had its impact on the identity of Christian ethics.[4] Thus the contemporary experience has brought to Christian consciousness, probably more so than in preceding times, the recognition that there are great similarities between Christian ethics and non-Christian ethics.

The second context in which the question of the identity of Christian ethics occurs is on the level of theological theory, especially involving a rethinking of three important sets of concepts—nature-supernature; creation-redemption; Church-world. An older Catholic theology seemed to hold a dualistic approach reserving some things for the area of nature and others for the area of supernature. Contemporary Roman Catholic thought has been trying to overcome that dichotomy. In a speculative context Karl Rahner has employed the concepts of the supernatural existential and the anonymous Christian to overcome the dichotomies between nature and supernature and between creation and redemption.[5]

On the level of action and moral theology, Gustavo Gutierrez emphasizes the concept of one history to overcome both the dichotomy of nature and supernature and the dualism of creation and redemption and thereby shows a proper relationship between the Church and the world. There are not two histories, one profound and one sacred, juxtaposed or closely linked. There is only one human history and human destiny irrevocably assumed by Christ, the Lord of history. Gutierrez himself recognizes that such an acceptance of only one history, a Christ-finalized history, raises the suspicion of not sufficiently safeguarding divine gratuitousness or the unique dimension of Christianity.[6]

Gutierrez then develops the reasons for his position. The Bible itself establishes a close link between creation and salvation. In this light the understanding of the relationship of Church and world must be changed. In an older approach it was thought that the salvific work of God was present primarily in the Church and not in the world, but such an approach can no longer be accepted. The building of the temporal city is not simply a stage of humanization or pre-evangelization as was held in theology until a few years ago; rather it is a part of a saving process which embraces the whole of man and all human history.[7] "The perspective we have indicated presupposes an uncentering of the Church, for the Church must cease considering itself as the exclusive place of salvation and orient itself toward a new and radical service of people."[8] The Church is the universal sacrament of salvation, but the work of salvation is a reality which occurs in the one history of the world.

While agreeing with the general thrust of such an approach, I personally have some problems and difficulties which might better be called amendments or modifications. Contemporary theology must overcome the dichotomies between nature and grace and between creation and redemption which were present in an older Catholic thought. But in overcoming the dichotomies there is the great danger of seeing everything in terms of the supernatural and of redemption. Roman Catholic theology, as well as Christian theology and human thought in general, in the late 1960's suffered from a naively optimistic approach that too often forgot about human limitations and sinfulness and mistakenly gave the impression that the fullness of the eschatological future was readily within our grasp. The stark realities of war, violence, hatred, and the inability of nations and individuals to live in peace and harmony have shattered such an illusion. My modifications to the approach taken by Gutierrez would insist that liberation is a long, hard, difficult process that will never be fully accomplished, but the Christian must be committed to strive to make liberation more present in our society. In my judgment much of the disillusion which characterizes life today, both in the world and in the Church, comes from the crushing of a naive optimism which forgot about the realities of limitation, sin and the eschaton as the absolute future. In addition, I have difficulty in accepting any one concept as being all controlling in ethical theory, even if that concept be liberation. In the past, for example, an overemphasis on freedom resulted in the doctrine of laissez-faire capitalism.

A third context in which the question of the identity of Christian and/or Catholic ethics arises refers to the methodological change which has occurred in Roman Catholic moral theology and which to some extent was influenced by the broader theological realities mentioned in the second context. To illustrate this changing methodology, compare the 1963 encyclical *Pacem in terris* of Pope John XXIII with the Pastoral Constitution on the Church in the Modern World.

Pacem in terris stands in the tradition of the papal social encyclicals beginning with *Rerum novarum* of Leo XIII, who decreed the teaching of thomistic philosophy and theology in Catholic universities and seminaries and employed the natural law concept to questions of the social and economic order. The sources of the papal teaching were often referred to as reason and revelation, but the heavy emphasis rested on reason and natural law.[9]

Pacem in terris, as mentioned above, was addressed not only to Catholics but to all men of good will. The methodology employed by the encyclical was in keeping with such an address, since the basic appeal was not to the Scripture and revelation but to human reason. At the very beginning of the encyclical Pope John insists that peace on earth can be firmly established only if men dutifully observe the order laid down by God the Creator. The Creator has imprinted an order in the universe in which we live and in the hearts of men. In the nature of man and the universe conscience can find the order and the norms by which men are guided to live together in peace and harmony. Appeal is thus made only to creation, human nature and human reason which all men share in common whether they are Christians or not.[10]

The revival of Catholic moral theology, which first appeared in the 1950's and can be illustrated in the pioneering work of Bernard Häring,[11] insisted that moral theology must be rooted in the Scriptures and in grace and not just in reason and in human nature. This newer emphasis was encouraged by the dialogue with other Christians which was beginning to occur at that time in a more regular and visible way. Protestant ethics had consistently emphasized the primary place of revelation and the need to see Christian ethics in this context. The Decree on Priestly Formation of Vatican II declared "special attention needs to be given to the development of moral theology. Its scientific exposition should be more thoroughly nourished by scriptural teaching. It should show the nobility of the Christian vocation of the faithful and their obligations to bring forth fruit in charity for the life of the world" (n. 16).

The Pastoral Constitution on the Church in the Modern World tries to propose such a new framework and methodology for its consideration of the political, social and economic problems of our day. No longer is the methodology based on creation alone or human nature alone, but the document addresses these questions in the light of the gospel and of human experience (n. 46). The methodological approach of the Pastoral Constitution on the Church in the Modern World can most adequately be described as a history of salvation approach which sees man's life in the world in the light of the whole history of salvation—creation, sin and redemption, and not merely on the basis of creation alone. Thus the tone and methodology of this document differ greatly from *Pacem in terris.*

At first sight the very obvious methodological differences between the older papal encyclicals and the Pastoral Constitution on the Church in the Modern World seem to indicate there is a heavy insistence on the distinctively Christian aspect in social ethics which was lacking in the approach of the hierarchical magisterium before that time. However, a deeper investigation of the question raises some contrary indications. The factors mentioned in the second context above—the overcoming of the dichotomy between nature and supernature and between creation and redemption—are also very much present in this document. There are also some startling individual statements about the identity of the fully human and the Christian. These questions will be discussed later in greater detail.

A fourth and final context refers to the specifically Catholic aspect of the question. Post *Humanae vitae* Catholic theology acknowledges the possibility and right of dissent to the authoritative or authentic, non-infallible teaching of the hierarchical magisterium. The possibility of dissent extends much more broadly than just to the specific question of the condemnation of artificial contraception which was proposed in *Humanae vitae*. Theoretically within Roman Catholicism today there are proposals going contrary to the official teaching of the Church on such questions as sexuality, abortion, euthanasia, and divorce.[12] In practice it also seems that many Catholics do not accept and follow the official teaching of the Catholic Church on specific moral questions.[13]

At the same time in the last few years many Catholics have expressed their belief that the Roman Catholic Church can and should speak out on any number of ethical questions facing our society. The war in Southeast Asia was the occasion on which many Catholics deplored the fact that the Catholic bishops of the United States did not give clear teaching to their people, although individual bishops made statements condemning American involvement in the war and finally the American bishops as a whole did issue a statement calling for the American withdrawal from Vietnam.[14] There have also been calls for explicit church teaching on questions such as prison reform, condemnation of the death penalty, backing particular groups of workers in their labor struggles, etc.

These two signs of the times, which in some ways appear to be conflicting, create the milieu in which theologians raise the question about a distinctive and specific Roman Catholic ethics.

II

A DISTINCTIVELY
CHRISTIAN ETHIC?

This paper will consider first the question of a distinctively Christian ethic and then only later the question of a distinctively Roman Catholic ethic. Any solution depends on a comparison between

Christian ethics and other religious and human ethics. In the past few years, particularly within Roman Catholicism, this question has been raised about the material content of Christian ethics. Does the material content of Christian ethics add anything distinctive to human ethics; and, if so, what?

One must be careful not to prejudice the argument. The question cannot be settled merely by comparing the ethical conduct proposed in the Scriptures with the ethical conduct exemplified in the lives of non-believers. In one sense Scripture proposes the objective and somewhat ideal teaching which all would have to admit is not always verified even in the lives of Christian believers. A comparison can be made by studying the content of the ethical teaching proposed in Scripture with the content of morality as expressed in the writings of another religion or of a philosopher. It is possible, for example, to compare the teaching of the Old Testament with the ethical content proposed by those who lived in the same historical circumstances. Some comparative studies have been made, but they are quite limited.[15] Comparative historical studies will always constitute an important aspect of the debate, but at the present time no one can claim to have made an exhaustive comparative study of the ethical teaching of the Old and New Testament with the teaching proposed by non-believers living in somewhat the same historical and cultural milieus.

In those discussions there can also be valuable data derived from experience and history. Does our own experience indicate that there is a specifically different Christian ethical content? Obviously our own personal experience is necessarily limited so that no conclusive answer can be drawn from experience alone although it can contribute insights to a final solution of the question. Can history itself indicate that the moral content of Christian ethics has differed from the moral content of non-Christian ethics? Here again it is very difficult, if not impossible, to do an exhaustive historical study to determine if there is a difference between the content of Christian ethics and of non-Christian ethics, but again some helpful insights can be obtained through history. In my judgment, the limited data we have from both experience and history give no clear evidence of indicating a distinctive content to Christian ethics. Even some who would admit to the existence of a different content recognize that history cannot prove the existence of a specifically Christian ethic as far as content is concerned.[16]

While all the above approaches to the question are helpful, they cannot at the present time give a definite and certain answer to the question of the existence of a specifically different content in Christian ethics. Such approaches unfortunately are necessarily incomplete. This paper will now concentrate on the more theological and theoretical approaches to the question of a specifically different material content in Christian ethics.

Some preliminary points deserve attention so that the question can be properly stated and pursued. Sometimes discussion about the specific contents of Christian ethics *vis-à-vis* others is only in terms of norms or precepts.[17] In my judgment such a description of the material content of ethics in general and of Christian ethics is much too narrow. The material content of ethics also includes other elements besides norms—attitudes, dispositions or virtues; goals and ideals; moral judgments. One cannot reduce the material content of ethics just to the question of rules and norms.

Secondly, it should be noted that the question about a distinctively Christian content to ethics and especially the denial of such a distinctive content in comparison with human ethics has arisen primarily in the context of Roman Catholic theology. There has been some discussion of the question among Protestants but comparatively little in the form of this specific question.[18]

This fact is not all that surprising but rather coheres with the basic theological thrust of Catholic and Protestant ethics. One, however, must be very careful in speaking about either Protestant ethics or Catholic ethics as if either were a monolithic system. This has been especially true of Protestant ethics throughout its history, but classical Protestant ethics has generally downplayed the human and the role of the human in Christian ethics. Roman Catholic ethics on the contrary has insisted on the goodness of the human, and its natural law tradition claimed that human reason on the basis of its understanding of humanity can arrive at true ethical wisdom and knowledge. Catholic ethics traditionally has given a very important place to the human, whereas classical Protestant ethics has seen Christian ethics as starting from God and his action and not from man.[19]

The Pastoral Constitution on the Church in the Modern World of Vatican II, despite the newer methodological approach mentioned above, still remains in basic continuity with the Catholic emphasis on the human. The acceptance of the goodness and importance of the human can be illustrated from a number of statements in the document itself. "Above all the Church knows that her message is in harmony with the most secret desires of the human heart when she champions the dignity of the human vocation restoring hope to those who have already despaired of anything higher than their present lives. Far from diminishing man, her message brings to his development light, life and freedom. Apart from this message nothing will avail to fill up the heart of man. 'Thou hast made us for Thyself, Oh Lord, and our hearts are restless till they rest in Thee'" (n. 21). A little further on, the document describes the ultimate vocation of man as in fact one and divine (n. 22). Jesus who entered world history as a perfect man revealed to us that God is love. "At the same time He taught us that the new command of love was the basic law of human perfection and hence of the world's transformation. To those therefore who believe in divine love he gives assurance that the way of love lies open to all men and that the effort to establish a universal brotherhood is not a hopeless one" (n. 38).

The encyclical letter *Populorum progressio* of Pope Paul VI follows the same general method of the Pastoral Constitution on the Church in the Modern World and also illustrates that the Catholic tradition has at the very least a high regard for the human. *Populorum progressio* builds its teaching around the concept of development. Since human beings, like all of creation, are ordered to their Creator, they should orientate their lives to God the first truth and supreme good. By reason of union with Christ man attains to a new fulfillment of himself, to a transcendent humanism which gives man his greatest possible perfection.[20] Later, the Pope comments that modern man is searching for a new humanism embracing the higher values of love and friendship, of prayer and contemplation, which will permit the fullness of authentic development (n. 20).

The discussion about a specific content of Christian ethics takes place at least in Roman Catholicism, in the light of this basic acceptance of the goodness and importance of the human as well as its continuity with grace. This paper does not intend to summarize all of the writing which has appeared on this question in the last few years. Rather, the different positions will be illustrated and criticized. Interestingly, many Catholic authors writing on this subject in the last few years have denied the existence of a specifically different material content in Christian ethics, although there have been two distinct and different approaches arriving at this conclusion. On the other hand there are also some authors who affirm a Christian ethic which does not contradict human ethics but does add a distinctively Christian content beyond the human. It is only in the last few years that the question has been raised in the exact terms which it has been raised now. For that reason, it would be an almost impossible task to determine how other thinkers in the past would have responded to this question because the question was not really posed exactly the same way as it is now.

The Position Affirming a Distinctively Christian Content.[21] One of the characteristics of Roman Catholic moral theology has been its heavy emphasis on anthropology as the starting point of Christian ethics, and the opinion affirming a specific material content to Christian ethics can readily find a basis in anthropology. The comparison, however, is not between the sinful nature of man and the redeemed nature of man. There is no doubt about the great contrast existing here as illustrated, for example, in Paul's description of those who walk according to the flesh and those who walk according to the spirit. Likewise, the call to conversion as it is frequently proposed in the Scriptures is not a call to man as such but rather to sinful human beings.

The human which is under discussion in the comparison of the human and the Christian must be that which pertains to the nature of man as such and not to the historical state of man after the fall. Since Catholic ethics has often accepted the axiom *agere sequitur esse,* then the starting point should be an anthropological understanding of the Christian as such. Christianity definitely adds a specific element in the area of anthropology. Faith and grace are the decisive elements in a Christian anthropology.

What do faith and grace add to ethics? A new way of being (life in grace) must result in a new way of acting. The teachings of Jesus indicate how he does extend the ambit of the human for those who are his followers. He calls for love of enemies, humility, renunciation, non-violence, virginity for the kingdom. The radical demands of gospel morality, including the cross and love of enemies, are not mere counsels but constitute ethical demands that go beyond the human and flow from the new life of those who are in Jesus Christ. The scriptural ethical teaching indicates that the gift of new life in Christ Jesus calls the Christian to act in a different way so that there is a specifically different material content in Christian ethics. However, the existence of an irreducibly specific Christian morality does not mean that such a morality stands in opposition to human morality. Christian morality goes beyond the human, but it is in the last analysis a fulfillment of the human and not in any way a contradiction of the human.

The above argumentation definitely shows the Catholic matrix out of which it comes. The Protestant approach would tend to see greater discontinuity between the human and the Christian; for example, human ethics is based on man giving his neighbor his due in accord with the rights of the neighbor, whereas Christian morality responds not to the rights of the neighbor but to the needs of the neighbor.[22]

Many theologians within the Protestant tradition do give some importance and value to the human. This more positive relationship between the Christian and the human can best be described in the model of the Christian transforming the human. This concept of transformation implies not only continuity between the human and the Christian but also some discontinuity so that occasionally the Christian ethical demands will go against the purely human demands.[23] However, it is important to point out that in Catholic thought the human or the natural is a metaphysical and ahistorical concept referring to the meaning of man as such apart from either the fall or grace, whereas the Protestant concept of the human is more historical referring to the actual human condition.[24] This difference of perspective is very significant but still does not completely explain away the divergencies between Catholic and classical Protestant thought on the relationship between the human and the Christian. On the other hand liberal Protestantism is often more willing to see a great continuity between the human and the Christian and at times even an identity.[25]

Denial of a Distinctively Christian Content. A comparatively large number of Catholic authors in the last few years denied the existence of a specifically different material content in Christian morality.[26] There are two possible ways of attempting to justify this assertion. The first approach which from a theological perspective is based on creation asserts that the material content of Christian morality adds nothing to the material content of human morality understood in a metaphysical way. The second approach which from a theological perspective is based on an understanding of redemption and grace asserts that the human as we know it today is already influenced by grace so that Christians cannot claim a distinctive content to their ethics which cannot be found in the ethics of non-Christians or others existing in this world.

The approach based on creation has been followed by most of the authors. Interestingly, some theologians (e.g., Aubert, Compagnoni, Fuchs) claim that Thomas Aquinas supported such a position even though he did not formulate the question as it has been proposed in the last few years.[27] Aubert arrives at this conclusion on the basis of Aquinas' teaching on the virtues and on the New Law. In his treatise on the virtues Thomas integrated the human virtues into the Christian perspective. Charity is the form of the virtues so that charity thus becomes the efficient and the final cause ordering the human virtues to their ultimate end. But charity is expressed in and through the moral virtues which thus constitute the material cause of Christian ethics. From the viewpoint of material causality the human and the Christian are the same. Aubert also points out that Aquinas acknowledges that the law of Christ introduces man into a radical newness, but the Angelic Doctor explicitly states that the law of Christ does not of itself add any new moral prescriptions to the human.[28]

The proponents of this position do not deny a specifically distinct Christian ethics as such, but they do deny that there is a distinctive material content to Christian ethics. Thus such a position makes a distinction between the material and the formal element in Christian ethics or between the transcendent and the categorical aspects.

In explaining this position, the paper will follow in general the exposition of Joseph Fuchs who has written more articles on this subject than any other Catholic author although other positions will also be mentioned. According to Fuchs there is a twofold aspect in morality. There are the particular, categorical moral values such as justice, fidelity or goodness which are present in the moral act itself. In addition, and even more importantly, in the realization of particular moral values in individual actions the person attains and realizes himself as a person before the Absolute who is God. The realization of the self occurs in every specific act but we are often conscious of it only in a non-thematic and non-reflexive way, whereas the realization of a particular moral value in an action usually occurs with a thematic and reflexive consciousness. The self-realization of the person which occurs usually in a non-thematic and non-reflexive way in every moral act is the more important and determining element of the individual moral act.[29]

The believer, however, can thematize his relationship as a person before the Absolute as his relationship to Jesus Christ and the Father of salvation. Although the Christian is not always reflexively conscious of this in every act, nevertheless this relationship is present as the most profound aspect in his moral life. Fuchs refers to this as Christian intentionality, understood as the decision for Christ and the Father, which is present and orientating the life of the believer as the most important aspect of Christian morality.[30]

The categorical content of Christian morality, as distinguished from Christian intentionality or the transcendental aspect, is fundamentally and substantially human or a morality of humanity. The Christian teaching on creation establishes the existence of man among men in this world with the Creator God requiring that men should live and act in accord with their multiple relationships.[31] Human morality, which Fuchs prefers to describe as *recto ratio* and not as natural law because of certain connotations connected with the concept of natural law, is the medium in which the Christian transcendentality realizes itself. Authentic human morality demands that the individual person live in accord with his relationships with God and with his interpersonal relationships with others working and striving with them for the formation of the world and of humanity. Fuchs goes on to indicate that the teachings of Scripture, as well as theologians such as Thomas Aquinas, Suarez, and even manualists such as Vermeersch and Zalba maintain that Christian ethics does not add anything to the material content of human ethics.[32]

Fuchs and other defenders of this position realize that they must respond to the strongest arguments proposed in favor of a specifically distinct Christian ethical content—the anthropological argument and the argument derived from the moral teachings of the Scripture. Fuchs believes that those who argue for a new Christian action based

on the new Christian being wrongly see Christ as a teacher of morality rather than as a redeemer of fallen man and correlatively see in
the Church the duty to teach morality rather than to enunciate and
communicate salvation. The newness that Jesus brings is not a new
moral teaching but rather a new man, born in the spirit rather than a
man of the flesh in the Pauline terms. To the new Christian *esse* there
does correspond a Christian *agere.* This new Christian being calls the
Christian person in faith, charity and the following of Christ to manifest his new existence by living in a Christian manner the true human morality. The material content remains the demands of human
morality as such.[33]

What about the biblical teaching on love of God and man, especially the love of enemies, self-denial even unto death, the role of the
cross in the life of the Christian, care for those people who are in
need and contribute nothing to society? Francesco Compagnoni devotes one chapter of his book, which was originally a doctoral dissertation, to show that the Scriptures do not add any moral content to
human morality.[34]

In what sense is the command of charity in the New Testament
a new commandment? Aubert responds to this question by citing
Pope Leo XIII who in the encyclical *Sapientiae Christianae* maintains that Jesus called his commandment new not because mutual
love was not prescribed by the law of nature itself but because the
manner of loving was completely new and unheard of. The newness
in the New Testament commandment of love arises from its relationship to the fallen nature of man—the flesh in the Pauline sense. If
one understands humanity in the metaphysical sense and not in the
sense of fallen man, then there is no fundamental difference in the
command to love. The natural law itself entails the precept of love of
God and of other men as the expression of the specifically human
tendency, for as a spiritual being man has as his end to tend toward
God and love him and to love his images who are other persons.[35]

Fuchs raises the question about a distinctive Christian content
in the teaching of the Sermon on the Mount and in the law of the
cross. But he points out that the antitheses in the Sermon on the
Mount are between the new man and sinful man and not between the
new man and humanity as such. Human nature or *recta ratio* does
call for man to love God and love neighbor. For fallen man this exi-

gency of humanity requires renunciation, sacrifice and the cross so that such a man can free himself from the egoism which is not a part of humanity as such. The law of the cross for fallen man does not add a new material content beyond the human but rather shows how the essential demand of humanity is to be achieved by fallen man.[36]

Interpretation and Critique. Although these two positions come to a different conclusion about the material content of Christian ethics, they are in no sense diametrically opposed. Obviously, within the Catholic tradition those who have proposed a specifically different content to Christian morality also recognize that much of the content is the same as that of human morality. Most of Catholic ethics in the past has been based on the natural law. Contemporary official Church documents speak of Christian morality as being the truly or fully or perfectly human so that even what is different from the human must not be opposed to the human but rather is in continuity with it and ultimately the fulfillment of the human.

On the other hand those who deny any specific Christian content in morality do admit that grace and the supernatural are necessary for man (fallen man in this historical situation) to live in accord with human morality.[37] In addition, Aubert recognizes that the demands of charity lead to the importance and place of some human virtues such as humility whose importance purely rational reflection is not able to perceive: He goes on to point out that man has need of these virtues even in his natural state and not only because he is marked by sin and in need of salvation.[38]

Compagnoni affirms that the precepts of the New Law add nothing to the material content of human morality, but they do bring about a radicalization of the precepts of human morality. Although the content of the moral precepts remains the same, they become more clearly manifest and their implications are seen more readily. Above all since grace now permits their realization, they are able to develop everything that is contained in them even virtually, as is evident in the Christian understanding of the virtue of humility.[39]

Fuchs himself is willing to admit that there are human moral truths which are *per se* accessible to human intelligence but in fact are not known by some men. He draws the comparison with what Vatican Council I said about man's natural knowledge of God. Reason is able to achieve this knowledge, but man because of his fallen state often does not acquire such knowledge.[40] These authors thus acknowledge some limitations in reason's ability to arrive at the full understanding of human morality.

Although I deny there is a specifically different content to Christian ethics that is not available to all other human beings and ethics, I prefer to propose the reasoning in a different manner. There are, in my judgment, difficulties with the argument based on creation and the metaphysical concept of humanity implied in such reasoning. Such a metaphysical concept of humanity is truly an abstraction which does not correspond to any given historical state of human existence. As a matter of fact, human beings are existing in the one order of creation and redemption in which all are called to a saving and loving union with God. It will always be difficult if not impossible to say what belongs to the metaphysical state of man as such because one can never abstract that perfectly from the influence of grace and sin that are always a part of human existence as we know it.

The proponents of this position admit that historical man cannot live according to such moral precepts without the help of grace and that existing human beings cannot even know these moral teachings expeditiously, with certitude and without any mixture of error without grace, if we are to fully apply the analogy Fuchs drew between reason's ability to know God as the beginning and end of all things and the ability to know human morality. One is thus employing reason to propose the content of human morality and at the same time admitting that human beings in this world will experience great difficulty in arriving at a knowledge of human morality. Likewise, one could bring an argument against the position proposed by Fuchs analogous to the argument brought against a natural knowledge of the existence of God.

The way in which these theorists have dealt with the questions of Christian love, the Sermon on the Mount and the law of the cross indicates a weakness in the approach itself. They assert the abstract content of human morality itself as calling for love of God and of neighbor and working together for the good of society. This nucleus then becomes present in different historical situations. The historical situations referred to here are not just the changing cultural and historical relativities of human history but also involve the changes in the so-called history of salvation.[41]

The condition of fallen man will somewhat change the materiality of human ethics. Love of neighbor for fallen man will now involve renunciation, sacrifice and the cross. Because of egoism, sin and selfishness, love of neighbor will be experienced as the cross and a self-emptying. Fuchs asserts that the non-Christian or the atheist experiencing his own egoism is able to recognize that in this situation renunciation, sacrifice and the cross are able to be part of the realization of humanity.[42] It seems difficult to assert that human reason, considered in the abstract even though it is present in human beings in the midst of a sinful world, can understand that in this situation humanity calls for sacrifice, renunciation and the cross.

There is another very possible alternative. Human beings might come to the conclusion that such a world is not rational and does not seem to make any sense on these grounds alone. At least many human beings historically have come to that conclusion and not the one proposed by Fuchs and others. I have grave doubts that suffering, sacrifice and the cross are historically verifiable as rational. Such an approach does not seem to give enough importance to the reality of sin and what effect it has on man and reality. There is such a thing as the mystery of evil and the mystery of iniquity which is so strong that in the midst of it rationality does not shine through. In the midst of suffering and unrequited love one could very easily conclude to the irrationality of the whole human enterprise. I do not want to say that sin totally does away with some aspects of the rational, but I do think sin has more effect than the proponents of this position are willing to admit. This approach to the question seems too abstract, ahistorical and overly rational to be fully satisfying.

One further point can be made. Aubert maintains that the material cause of Christian morality is the same as human morality, but the final and formal causes are different. Fuchs writes of a specific Christian intentionality and Christian motivation but this is expressed in the medium of human morality. In the light of the Thomist reasoning explicitly employed by Aubert one can ask if the formal element should not have some effect on the material element. Is there not a reciprocal causality between them so that the form in some way does effect the matter? The thrust of my critical remarks is that the second approach does not seem able conclusively to prove the thesis that human morality understood in the metaphysical sense has the same content as Christian morality.

Another approach. My own approach to this question begins with the actual historical order in which we live and not with an abstract concept of the metaphysical notion of the human. The Christian knows only one historical order—man created, fallen and redeemed. The human beings that we know are under all these influences. Roman Catholic theology has consistently acknowledged the universal salvific will of God by which a loving Father calls all men to salvation. Redemption and saving grace are offered to all men and exist outside the pale of the Catholic and the Christian.[43] Theologians have developed various theories to explain precisely how the reality of God's saving gift occurs, but it is not necessary for us to mention these at the present time. One theory, for example, maintains that in moral choice man is ultimately confronted with the absolute and in this way the saving gift of God can come to him.[44]

By understanding the human in this historical sense of man existing as created, fallen and redeemed, the specifically Christian aspect of morality is going to be even less than that proposed by the second approach to the question. The human can also share in the intentionality and motivation corresponding to the redeeming gift of God's love even though these are not present in a thematic way or in an explicitly Christian manner. The specific aspect of Christian morality is the explicitly Christian way in which this is known and manifested. But what the Christian knows with an explicit Christian dimension is and can be known by all others. The difference lies in the fact that for the Christian his ethics is thematically and explicitly Christian. Earlier I stated my conclusion in this way. "Obviously a personal acknowledgement of Jesus as Lord affects at least the consciousness of the individual and his thematic reflection on his consciousness, but the Christian and the explicitly non-Christian can and do arrive at the same ethical conclusions and can and do share the same general ethical attitudes, dispositions and goals. Thus, explicit Christians do not have a monopoly on such proximate ethical attitudes, goals and dispositions as self-sacrificing love, freedom, hope, concern for the neighbor in need or even the realization that one finds his life only in losing it."[45]

Again, it should be pointed out that this position is not in total opposition with, and in some ways might even be reconciled with, the other two approaches to this question. For example, Dionigi Tettamanzi admits that if human ethics refers to the metaphysical concept of man as such, then Christian ethics does have a distinctive content; but if human ethics refers to man historically existing in the one given order, then the human and the Christian coincide.[46]

Joseph Fuchs has also insisted upon the fact that grace and salvation are offered to all men even those outside the pale of explicit Christianity. Fuchs' latest article on the question is entitled: "Is there a Non-Christian Morality?" Just as in the case of the question about Christian morality, his answer is both yes and no. Fuchs maintains that in the last analysis there is only one historical moral order and the ultimate meaning of the human is Christian.[47]

Norbert Rigali has pointed out that the above approach is true of "essential" ethics but not of existential ethics. Existential, personal or individual ethics has to be taken into account. The Christian as an individual belongs to the Christian community (the Church) and recognizes moral obligations existing within this particular framework. Such an example illustrates that individuals precisely because of their individuality will experience different moral calls and obligations.[48] Certainly one must accept the existence of such a personal and individual aspect of morality. I merely want to recall that the non-Christian too can perceive personal obligations of self-sacrificing love and service which are to be carried out in accord with his own individuality and circumstances.

Although this study has outlined three different approaches to the question of the specific content of Christian morality, it must always be recalled that there is general agreement within the Roman Catholic tradition that the human plays a large role in Christian morality. The practical differences between the second and third approach are not that great, and they result primarily from the different concept of the human. In the second opinion the human is understood in a metaphysical way as referring to humanity as such apart from the realities of the history of salvation, whereas in the third opinion the human is understood as that which is historically existing here and now in terms of human beings created, fallen and redeemed. When speaking of the content of Christian ethics being the same as human ethics, I have frequently used the terminology fully, truly or authentically human so that the sinful element does not enter in.

The moral theology of the manuals of theology also gave very great importance to the role of the human in Christian ethics. Even those who assert that there is a specifically different Christian content to ethics will also recognize and accept the fact that there is much content which the Christian shares with the human. As pointed out before, the teaching of the hierarchical magisterium on social matters was explained almost exclusively in terms of the natural law which is common to all mankind. In addition, those teachings which can be looked upon as most distinctively Catholic, such as the condemnation of contraception, sterilization, abortion, euthanasia, as well as the principle of the double effect, have all been based on natural law which is available to all mankind. Even the Catholic teaching on divorce has been proposed in the name of the natural law. Thus within the Roman Catholic tradition all would have to admit that a very large place in Christian morality has been granted to a human morality. Translated into other terms this means that Christian morality must always be open to and learn from the true insights of a human morality. Christian morality in no way can ignore the meaning of the human but must work together with all other sciences and human experiences in trying to discern what precisely is the human.

There is one final point which must be mentioned. The reasoning as developed in this section has talked in theory about the fact that truly human ethics and Christian ethics are the same with the Christian just adding the explicitly Christian understanding of ethical reality. However, in practice it must be admitted that Christians and all others fall far short of the fullness of the ethical ideal. Without in any way claiming superiority, the Christian emphasis must make explicit those aspects of the ethical teaching which can so easily be obscured and forgotten by Christians and non-Christians alike. Christian ethics must continually recall the reality of sin and the call to conversion on the part of all individuals and societies. Likewise the paschal mystery must be uppermost in the explicit understanding of ethics for one who is trying to follow Jesus. A proper understanding of the paschal mystery in the life of the Christian will show forth the need for the ethical realities of self-sacrificing love, suffering and hope in the Christian life.

One must also be careful not to understand the paschal mystery in a one-sided way. It is true that in Jesus the paschal mystery involves the triumph of life in the midst of death, of power in the midst of weakness, of joy in the midst of sorrow and of light in the midst of darkness. The Christian, however, already shares in the first fruits of redemption so that one already knows the joy, the happiness and the peace that come from the redemption itself.

I propose a transformationist interpretation of the paschal mystery and not merely a paradoxical or dialectical interpretation. Since we live between the two comings of Jesus, his life, his victory, and his love are already present but not yet fully. Sometimes God's love is made known in human love; God's joy in human joy; but at other times the paradoxical element predominates so that his power is made known in weakness and his joy in sorrow. The paradoxical motif cannot be the ultimate explanation of the paschal mystery, but a transformationist interpretation properly understands that there will be some paradoxical aspects as brought out especially in the Christian realities of suffering and hope. This in no way denies that the non-Christian can also come to a realization of these same aspects of the ethical life, but it is necessary for the Christian to emphasize them because both the Christian and the non-Christian often tend to forget these important but by no means only aspects of the ethical life.

III
A Distinctively Catholic Ethic?

Is Catholic ethics different from Christian and human ethics; and if so, what are the specifically different characteristics? An adequate response to this question must distinguish between Catholic ethics in practice as lived and proclaimed by the Church and reflective ethics which as a theologian discipline takes place in the Catholic tradition.

On the practical level of the ethics as taught by the Catholic Church one can point to certain specific teachings proposed by the hierarchical teaching office in the Church and at times denied by many other people in contemporary society. In discussing the question of a specifically Catholic ethics, G. B. Guzzetti proposes some of these ethical teachings as what specifies and distinguishes Catholic ethics from all others—the indissolubility of every true marriage, the purity of marriage against all onanism, the inviolability of any human life from direct attack, especially the condemnation of abortion and euthanasia.[49] One could add to this list other specific moral teachings that have been proposed by the hierarchical teaching office in the Catholic Church, but Guzzetti does mention those which are well known and in the popular mind represent what is specific and distinctive about Catholic ethics.

A further investigation of these distinctive moral teachings in the Roman Catholic Church reveals two other distinctive aspects of Catholic ethics. These teachings are proposed by the authoritative, hierarchical teaching office in the Church. They have their force, therefore, not only on the basis of ethical arguments but also because they are proposed authoritatively by the Church. In addition, the hierarchical magisterium proposed all these specific teachings as being based on the natural law. It is true that in the case of divorce references are also made to the scriptural teaching,[50] but the specific and distinctive teachings proposed in Catholic ethics are based on the natural law.

At the present time, however, these three aspects—the specific teachings themselves, the natural law basis and the authoritative teaching role of the Church are being questioned within Roman Catholicism. In terms of the specific teachings mentioned by Guzzetti and popularly understood as what specifies Catholic moral teachings, many Catholic theologians are expressing their disagreement with the official teaching of the Church. Responsible Roman Catholic theologians have called for changes in the teaching of the Church on artificial contraception, sterilization, divorce, abortion, euthanasia, the principle of the double effect with its prohibition of direct killing, and even in other matters of sexuality. In addition samplings of public opinion indicate that many individual Catholics disagree with the official teaching of the Church on these positions.[51] These specific teachings can no longer be regarded as what is distinctive about Catholic ethics.

The natural law invoked by the hierarchical teaching office in arriving at these conclusions has in theory always occasioned some question and uneasiness on the part of Catholics. On the one hand the natural law is said to be available to all men because all share human nature and human reason, but on the other hand on the basis of such a natural law the hierarchical teaching office in the Church has arrived at ethical conclusions which many people in our society do not accept.

The key to the understanding of this apparent dilemma lies in the ambiguous concept of natural law. Natural law in the broad sense of the term refers to the humanity and reason which all men share in common. Natural law in the more restricted sense of the term refers to a particular understanding of humanity based on nature as a principle of operation in every living thing including human beings. Man's nature thus determines how he should act. The official teaching office used the more restricted concept of natural law to arrive at its ethical conclusions. Such an understanding of natural law resulted in a moral methodology which was primarily deductive, somewhat ahistorical and tending toward the possibility of absolute certitude in moral matters. The problem was intensified by the fact that such a restricted notion of natural law was authoritatively imposed as the methodology to be followed in Catholic moral theology and thus did constitute a distinctive characteristic of Catholic ethics.[52]

Today Catholic theologians are rejecting this very restricted notion of natural law so that it no longer is the characteristic and distinctive aspect of Catholic ethics. In the place of a monolithic ethical theory there now exists a plurality of ethical methodologies within Roman Catholicism with a greater emphasis on induction, *a posteriori* argumentation, experience and a recognition of the lack of absolute certitude on specific moral issues. Thus what at one time, especially from the end of the nineteenth century, was distinctive about Roman Catholic ethical teaching no longer holds today.

The third distinctive aspect which characterized Catholic moral teaching in the recent past was the authoritative teaching of the hierarchical teaching office on these matters. The post *Humanae vitae* Church now realizes that the possibility of dissent from specific moral teachings was present even in the manualistic understanding of the role of the hierarchical teaching office although it was not popularly known by the vast majority of Roman Catholics.[53] It is important to understand the ultimate reason for the possibility of dissent so that the ramifications of such dissent on the future developments of ethics in the Catholic Church can be properly judged. The ultimate theo-

and in some way all members of the Church do participate in that teaching function. Unfortunate consequences have arisen from associating the teaching function with the juridical aspect of the Church and from restricting the teaching office to giving authoritative answers to particular problems. In this connection it is necessary to recognize the need for the personal responsibility of the individual but also the limitations and sinfulness that can affect every individual. Within the community of the Church the individual can find help and guidance in conscience formation. This is not the place to develop in detail how the Church should carry out its teaching function in the area of morality, but what has been said here and elsewhere sketches some possible approaches.[55]

This section has been content to prove that those aspects most often proposed as distinctive of Roman Catholic ethics—the specific teaching on certain questions, natural law methodology and the authoritative teaching of the hierarchical Church—are no longer the distinguishing characteristics of Catholic ethics. In fact, on the level of Catholic ethics as lived in the Catholic community I do not see any distinctive aspects. Perhaps a Catholic gives more weight to the teaching function of the Church, but the fact that dissent on specific moral teachings is a possibility means that this aspect is no longer absolutized.

From the perspective of moral theology or Christian ethics as a thematic and reflexive discipline, I believe there is one characteristic which has consistently been a part of the Roman Catholic theological tradition. This distinctive characteristic can best be described as an acceptance of mediation. Christian ethics like any theological or religious ethics ultimately sees man's ethical behavior in terms of his relation to God, and more specifically at times, to the will of God. Catholic ethics has generally seen God's will as mediated through other things; for example, the older concept of natural law as the participation of the eternal law in the rational creature is an excellent illustration of such mediation. The anthropological basis which has been a traditional starting point for Roman Catholic ethics likewise illustrates the reality of mediation. The generic emphasis on the human in Catholic moral theology illustrates the practical consequences of mediation.

In an analogous manner the role of the Church in moral matters logical reason for the possibility of dissent on specific moral teach ings comes from the impossibility of achieving absolute certitude i the light of the complex elements involved in any specific mora judgment or teaching. The older and restricted natural law approach characteristic of past Roman Catholic theology added weight to the argument that absolute certitude could be achieved on such issues.

It is no coincidence that the three elements which were distinctive characteristics of Catholic ethical teaching in the past are breaking down today and no longer true. Newer ethical methodologies only underline the reasons supporting the possibilities of dissent from authoritative Church teaching and at the same time argue against the specific teachings that have often been proposed by the hierarchical magisterium in the name of a restricted concept of natural law in the past. Even at the present time one can no longer say that any or all of these three characteristics are distinctive of Roman Catholic ethics.[54] In the future it will be even more evident that these three characteristics do not distinguish Roman Catholic ethics from other Christian ethics.

Such an understanding with its heavy ecclesiological overtones calls for a marked change in the way in which the Catholic Church understands and carries out its teaching function in the area of morality. At the present time the hierarchical Church still appears to cling to the older understanding. The American mentality and the experience of the Catholic Church in this country have tended to emphasize Catholic identity primarily in terms of the observance of the moral teachings which have been proposed by the Church and thought to be the distinctive sign of being Catholic. If one insists on seeing the unity of the Catholic Church in terms of specific moral teachings, that unity will quickly be shattered. This is not the place to find either the unity of the Catholic Church or the distinctive aspect of Roman Catholicism. This same warning applies to those who want the Church to give absolutely certain answers on specific social and political questions facing society. In all these matters I think tha the Church at times should teach on specific moral questions but i so doing cannot exclude the possibility that other members of th Church might come to different conclusions. From an ecclesiologica perspective it is necessary to recognize that the hierarchical magi terium is only one part of the total teaching function of the Chur again exemplifies mediation. The Church mediates the presence of the risen Lord to all mankind. The same basic concept of mediation can be found in the traditional Catholic emphasis on Scripture *and* tradition. Such a concept of mediation is opposed to a direct and immediate approach to God and the will of God. Even in the transcendental approaches in which there is no reflexively conscious knowledge of an object as such, the presence of God is still mediated through the consciousness of the subject. One can legitimately affirm that in general the Roman Catholic theological tradition in the area of morality has been characterized by its insistence on mediation.[56]

In conclusion, this paper has maintained that there is a Christian ethic in so far as Christians are called to act and Christian ethicists reflect on action in the light of their explicitly Christian understanding of moral data, but Christians and non-Christians can and do share the same general goals and intentions, attitudes and dispositions, as well as norms and concrete actions. The difference is in terms of the explicitly Christian aspect as such. Likewise there is a Catholic ethic in so far as Catholics act and Catholic theology reflects on action in the light of a Catholic self-understanding, but this results in no different moral data although more importance might be given to certain aspects such as the ecclesial element. From the theoretical viewpoint of moral theology as a theological discipline, an emphasis on mediation has characterized the Roman Catholic approach.

Notes

1. Pope John XXIII, *Pacem in terris, Acta Apostolicae Sedis* 55 (1963), 257. For a readily available English translation: *Pacem in terris*, ed. by William J. Gibbons (New York: Paulist Press, 1963).

2. Pastoral Constitution on the Church in the Modern World, nn. 19–21. The most available and reliable English translation of the documents of Vatican Council II is *The Documents of Vatican II*, ed. by Walter M. Abbott (New York: Guild Press, 1966).

3. For theoretical aspects of this dialogue, see Roger Garaudy and Quentin Lauer, *A Christian-Communist Dialogue* (Garden City, N.Y.: Doubleday, 1968). For practical aspects of this dialogue, see Peruvian Bishops' Commission for Social Action, *Between Honesty and Hope: Documents*

From and About the Church in Latin America (Maryknoll, N.Y.: Maryknoll Publications, 1970).

4. Coenraad van Ouwerkerk, "Secularism and Christian Ethics," *Concilium* 25 (1967), 97–139.

5. For an exposition of Rahner's thought, see William C. Shepherd, *Man's Condition: God and the World Process* (New York: Herder and Herder, 1969).

6. Gustavo Gutierrez, *A Theology of Liberation: History, Politics and Salvation* (Maryknoll, N.Y.: Orbis Books, 1973), p. 153.

7. *Ibid.,* pp. 153–60.

8. *Ibid.,* p. 256.

9. For explanations and commentaries on the papal social encyclicals see J. Y. Calvez and J. Perrin, *The Church and Social Justice* (Chicago: Henry Regnery Co., 1961); John F. Cronin, *Social Principles and Economic Life* (Milwaukee: Bruce Publishing Co., 1959); John F. Cronin, *The Social Teaching of Pope John XXIII* (Milwaukee: Bruce Publishing Co., 1963).

10. *Pacem in terris,* nn. 1–7.

11. Bernard Häring, *The Law of Christ,* trans. by Edwin G. Kaiser, 3 vols. (Westminster, Md.: Newman Press, 1961, 1963, 1966).

12. For a survey of recent developments in moral theology consult the "Notes on Moral Theology" which usually appear twice a year in *Theological Studies.*

13. For references to European questionnaires showing such divergencies from the official teaching of the hierarchical magisterium, see Franz Böckle, "La Morale Fondamentale," *Recherches de Science Religieuse* 59 (1971), 331, 332.

14. "Resolution on Southeast Asia," a statement issued by the Roman Catholic Bishops of the United States in November, 1971, is available from the Division of Justice and Peace, USCC, 1312 Mass. Ave., N.W., Washington, D.C. 20005.

15. Francesco Compagnoni, *La specificità della morale cristiana* (Bologna: Edizioni Dehoniane, 1972), pp. 27–61; Carroll Stulhmueller, "The Natural Law Question the Bible Never Asked," *Cross Currents* 19 (1969), 55–67.

16. James M. Gustafson, *Christ and the Moral Life* (New York: Harper and Row, 1968), p. 238; Donald Evans, "A Reasonable Scream of Protest," in *Peace, Power and Protest,* ed. by Donald Evans (Toronto: The Ryerson Press, 1967), p. 5.

17. Compagnoni, *La specificità della morale cristiana* pp. 17, 18.

18. For one Protestant author who denies the existence of a distinctively Christian content in ethics, see John Macquarrie, *Three Issues in Ethics* (New York: Harper and Row, 1970), pp. 87–91. Macquarrie as an Anglican theologian with a strong emphasis on philosophy is very much in the mainstream of the Roman Catholic tradition on this question. For a Protestant critique of his position, see Hideo Ohki, "A New Approach to Christian Ethics," *Lexington Theological Quarterly* 7 (1973), 11–26.

19. Paul Lehmann, *Ethics in a Christian Context* (New York and Evanston: Harper and Row, 1963), especially pp. 165–367.

20. Pope Paul VI, *Populorum progressio, Acta Apostolicae Sedis* 59 (1967), 265, n. 16. For an available English translation see *On the Development of Peoples,* commentary by Barbara Ward (New York: Paulist Press, 1967).

21. The following section, while bringing in other aspects, will basically follow the position proposed in an unsigned article "Esiste una morale 'cristiana'?" *La Civiltà Cattolica* 123, No. 3 (1972), 449– 55. As illustrations of the wide attention given to this problem in different countries and of the position affirming a distinctive content in Christian ethics, see René Coste, "Loi naturelle et loi évangelique," *Nouvelle Revue Théologique* 92 (1970), 76–89; J. Gründel, "Ethik ohne Normen? Zur Begründung und Struktur christlicher Ethik," in *Ethik ohne Normen?* ed. by Gründel-Van Oyen (Freiburg: Herder, 1970), pp. 11–88; Dionigi Tettamanzi, "Esiste un'etica cristiana?" *La Scuola Cattolica* 99 (1971), 163–93.

22. Paul Ramsey, *Basic Christian Ethics* (New York: Charles Scribner's Sons, 1950), pp. 1–152.

23. For an explanation of this model in contrast to other possible models, see H. Richard Niebuhr, *Christ and Culture* (New York: Harper Torchbooks, 1956). Paul Ramsey has explicitly adopted such a model of transformism in his later writings, especially *Nine Modern Moralists* (Englewood Cliffs, N.J.: Prentice-Hall, 1962).

24. Josef Fuchs, *Natural Law: A Theological Perspective* (New York: Sheed and Ward, 1965), pp. 85–122.

25. Lloyd J. Averill, *American Theology in the Liberal Tradition* (Philadelphia: Westminster Press, 1967).

26. The following list is illustrative and does not intend to be a complete bibliography on the subject. The authors cited do refer to other references to the question. Jean-Marie Aubert, "La spécificité de la morale chrétienne selon Saint Thomas." *Le Supplément* 23 (1970), 55–73; Franz Böckle, "Was ist das Proprium einer christlichen Ethik," *Zeitschrift für Evangelische Ethik* 11 (1967), 148–58; James F. Bresnahan, "Rahner's Christian Ethics," *America* 123 (1970), 351–4; Josef Fuchs, *Human Values and Christian Morality* (Dublin: Gill and Macmillan, 1970), esp. pp. 112–47; Fuchs, "Gibt es eine spezifisch christliche Moral?" *Stimmen der Zeit* 95 (1970), 99–112. The same article appears in Fuchs, *Esiste una morale cristiana?* (Rome: Herder, 1970), pp. 13–44; Fuchs, "Esiste una morale noncristiana?" *Rassegna di teologia* 14 (1973), 361–73. Richard A. McCormick, "Notes on Moral Theology," *Theological Studies* 32 (1971), 71–8; Bruno Schüller, "Typen ethischer Argumentation in der katholischen Moraltheologie," *Theologie und Philosophie* 45 (1970), 526–50; René Simon, "Spècificite de Pethique chretienne," *Le Supplément* 23 (1970), 74–104. For a more complete bibliography, see Compagnoni, *La specificità della morale cristiana,* pp. 172–82.

27. Aubert, *Le Supplément* 23 (1970), 55–73; Compagnoni, *La specificità della morale cristiana*, pp. 63–96, Fuchs, *Rassegna di teologia* 14 (1973), 306.

28. Aubert, *Le Supplément* 23 (1970), 64–70.

29. Fuchs, *Esiste una morale cristiana?* pp. 17, 18.

30. *Ibid.*, pp. 18, 19.

31. *Ibid.*, pp. 22, 23.

32. Fuchs, *Rassegna di teologia* 14 (1973), 364–7.

33. *Ibid.*, p. 369.

34. Compagnoni, *La specificità della morale cristiana*, pp. 27–61.

35. Aubert, *Le Supplément* 23 (1970), 67.

36. Fuchs, *Esiste una morale cristiana?* pp. 25–7.

37. Fuchs, *La Rassegna di teologia* 14 (1973), 373.

38. Aubert, *Le Supplément* 23 (1970), 64.

39. Compagnoni, *La specificità della morale cristiana*, p. 95.

40. Fuchs, *Rassegna di teologia* 14 (1973), 373.

41. Fuchs, *Esiste una morale cristiana?* p. 26.

42. *Ibid.*, pp. 26, 27.

43. Pastoral Constitution on the Church in the Modern World, n. 22.

44. Compagnoni (*La specificità della morale cristiana*, pp. 121, 122) criticizes Fuchs, with whom he is in fundamental agreement, for basing his argument on theological hypotheses when it is not necessary.

45. *Catholic Moral Theology in Dialogue* (Notre Dame: Fides Publishers, 1972), p. 20.

46. Tettamanzi, *La Scuola Cattolica* 99 (1971), 193.

47. Fuchs, *Rassegna di teologia* 14 (1973), 361–73.

48. Norbert J. Rigali, "On Christian Ethics," *Chicago Studies* 10 (1971), 227–47. For a similar emphasis see Richard Roach, "Christian and Human," *The Way* 13 (1973), 112–25.

49. G. B. Guzzetti, "C'e una moral cristiana?" *Seminarium* 11 (1971), 549.

50. For documentation of the comparatively late (nineteenth and twentieth centuries) emphasis on natural law as the basis for the prohibition of divorce, see John T. Noonan, Jr., "Indissolubility of Marriage and Natural Law," *The American Journal of Jurisprudence* 14 (1969), 79–88.

51. See footnote 13.

52. For a somewhat typical overview of the question of natural law with a bibliography, see Jean-Marie Aubert, "Pour une herméneutique du droit natural," *Recherches de Science Religieuse* 59 (1971), 449–92.

53. For a summary of much of the literature which appeared on the occasion of *Humanae vitae*, see Richard A. McCormick, "Notes on Moral Theology," *Theological Studies* 30 (1969), 645–68.

54. A more detailed development on these three points is found in my article, "Moral Theology: The Present State of the Discipline," *Theological Studies* 34 (1973), 446–67.

55. Daniel C. Maguire, "Moral Absolutes and the Magisterium," in *Absolutes in Moral Theology?* ed. by Charles E. Curran (Washington: Corpus Books, 1968), pp. 57–107; Maguire, "Moral Inquiry and Religious Assent," in *Contraception: Authority and Dissent,* ed. by Charles E. Curran (New York: Herder, 1969), pp. 127–48; Maguire, "Teaching, Authority and Authenticity," *Living Light* 6 (1969), 6–18. For helpful insights on the same question from a Protestant perspective, see James M. Gustafson, *The Church as Moral Decision Maker* (Philadelphia: Pilgrim Press, 1970).

56. As an illustration of this point, see Eric D'Arcy, " 'Worthy of Worship': A Catholic Contribution," in *Religion and Morality: A Collection of Essays,* ed. by Gene Outka and John P. Reeder, Jr. (Garden City, N.Y.: Doubleday, 1973), pp. 173–203.

Christian Ethics:
Distinctive and Specific?

James J. Walter

Down through the ages, Christian theologians have asked this question in order to reflect upon the identity of Christian ethics. Although the context in which this inquiry has taken place has varied, nevertheless, there is evidence that such an endeavor has taken place since the time of Saint Paul. The purpose of this paper, however, will not be to analyze the history of this problem. Much has been written on this topic within the last few years by both Catholic and Protestant theologians,[1] and thus it does not appear fruitful to add one more study alongside others. Rather, it seems to me that what is extremely necessary at this stage is for someone to further clarify a few of the important issues involved in the discussion. I would submit that in addition to some conceptual differences among authors there are a few linguistic stumbling blocks that are operative in the debate; and thus my purpose will be to help clarify these issues, while making reference to other authors who have written papers on the identity of Christian ethics. I trust that my own position in the debate will become clear as I proceed.

The title which I have given to this paper contains the key words and concepts which I would like to discuss and clarify. First of all, it is my contention that most authors seem to presume that the reader understands what is meant by the word "ethics." I believe that this presumption is not only unwarranted, but that such a presumption has in fact led to a number of misunderstandings in the whole debate. Thus, in the initial section of this paper, my purpose will be to discuss the meaning of "ethics" and to delineate what I consider to be the various levels or orders of ethical discourse relative to our topic. Secondly, I believe that it is necessary to describe what the function of the adjective "Christian" is in the whole context of this problem. In other words, I will be inquiring into the meaning which we attribute to "ethics" when we qualify that word by attaching the adjective "Christian" to it. It seems to me that it is only by answering the above two considerations that we can even begin to answer whether or not there is anything distinctive and/or specific to Christian ethics. Although several authors seem to use the words "distinctive" and "specific" interchangeably, I feel that this too has led to misunderstandings in the debate. My purpose, therefore, in the last section of my analysis will be to call for a distinction in the use of these words.

Ethics and the Levels of Ethical Discourse

As was stated above, I feel that many, but not all, of the differences of opinion among authors in this debate have stemmed from the way one defines "ethics" and delineates the various levels or orders of ethical discourse. A univocal definition of ethics would not obviously solve the problem of various ethical methodologies[2] and models[3] within Christian thought, but at the very least I believe that such an agreement on a basic definition could aid authors to specify more clearly where their positions actually rest within the debate. In other words, I believe that there would be greater explicit agreement among scholars on this issue if they were able to agree upon a given set of "ground rules" at the very beginning. Although I do believe that many authors' positions may be ultimately reconcilable, a point which I hope to adumbrate in my analysis below, nevertheless, I feel that each author's position lacks a certain clarity with regard to this issue of how one goes about discussing the meaning of ethics and the levels or orders of ethical discourse.

It seems to me that the first step that one must take in untangling the problems in this debate is to draw a clear distinction between the words "ethics" and "morals." Several authors have used these words interchangeably, and thus they may have confused the discussion to a certain extent. A few examples might be helpful to illustrate my point.

Over the last few years Charles E. Curran has strongly advocated that the Christian and the explicitly non-Christian can and do arrive at the same ethical conclusions. He believes that both the Christian and the explicitly non-Christian can and do share the same proximate motives, virtues, goals, attitudes and dispositions; and thus on this level, Christian "ethics" and authentically human ethics can be considered identical.[4] The major thrust of Curran's argument is that one cannot prove that there is any specificity to Christian "ethics" by reference to types of actions, goals, ideals or dispositions which only the Christian does or possesses. Rather, he defines the specificity of "Christian ethics" in terms of the Christian's explicit reference to Jesus Christ.[5]

In a similar fashion Josef Fuchs denies that there is any specificity to Christian "morality" on the level of conduct. He maintains that Christian conduct is "substantially identical with human conduct as such," but he does believe that what is specific to "Christian morality" is Christian intentionality.[6]

My purpose above was not obviously to give an in-depth study of either Curran's or Fuch's position on the specificity in Christian ethics/morality, but rather it was to indicate that the words "ethics" and "morality" or "morals" have been used almost synonymously in the discussion of this problem. Whereas Curran has used the word "ethics" in his discussion, Fuchs has employed the word "morality." This non-distinction between "ethics" and "morality" is not just limited to English publications, but it is also somewhat widespread in French articles on this topic. For example, Abbé Jean-Jacques Latour maintains that the appellation of Christian morality *(morale chrétienne)* is well founded because of an infusion of a "second sense" by faith into ethics *(l'éthique).*[7]

I tend to agree with James M. Gustafson that a clear distinction should be made between these words in order to differentiate the two tasks that are involved in Christian ethics and in ethics in general. He maintains that "ethics" should refer to "a task of careful reflection several steps removed from the actual conduct of men."[8] In other words, Gustafson believes that "ethics" is a theoretical task which reflects on the various ways in which moral action occurs, the assumptions and presuppositions of moral life. Thus, at the level of "ethics" one is seeking answers to the questions, "What fundamental principles are involved in determining an answer to the moral questions?"; "What is the nature of obligation?"; "What is the nature of the good?"[9] On the other hand, "morals" or "morality" should be used to refer to the actual conduct of men. "It is a practical task: giving directions to human behavior in the light of what one believes to be right, or good."[10] Therefore, at the level of "morals" one is seeking to give answers to the following questions: "What ought I do in this place of responsibility?"; "Is what I am interested in *really* good?"[11] Gustafson's position, then, is that there is a bifocal character to the study of Christian ethics. On the one hand, there is the task to clarify the fundamental principles of the Christian life (ethics), and on the other hand, there is the task to interpret how the Christian and the Christian community need to make moral judgments and to act in accordance with faith (morals).[12]

This distinction between "ethics" and "morals" might seem quite elementary, and indeed it is; but it seems to me that much confusion has been caused precisely because it has not been made. Why this is so cannot be clarified here, but it must wait until we have fleshed out a few more problems. Suffice it to say here that this distinction would not in any way distort the positions mentioned above (Curran, Fuchs and Latour), but rather it would seem to help clarify the issues at stake in the discussion for authors like Gustafson and others.[13]

Beyond this problem of distinguishing ethics from morals, I believe that there is another problem which arises in the discussion over the specificity of Christian ethics due to a lack of an essential distinction. It seems to me that in asking the question, "Is there anything that is distinctive and/or specific about Christian ethics?", one must clearly distinguish the ground of ethics, on the one hand, from the reality of principles and presuppositions (ethics) and moral conduct (morals), on the other hand. In other words, I am proposing that we are actually dealing with three distinguishable but interrelated levels in our discussion of this topic, namely, 1) the ground of ethics, 2) ethics as such; and 3) morals. None of these levels can be identified nor conflated with any of the other levels in ethical discourse.

The ground of ethics to which I have referred pertains to the reality of being wherein lie the very possibilities and potentialities for man as such to not only become a moral subject but also to formulate a given set of ethical principles and judgments to guide his moral conduct. The ground of ethics, thus, refers to the transcendental level of man's existence. Man as such is not a moral subject because he erects a set of ethical principles and judgments to guide his moral life, but rather he becomes a moral subject because he has the capacity at the very root (ground) of his being to act responsibly. In other words, inasmuch as man has the capacity and possibility to be free and conscious of self, he necessarily has a concomitant capacity and possibility to become responsible.

Ethics as such, or ethics as a theoretical task which is several steps removed form the actual conduct of man, refers to the reality of a set of principles and judgments which one *thematically* uses in determining his moral action. I emphasize the word "thematic" here because I wish to make it clear that it is at this level that an individual or group of individuals reflect upon experience in order to thematize it into a particular pattern or style of life. It is at this thematic or categorical level, where ethics as a science takes place, that man attempts to understand and judge his experience in the world. This understanding and judging of experience eventually leads to the formulation of various principles which then in turn become normative for deciding about moral actions.[14]

The distinction between the ground of ethics and ethics as such is extremely important in our analysis of whether or not there is anything distinctive and/or specific to Christian ethics. This is so because we are better able to situate the discussion of this topic. In other words, when one asks the question, "Is there anything distinctive and/or specific to Christian ethics?", is one inquiring about distinctiveness and/or specificity at the level of the ground of ethics or at the levels of ethics and morality? I would maintain that, although most authors writing on this topic focus their attention on the latter, viz., on the levels of ethics and morality, this focus is not always clear from their publications because the distinction is not made explicitly. Whereas this creates problems not only for the inexperienced reader but also for some who are avidly involved in the debate, the real problem seems to lie with the issue of whether one believes there is only one moral order or two. Those who maintain that there is only one possible moral order (an engraced ground of ethics) tend to agree that there is no distinctiveness and/or specificity to Christian ethics at the level of dispositions, intentions, actions, principles and norms. On the other hand, those who tend to maintain that there are two orders operative in man's moral life, one based upon creation and the other based upon redemption, tend to believe that there is indeed distinctiveness and/or specificity on the level of dispositions, intentions, etc.[15] A few examples of each of these positions might be helpful before I delineate my own position on this matter.

In an article dealing with the relationship between the natural law and the evangelical law, René Coste states that there is neither a contradiction nor a simple going beyond *(dépassement)* between these two laws. In the same section of his article, however, he makes a statement about evangelical charity belonging to a whole other essence than the demand to love in the natural law.[16] In another place Coste exclaims what an astronomic distance there is between the New Testament notion of *agape* and the natural law. This New Testament notion of *agape* he calls the ethic of the resurrection.[17] My intention here is not to quarrel with Coste's estimation of the natural law, but rather to indicate how he seems to implicitly work out his position based upon a dual order of morality. Although he does not state it explicitly, it seems that for him the natural law, which is founded upon creation, provides one order of morality, and the New Testament notion of *agape,* which is founded upon the cross and the resurrection of Jesus, provides another order of moral conduct.

On the other hand, there are a number of authors who maintain that there is only one possible moral order. However, not all of these authors seem to arrive at this conclusion from the same vantage point. Several authors have come to this conclusion after discussing the problem from a metaphysical stance;[18] and some of them have based their conclusion on the fact that, since there can only be one end of man, there is essentially only one moral order available to all men.[19] In the final analysis there is a common approach taken by all of these authors. In each case the assertions which are made are based upon a notion or doctrine of creation. In other words, they all maintain to one degree or another that creation (reason) provides the principal basis for ethics and morality. For example, John Macquarrie states quite plainly that, "I am trying to link Christian and non-Christian moral striving not on the ground of a doctrine of redemption but on the ground of a doctrine of creation."[20] They certainly do not believe that the coming of Jesus brings with it another type of morality; but rather they seem to all agree that Jesus makes explicit that which is already implicit in creation.

Charles Curran has proposed an alternative approach to this problem, and it differs somewhat from the approach taken by the group of authors who base their conclusion on a metaphysical stance. For him, the human as we know it today is already influenced by grace and redemption at the transcendental level of man's existence.[21] In other words, Curran believes that the Christian really only knows one historical order, and that order is the order of man created, fallen and redeemed.[22] In light of this presupposition, Curran maintains that all human being are constantly under these influences, whether they are aware of them or not.[23]

Of all the approaches mentioned above I tend to agree with Curran's the most. I personally reject any particular approach which is based upon a dual morality, whether this is representative of a Catholic natural law theory or a classic reformation two-realm theory. It seems to me that when one speaks of the ground of ethics one is necessarily speaking of a common ground of ethics for all mankind. With Curran, I believe that this one common ground of ethics is an engraced ground of ethics. In other words, I do not contend that there is an order of creation which refers to pure nature and an order which refers to redemption. As "The Pastoral Constitution on the Church in the Modern World" states, there is a co-penetration between human history and salvation history.[24] This co-penetration is not just limited to Christians, but it is also operative in the lives of explicitly non-Christians. What this implies is that God's grace is available and is given to all men, whether or not they accept this divine gift. The gift and acceptance or rejection of God's love occurs on the level of the ground of ethics, i.e., at the transcendental.[25] Since it seems to me that there is only one common ground of ethics, namely an engraced reality that situates all the possibilities of man to become moral and to develop ethics as such at the thematic level, there is no possibility of speaking of a distinctiveness and/or specificity to Christian ethics at this level. Because there is only one common ground of possibilities and potentialities available to man, there necessarily is only one end of man's ethical and moral activity.

That one end of man's ethical and moral activity is the acceptance and loving of the neighbor; the opposite being the rejection and turning away from the neighbor. Karl Rahner, it seems to me, has adequately shown this position to be true and acceptable by ontologically unifying the loving of one's neighbor with the loving of God.[26]

Before continuing any further let me state here that the position which I have taken does not in any way preclude the possibility of an existential ethic and/or morality. It is true that in most of the publications on this topic authors have neglected to address themselves to an existential ethic and/or morality—a fact which Norbert Rigali illustrated a few years ago.[27] What I have stated above only sustains the position that there is a common ground of ethics which forms the basis for pointing to and developing an essentialist ethic and an essentialist morality. In other words, my position is that all ethics and moralities, no matter how divergent they may seem or be, receive their possibility for formulation because of and from the ground of being which is common to all mankind. This affirmation does not imply that each ethic and/or morality is as truly human as the next, because we know that this is not the case. Some ethics and moralities respond to the true ground of man's being, and others do not.

Although my position does not preclude the formulation of an existential ethic and/or morality, I do not believe that such an ethic and/or morality can arise at the transcendental level of man's being. Rather, existential ethics and/or morality become operative at the thematic level where man attempts to understand, judge, and decide about his experience in his own particular situation.[28] While admitting that there is indeed such a thing as an existential ethics and/or morality, I must also affirm that the very possibility for such an ethics and/or morality to exist is rooted in the one common ground of all ethics.

Because there is only one ground of ethics, it seems to me that one must look elsewhere for establishing any distinctiveness and/or specificity to Christian ethics. It seems that it is at the thematic or categorical level, where man is able to objectify the contents of his experience, that one could point to a distinctiveness and/or specificity to Christian ethics. It is precisely at the thematic or categorical level of ethics as such that one thematizes his experience into a certain pattern or style of life. This thematization ultimately results in the development and formulation of principles and judgments to guide one's moral activity.

Now, there are obviously many ways in which one could thematize his experience in relation to reality. In an ethical frame work, for example, one could thematize his experience in terms of a utilitarian ethic, or in terms of a Kantian ethic, or in terms of a religious ethic as such. In each of these cases an individual or a group of individuals understands and judges the experiences of reality in a different way, and consequently relate themselves to reality differently. The utilitarian understands and judges reality in terms of things and actions as being means to further ends; the Kantian understands and judges reality in terms of duty; the religious man understands and judges reality in terms of God.[29] To be more precise, one could say that the intentionalities of each of these groups are different. By intentionality I mean the process by which man gives meaning to his experience. Intentionality cannot and should not be identified with specific intentions of an agent, but rather it is the capacity to have intentions. Obviously some intentions are more congruent or consonant with a particular intentionality than others, and so to a certain extent one should expect that any given intentionality should produce intentions which are representative of one's stance toward reality.

Function of the Adjective "Christian"

It is precisely this discussion of intentionality that leads us now into the next problem of our study, namely, what function does the word "Christian" play when we qualify "ethics" by this adjective?

As was stated above, ethics as such should refer to the theoretical task of ethical discourse and inquiry. By its very nature ethics can only refer to the thematic or categorical level, since it is only at this level that one can objectify the contents of experience. Ethics as such is an attempt to thematize the conscious experience of a group of individuals who share in common a given consciousness of reality. Because, as we established above, there are different ways in which groups of individuals relate themselves to reality, it follows necessarily that each ethic will answer the theoretical questions of ethics differently. For example, the question, "What is the good?", is answered by the utilitarian as the "end"; for the Kantian, it is answered by "duty"; and for the religous man, it is answered by "doing God's will." In each case, then, the consciousness of the group of individuals determines not only the answers to the theoretical questions of ethics but also the type of methodology which will be employed to express the conceptual understanding of experience.

What function, then, do "utilitarian," "Kantian," and "Christian" play when they are placed in front of the word "ethics." It seems to me that those adjectives specify certain horizons or thematizations of experience. Each one of them denotes a peculiar consciousness, a peculiar way of relating oneself to reality. This being the case, the Christian who adheres to a Christian ethic is saying that he has thematized his experience in terms of Jesus Christ, the Lord. Not all adjectives which are placed in front of the word "ethics" necessarily specify a certain horizon or thematization of experience. Adjectives such as "social" or "medical" do not qualify ethics in terms of consciousness but only delineate or specify a body of knowledge or subject area. The principles and judgments which are formulated in light of a given consciousness, e.g., Christian, would then be applied to the subject area in question.

Several authors have already referred to the fact that what is distinctive and/or specific to Christianity is its intentionality.[30] I would imagine that most, if not all, of these authors would also speak of a distinctive and/or specific Hindu, Buddhist, etc. intentionality.[31] All of these authors, however, have made it quite explicit that there is nothing else which could be classified distinctive and/or specific to Christian ethics. For example, as we recall, Curran has strongly advocated that Christians and explicitly non-Christians can and do share the same proximate dispositions, intentions, and goals; and they can and do arrive at the same ethical conclusions.[32] Several authors, such as Gustafson, have reacted against this position taken by Curran and others. Gustafson's reaction is based upon his contention that faith in Jesus often does make, can make, and ought to make some difference in the moral lives of Christians.[33] Because I believe that one of the major stumbling blocks to a possible reconciliation between Curran's and Gustafson's positions lies in a lack of an essential distinction between the words "distinctive" and "specific," let me now address myself to this problem.

Distinctiveness and Specificity in Christian Ethics

It is a fact that a lack of a distinction between these two words has been widespread throughout the entire debate concerning the distinctiveness and/or specificity to Christian ethics. As a matter of fact, I do not know of one author in the debate who has attempted to untangle the problem by making this distinction. A few examples might be helpful in illustrating my point that some confusion has been injected into this discussion because of a non-distinction between these two terms.

In one of his articles Josef Fuchs states, "This distinctive element of Christian morality is that specific Christian intentionality which transcends and fulfills all human moral values."[34] As we can see here Fuchs is saying that that which is *distinctive* of Christian morality is that which is *specific*. By using these words interchangeably I believe that Fuchs is not able to qualify his position to the degree that it could be qualified.

Michael Simpson asks in his article, "What are the distinctive features of the Christian ethic arising from the common religious awareness of Christians which is not shared, in general, by non-Christians?" He answers this question by enumerating two distinctive characteristics in Christian ethics:

> 1) the Christian awareness of death-resurrection, which was first realized historically in the person of Christ, 'the first-born from the dead', but which is taken to express the situation of every human person; 2) the love and self-giving of Christ expressed principally in his acceptance of suffering and death for all men.[35]

After delineating these two distinctive characteristics, Simpson mentions a few moral demands which could be derived from these characteristics, e.g., the Christian must be concerned about the value of the present life. It becomes quite clear later in Simpson's article that when he uses the word "distinctive" he in no way implies exclusivity. The moral demands which he has deduced from the distinctive characteristics of Christian ethics are also available to non-Christians, but "these demands may be said to constitute a distinctively Christian ethic"[36] because they are experienced consistently, and not in exceptional circumstances, by Christians who have a distinctive religious awareness. If Simpson believes, and I think that he does, that there is something peculiar only to Christian experience, then he should not use the word "distinctive" to express this reality, especially since he uses "distinctive" in reference to moral demands which are not exclusively maintained by Christians.

In my own position, I would distinguish the words "distinctive" and "specific" along the following lines. I would submit that the term "specific" should be restricted to something that is by nature reserved to a particular individual, situation, relation or system. In other words, "specific" should refer to something which is peculiar to a thing or a relation that is in question. Thus, when one speaks of a "specifically Christian element in ethics," one should mean something that is peculiar only to Christianity and cannot be found or discovered in other ethical systems. On the other hand, the word "distinctive" should be used in the context of something being set apart or distinguished from other things. In other words, "distinctive" connotes a certain style or pattern. Thus, when Christian ethics are said to be "distinctive," one should mean to imply that they have a certain quality or style or pattern; that they are set apart from ethics that are distinguished by another adjective, e.g., utilitarian or Kantian. In summary, I would maintain that whereas the term "specific" connotes exclusivity, the term "distinctive" only connotes a characteristic quality or set of relations which are typically associated with any given reality. For example, whereas it is specific to man that he has rational powers and self-consciousness, it is only distinctive of man that he can bear his offspring alive from the womb.

With this distinction in mind I would now like to discuss some of the aspects of Christian ethics which I believe are either specific to or distinctive of Christian ethics. In performing such a task as this, it must be made clear from the beginning that it would be extremely difficult, if not totally impossible, to discover either specificity or distinctiveness to Christian ethics based upon an empirical analysis of the moral conduct of Christians.[37] The principal reason for this is because of the difficulty to isolate, compare and contrast all of the factors which form part of the ethical beliefs of Christians and non-Christians in the past and in the contemporary world.

Is there anything which is specific to Christian ethics? I believe that an affirmative answer must be given to this question. The specific element in Christian ethics is the way in which the Christian perceives himself and the world; the way in which the Christian believer relates himself to others and the world. Stated in other words, it is the intentionality of the Christian which is specific or exclusive. Christian intentionality is specific because of its direct reference to Jesus Christ, the Lord. The consciousness of all explicitly non-Christians lacks this reference, and thus their explicit relation to others and the world is worked out in terms of other reference points, such as atheism, Buddhism, Hinduism, etc. The key element which underlies this specific intentionality and consciousness is the Christian faith.[38] The Christian faith, although it is only one factor in the total development of self-awareness, is or should be the pervasive context in which the Christian understands, judges and decides about reality. It is within the context of Christian faith that the Christian is opened to a vertical dimension in his ethical and moral activity.[39] This vertical dimension allows the Christian to perceive the eschatological vision of ethical and moral activity,[40] and thus the Christian does not identify the end of human existence in terms of the world as it exists now. In addition, Christian faith gives an insight and dimension to knowledge of what it means to be authentically human in the sense that the faith illuminates and interprets man to himself in the plan of his humanity and his history.[41] This illumination does not, in my opinion, result in various norms and principles which could be considered specific only to Christianity. Rather, the point which I am making is that faith in Jesus Christ provides the Christian the fullest interpretation of authentic humanity in a general sense through the writings of the Gospel. It does this by furnishing the Christian with a global view of human existence which is interpreted Christologically. Furthermore, many authors have pointed to the fact that faith in Jesus Christ functions on a socio-critical level.[42] In other words, faith in Jesus Christ contains an eschatological proviso which forces the Christian to stand back from his social context and interpret it from the context of the Kingdom of God which is breaking into human history.

My intention in the above section was certainly not to lay out in detail all of the implications of the Christian faith on the consciousness of the Christian believer. Moreover, it was not my intention to imply that each one of the perspectives which are derived from one's faith in Christ Jesus could only be sustained by a Christian believer. Rather, my purpose was to indicate that the Christian faith can, does and ought to relate the Christian to others and the world in a specific way. The reality of Jesus in the Christian's life becomes the context in which the Christian understands, judges and decides the meaning of human existence, and this way of understanding, judging and deciding is exclusive to a Christian consciousness. It is my contention that in the last analysis this is the key element which remains specific to Christian ethics. However, contrary to many authors I also believe that there are several other elements which may be considered specific to Christian ethics.

It seems to me that many ethical systems contain common components, presuppositions and principles. For example, all religious ethics somehow or other attempt to integrate the assumption that there is some kind of superior being into their ethical systems. In addition, both Kantian and Christian ethics adhere to the principle that a person should never be treated merely as a means. Although there may be different interpretations of these principles, nevertheless there is sufficient evidence that many ethical systems do explicitly utilize such common principles. The reason why it is even possible for a commonality to exist on this level is because of man's ability to reason and have consciousness of self. However, it is also a fact that not every ethical system employs nor arranges these presuppositions and principles in the same fashion. This is so because the use and arrangement of these elements are determined to a great extent by the consciousness of the members who adhere to a particular system. It seems to me that because of the specific Christian intentionality the use (choice), arrangement, and importance given to various assumptions, presuppositions, principles and judgments that make up the theoretical task of ethics as such might also be considered specific to Christian ethics. This should not be surprising, since a similar conclusion would also necessarily follow from the fact that there are specifically Buddhist and Hindu intentionalities.

Furthermore, I am also in agreement with Michael Simpson when he states that certain moral demands could be considered specifically Christian, not simply in the way they are psychologically formed but in the way the demands are justified.[43] Although I also agree with Gerard Hughes that most of the demands which the Christian experiences are not and cannot be directly justified by reference to the teaching and example of Jesus.[44] I do believe that they are justified, and indeed *ought* to be justified, by reference to the specifically Christian awareness. In making these statements I do not intend to imply that the process of justification of moral demands as such is specific to Christianity, since many ethical systems utilize this very same process; but rather my point is that the contents of a specifically Christian consciousness become the warrants for justifying moral demands in the Christian life.

Finally, I think that one could point to specifically Christian moral demands as such. As Norbert Rigali indicated a few years ago, there could be and probably are moral demands which arise out of an individual's consciousness and commitment to a particular community, e.g., Christian Church, that would not be experienced by any non-member. For example, Rigali mentioned the religious demand to receive the sacraments on a regular basis in the Christian community; a demand which obviously would be outside the experience of a non-Christian.[45] Whereas I do believe that Rigali's insights are very worthwhile and accurate, as I stated above I believe that these demands would be operative only at the level of existential ethics. In any case, it is not my purpose here to delineate all of the possible moral demands which might be considered specific to Christianity, but rather to make it clear that my position would accept such a possibility for developing specificity to Christian ethics at this level of ethical discourse.

Thus far I have delineated four aspects which I consider to be specific to Christian ethics. The aspect of intentionality is certainly the most important, since it seems that it is this element which forms the basis for establishing specificity to the other three elements. There may indeed be other elements which are specific to Christianity, but I leave this question open for further research in this area. It now remains for us, however, to see whether or not there is anything which is distinctive, i.e., characteristic of, but not exclusive to, Christian ethics.

I have stated above that I believe that the Christian's use (choice), arrangement and importance given to various assumptions, presuppositions, principles and judgments that make up the theoretical task of ethics as such might be considered as specific to Christian ethics. In making this particular statement, I did not mean to imply that the various assumptions, presuppositions, principles and judgments themselves are necessarily specific to Christian ethics. It seems to me that it is only to the extent that various assumptions and presuppositions can be directly derived from the Christian faith that they can be considered specific to Christianity. For example, whereas the assumption that there is a supreme being whose activity situates the context for man's moral activity cannot be considered to be specific to Christianity, the belief that this supreme being is incarnate in the person of Christ Jesus qualfies this assumption to such an extent that one could consider it as specific to Christianity. Furthermore, to the extent that a particular judgment about what one is to do in a situation could only arise within the context of a Christian's consciousness, it is to that extent that a particular judgment could be considered specific to Christianity. For example, whereas the judgment that one should praise God could not be considered specific to Christianity, the judgment to praise God in terms of the Eucharist would be considered as being specific to Christianity. It seems to me that for the most part there is very little which could be pointed to as being specific to Christian ethics at this level. This applies particularly to the question of principles, norms, rules and laws. Even though this is the case, in my opinion, it does not preclude the fact that one could consider these things as being distinctive to Christian ethics.

My own position on this matter is very close to Curran's in that I would contend that in principle the Christian and explicitly non-Christian can and do share the same general ethical attitudes, dispositions and goals.[46] In making this statement I do not mean to imply that the Christian and explicitly non-Christian both consistently and characteristically utilize the same attitudes, dispositions and goals. My conclusion, as is Curran's, is based upon an "in principle" argument, rather than upon a phenomenological investigation of moral experience.[47] Although I do not contend that the Christian alone possesses a certain number of ethical attitudes, dispositions and goals which would be inaccessible to explicitly non-Christians, it certainly seems to me that a disposition such as self-sacrificing love of neighbor could be considered distinctive of Christian ethics. This disposition would be distinctive of Christian ethics because it is most characteristic of the Christian ethics, and because it properly delineates the style or pattern of life of the Christian. In other words, the disciples of Jesus are known as such because of their distinctive style or pattern of life toward the neighbor. In addition, it seems to me that one could describe certain attitudes toward nascent life, war, suffering, etc., as being distinctive or characteristic of a Christian ethic.

It does not seem to me that my position substantially contravenes the one of Gustafson. As I stated above Gustafson believes that faith in Jesus Christ can, does, and ought to make a difference in the lives of members of the Christian community. For him the difference Jesus makes for the Christian is specified in terms of perspective, intentions and dispositions. As we recall, my own position contends that there is a perspective or horizon which is specific to Christian ethics. This perspective is the thematization of the contents of Christian consciousness. Derived from this specific perspective are distinctive intentions and dispositions which are consistent with the thematization of a Christian consciousness. In this regard, belief in Jesus Christ can, does, and ought to result in certain intentions and dispositions commensurate with the specific perspective of Christianity.

Does all of this mean that a Christian will behave or act differently than an explicitly non-Christian? Here we are questioning whether there is a difference on the level of morals or morality as such. Once again I would say that "in principle" there would be specificity to a Christian's moral activity only to the extent that a particular moral activity would be outside the consciousness of an explicitly non-Christian. For example, the decision to become a Christian minister or to receive the Christian sacraments would be specific to Christians. For the most part then, I would contend that Christians and non-Christians can and do arrive at the same conclusions about what must be done in a situation. However, I believe that there are or should be distinctive features to the Christian's moral decisions. Although there is always a pluralism within the Christian community about what should be done in a particular situation, this pluralism should not contain diametrically opposed views. Some views about moral action are not consonant with Gospel ideals and perspectives, and thus these views should be abandoned in favor of others more commensurate with the Gospel message. In any case, the distinctiveness of certain ways of acting would be derived from the specific acknowledgement of Jesus as Lord. It seems to me that it has been and still is the duty of Christian theologians to delineate and discuss those types of moral judgments and actions which are most consonant with, and therefore distinctive of, the Christian life.

Conclusion

It has been my purpose to lay bare and clarify some of the confusions which have been operative in the discussion over the distinctiveness and/or specificity in Christian ethics. It has been my contention that there is neither anything distinctive nor specific to Christian ethics at the level of ground of ethics. However, I have maintained that the primary focus of specificity to Christian ethics is at the level of intentionality. Ethics as a theoretical task becomes specifically qualified by the adjective "Christian" at this point, since this adjective specifies a certain given perspective, horizon or stance within the general realm of ethical inquiry or discourse. This specific perspective can, does, and ought to issue forth in distinctive intentions, dispositions, goals and ways of acting that are consonant with the Gospel message. In the final analysis, it will only be by further investigation and inquiry that students of Christian ethics will be able to articulate more clearly the identity of the Christian in the modern world in order that he might live more faithfully the Gospel of Jesus Christ.

Notes

1. For a somewhat complete bibliography, see Richard McCormick, "Notes on Moral Theology," *Theological Studies* XXXII (1971), 71–78; and XXXIV (1973), 58–61.
2. Here I am referring to the four most common methodologies which have been utilized in the history of Christian ethics: 1) Catholic natural law; 2) Classic reformation; 3) Liberal Protestant; and 4) Neo-orthodox.
3. Here I am referring to the three most common models which have

been utilized in Christian ethics: 1) Teleology; 2) Deontology; and 3) Relational-responsibility.

4. Charles E. Curran, "Dialogue with Humanism: Is There a Distinctively Christian Ethic?," *Catholic Moral Theology in Dialogue* (Notre Dame: Fides, 1972), 20–21.

5. *Ibid.*, 62.

6. Joseph Fuchs, "Humanist and the Christian Morality," *Human Values and Christian Morality* (Dublin: Gill and Macmillan, 1970), 123.

7. Abbé Jean-Jacques Latour, "Morale, métaphysique et religion," *Recherches et Débats* LV (1966), 125. A. Jousten also employs both of these terms without distinguishing their content. See A. Jousten, "Morale humaine ou morale chrétienne?" *La Foi et Le Temps* I (1968), 428.

8. James M. Gustafson, *Christian Ethics and the Community* (Philadelphia: Pilgrim Press, 1971), 85.

9. *Ibid.*

10. *Ibid.*

11. *Ibid.*

12. *Ibid.*

13. Gustafson has criticized Curran's position precisely on this topic in his response to Curran's paper delivered at the CTSA convention in June, 1974. See, the *CTSA Proceedings,* XXIX (June, 1974), 155–160.

14. Bernard Longeran has maintained that the movement from experience, through understanding and judgment, to decision occurs spontaneously in consciousness. For further implications of my brief remarks on this subject, I refer the reader to Longeran's notion of the different levels or operations of consciousness and intentionality. Bernard Longeran, *Method in Theology* (New York: Herder and Herder, 1972), 9–25.

15. This categorization must be somewhat flexible due to the fact that some authors have been more concerned with discussing a phenomenology of moral experience in light of a belief in Jesus Christ than with discussing the theoretical implications of the distinctiveness and/or specificity of Christian ethics. I would include James M. Gustafson and Stanley Hauerwas as being representative of this very position. See James M. Gustafson, *Christ and the Moral Life* (New York: Harper and Row, 1968) and Stanley Hauerwas, "The Self As Story: Religion and Morality From the Agent's Perspective," *The Journal of Religious Ethics* I (1973), 73–85.

16. Rene Coste, "Loi naturelle et loi évangelique," *Nouvelle Revue Theologique* XCII (1970), 84.

17. *Ibid.*, 85.

18. See, for example, Francis Jeanson, "Morale, métaphysique et religion," *Recherches et Débats* L V (1966), 118–125.

19. See, for example, J. M. Aubert, "La spécificité de la morale chrétienne selon Saint Thomas," *Le Supplement,* XXIII (1970), 71, and John Macquarrie, *Three Issues in Ethics* (London: SCM Press, 1970), 82–110.

20. Macquarrie, *op. cit.,* 88.

21. Charles E. Curran, "Is There A Catholic and/or Christian Ethic?", *CTSA Proceedings* XXIX (June 1974), 142–148.

22. *Ibid.*, 144. See also Curran's article "Dialogue with Humanism: Is There a Distinctively Christian Ethic?", *Catholic Moral Theology in Dialogue, op. cit.*, 1–23.

23. *Ibid.*

24. "The Pastoral Constitution on the Church in the Modern World," n. 40, *The Documents of Vatican II*, ed. Walter M. Abbott (New York: Guild Press, 1966).

25. See, Karl Rahner, "Atheism and Implicit Christianity," *Theology Digest, Supplement*, Vol. 16 (1968), 43–56.

26. Karl Rahner, "The Unity of Love of God and Love of Neighbor," *Theology Digest* XV (1967), 87–93.

27. Norbert Rigali, "On Christian Ethics," *Chicago Studies* X (1971), 227–247.

28. See, Karl Rahner, "On the Question of a Formal Existential Ethics," *Theological Investigations*, Vol. II (Baltimore: Helicon Press, 1964), 217–234.

29. It must be noted here that in each one of these instances there could be and generally is a diversity of opinion among those who maintain a particular stance when one reaches the level of the conceptual formulation of the stance. For example, all religious men who understand and judge their experience in terms of God do not all agree upon the concepts which are used to communicate their experience of God in the world and in their lives.

30. See, for example, Aubert, *art. cit.*, 71; René Simon, "Spécificité de l'éthique chrétienne," *Le Supplément* XXIII (1970), 82; Fuchs, *op. cit.*, 124; James Bresnahan, "Rahner's Christian Ethics," *America* CXXIII (1970), 353; and Curran, "Dialogue with Humanism," 20–21.

31. Michael Simpson is one author who has explicitly made this clear in his article. See, Michael Simpson, "A Christian Basis For Ethics?", *The Heythrop Journal* XV (July, 1974), 290.

32. Curran, "Dialogue with Humanism," 20.

33. Gustafson, *Christ and the Moral Life*, 240. For a similar position, see Hauerwas, *art. cit.*, 73–85.

34. Fuchs, *op. cit.*, 123.

35. Simpson, *art. cit.*, 290.

36. *Ibid.*, 292.

37. Several other authors have also indicated that an empirical study would be an almost impossible task. See, for example, Curran, "Is There A Catholic and/or Christian Ethic?", 10–11; Gustafson, *Christ and the Moral Life*, 238; Laurence Bright, "Humanist and Christian in Action," *Theology* LXXV (1972), 525; and Gerard J. Hughes, "A Christian Basis For Ethics," *Heythrop Journal* XIII (1972), 27.

38. Many other authors have explicitly pointed to intentionality or Christian faith as being the specific element in Christian ethics. See, for ex-

ample, Aubert, *art. cit.,* 71; Curran, "Dialogue with Humanism," 20; Fuchs, *art. cit.,* 123; and Macquarrie, *op. cit.,* 89.

39. See "Lacroix, Morale, métaphysique et religion," *Recherches et Débats* LV (1966), p. 115 and Jousten, *art. cit.,* 427.

40. See, Aubert, *art. cit.,* 72–73.

41. See, Simon, *art. cit.,* 82.

42. See, for example, Edward Schillebeeckx, *God the Future of Man,* Trans. N. D. Smith (London: Sheed & Ward, 1969), 143–166; Johannes B. Metz, *Theology of the World,* Trans. William Glen-Doepel (New York: Herder and Herder, 1971); and Simon, *art. cit.,* 90–95.

43. Simpson, *art. cit.,* 292.

44. Hughes, *art. cit.,* 29–31.

45. Rigali, *art. cit.,* 241–243.

46. See, Curran, "Dialogue with Humanism," 20.

47. Several other authors have based their conclusion upon this same "in principle" argument. See, for example, Hughes, *art. cit.,* 39; Simpson, *art. cit.,* 290 and 294; and Bresnahan, *art. cit.,* 353.

Christ and Morality

Norbert Rigali, S.J.

The question of whether there is a specifically Christian ethic has continued to exercise theologians in Europe and America in the wake of the Second Vatican Council. Although Richard McCormick could rightly note earlier in the discussion that, according to "nearly everyone" "human morality (natural law) and Christian morality are materially identical" but formally different,[1] the virtual consensus of the time was strangely disquieting and failed to lay the question to rest. The discussion has recently reached the point where a theologian suspects that the recent abundance of literature on the subject is indicative of theologians' inability to locate adequately the *real* problem.[2]

It is indeed unfortunate that the problem has been formulated for contemporary theology in the question, Is there a specifically Christian morality or ethics? The question means, as McCormick's comment illustrates: Is Christian morality (or ethics) one and the same thing as human morality (or ethics), or are they two things? The question first presupposes that "Christian morality" and "human morality" are *essences* and then asks whether or to what extent the one essence is identical with the other. In short, the question itself of whether there is a specifically Christian ethic is born of a certain metaphysical viewpoint, indeed the static understanding of the classical worldview.

The classical worldview, antedating both the dawn of historical consciousness and the development of philosophical personalism, yielded its connatural "faculty psychology," the so-called rational psychology of the scholastic manuals, and a corresponding essentialistic ethics, centred on individual acts (exterior actions and interior intentions). *Moralitas essentialis et substantialis* was located in the object or *finis operis* of the individual action, and *moralitas secundaria et accidentalis* was to be found in its circumstances and intention or *finis extrinsecus, finis operantis.*[3]

Generated out of the classical worldview, the question of whether there is a specifically Christian ethic has meant: Does the essence "Christian morality" contain individual actions and/or intentions that are not included in the essence "human morality"? Accordingly, Charles Curran expressed his negative answer to the question about a specifically Christian ethic by noting that "others who have never accepted or even heard of Christ Jesus are able to arrive not only at the same *ethical decisions about particular matters* but are also able to have for all practical purposes the same *general dispositions and attitudes* such as hope, freedom and love for others even to the point of sacrificing self."[4]

In a later presentation of this thesis, Curran distinguished his own approach to the question from that of some other contemporary theologians. The latter approach uses "an abstract concept of the metaphysical notion of the human" while his own approach understands the human in "the actual historical order in which we live," i.e., in the "historical sense of man existing as created, fallen and redeemed."[5] Nevertheless, he rightly notes that, inasmuch as both approaches lead to the same conclusion, there are no great "practical differences" between them.[6] Indeed, it makes little difference which approach is used. Both conceptions of the human being are standard conceptual tools of the classical worldview. Curran's approach is no more within historical consciousness than is the other.

Whereas the classical worldview inclines toward locating morality primarily, if not exclusively, within individual acts, a contemporary worldview sees it as lodged essentially in the totality of the person, i.e., in the unity that is a person's temporal existence. Morality, on this view, is basically in the continuing fundamental option "between a 'yes' and a 'no' in which man, as a spirit, unconditionally commits or refuses himself."[7] Morality is, quintessentially, the person *as person,* i.e., the person in his or her enduring choice "with respect to the totality of existence, its meaning and its direction."[8]

At its best, the classical worldview, with its traditional doctrine of the virtues, approximates the contemporary view of morality that locates it primarily in persons and only secondarily in individual acts. Nevertheless, all too frequently the virtues themselves have been understood as only so many different human capacities enabling a person to perform individual acts or to perform them more easily. In any case, introducing a restatement of the traditional doctrine of the virtues into the discussion of whether there is a specifically Christian ethic cannot transform the question itself into being anything other than a question of the classical worldview, which as such can never receive a satisfactory answer today.[9]

It is understandable, then, that the moralist who situates himself or herself within a horizon of historical consciousness responds, when confronted with the question of whether there is a specifically Christian morality, differing from human morality, with a trace of impatience: Of course, there is; in fact, there are many.[10]

The time has come, therefore, for moralists to reject decisively the question focused on specificity, which despite good intentions is at best a form of inverse parochialism. The question for theologians is the wide-open question: What should Christian ethics be today?

Our question here is an aspect of this wide-open question. What can and should Christ mean, if anything, in the moral lives of Christians? This question, of course, can be answered only by answering another, which it presupposes: Who and what is Jesus Christ? From this perspective it is evident that moral theology should be a science that seeks to relate Christology to the moral lives of Christians.[11]

Jesus Is "Our Law," "Our Norm Itself"

Jesus as Son of God, as God who is incarnated in him, is the Truth (Jn. 14:6), God's revelation of himself and the divine revelation of the human. Because of his hypostatic union or privileged relation to the Father, because of his being filled with God in a unique way—and not despite this uniqueness—he is God's absolute and definitive revelation of the human. As such, he is the absolute and definitive norm of the *humanum.* He is "our Law," "our Norm itself."[12]

What does it mean that Jesus Christ is our law or norm, the

norm of the *humanum?* Two clarifications are needed here: the *humanum* and law or norm.

As traditional theology distinguished between *actus hominis* and *actus humanus,* the *humanum* revealed in Jesus must, of course, be distinguished from a physical or ontic notion of the human being. The revealed *humanum* is *personal* reality.

The *humanum* in this personal or moral sense has always been the object of ethics. However, in the ethics of the classical, prepersonalist worldview there was undeniably a tendency to locate morality primarily in the *actus humanus,* as noted earlier, rather than in the *vita humana.* Accordingly, classical moral theology had no need to distinguish *vita humana* from *vita hominis* in the way in which it distinguished acts and to employ "*vita humana*" as a key concept. The *humanum* revealed in Jesus, nevertheless, must be recognized as the totality that it is, namely, a human life, a personal existence in the world.

It is not enough that the contemporary moralist be explicitly and constantly aware that the *humanum* or *morale* of an act is secondary to and derived from the primary *humanum* or *morale* that is personal existence in the world. Since personal existence is radically and essentially interpersonal and unrestrictedly open in principle to the other, the *humanum,* to be understood and located adequately, must be seen in its ultimate context, the entire human race throughout the past and into the future. In other words, the *humanum* of an act can be seen only in the *humanum* of a life, and the *humanum* of a life exists only in relation to the *humanum* that is the history-in-progress of the human race.

Traditionally in moral theology the term "law" connotes immediately and directly human acts. In accord with the classical worldview's inclination to see the *humanum* or *morale* primarily in acts is its tendency to understand law as primarily referred to *doing.* Even "natural law" has frequently seemed to be ultimately no more than a law of doing or not doing when its "primary precept" was formulated: *bonum est faciendum et prosequendum, et malum vitandum.*[13] On a contemporary view, however, natural law can be clearly seen as referring directly and primarily to human life, personal existence, as the unity and whole that it is rather than to human acts or even the sum-total of human acts. It can be seen as the law of being and becoming; for it is the "dynamically inviting possibility" confronting human freedom, "Become what thou art," in which "man's 'self' presents its demands to an 'ego' consciously realizing itself."[14]

That Jesus Christ is the law of morality means that his human life is the standard by which every human life is to be measured. The task of trying to understand Jesus as the norm of the *humanum*, then, is not directly one of collecting his teachings about what people should or should not do—for example, in the Sermon on the Mount. Nor is it directly the effort of trying to discern in Jesus' individual acts and reactions to situations models to be copied or repeated. The task is, rather, that of trying to discern the unity, the unified meaning, of the human life that is Jesus himself. In a word, that Jesus is the norm of the *humanum* means that his meaning, the meaning that he freely gave to his life (or, more precisely, that he freely chose to accept for his life), the meaning that he freely created out of his life—this is the norm of what every *vita humana* should mean.

There is, of course, a great philosophico-theological problem in saying of a particular human life that this is the absolute and definitive norm in history of what every human life should be and mean. Since historicity is of the essence of a human life, to designate a human life as the absolute, definitive norm of the *humanum* in history is to say, paradoxically, that this human life, this historical reality *as such,* transcends all historical reality as its norm or ideal.

We should emphasise the paradox here. It is not paradox but mystery that Christ *as divine* transcends history or that his grace is offered universally to all persons. It is a paradox, however, that Jesus Christ *as human,* as the particular *historical reality* that his human life is, transcends history as its norm. More sharply stated, the paradox is that Jesus Christ *precisely as historical, precisely as humanum,* transcends the *humanum* of history-in-progress; as *humanum,* he is "the concrete universal."

A human life can be reasonably believed to transcend history-in-progress as its absolute, definitive norm only if this life is believed to be a revelation of the *humanum* by the absolute God. On the other hand, to believe reasonably (in line with the Catholic tradition that faith is reasonable) that a particular human life is the absolute, definitive norm of the *humanum,* one must be able to perceive in this human life the quality of absoluteness.

The Absoluteness of Jesus' Life
Is the Absolute Norm of the Humanum

As Christology in recent years has increasingly emphasized Christology "from below," some theologians have sought to capture the absoluteness of the humanity of Christ in the phrase, "the man for others":

> Jesus is "the man for others," the one in whom Love has completely taken over, the one who is utterly open to, and united with, the Ground of his being. And this "life for others, through participation in the Being of God," is transcendence. . . . Because Christ was utterly and completely "the man for others," because he *was* love, he was "one with the Father," because "God is love."[15]

In Jesus "there is nothing of self to be seen, but solely the ultimate, unconditional love of God" which constitutes him absolutely as "the man for others and the man for God."[16] Jesus is he who emptied himself in the self-giving love of unconditional commitment to God that grounds his unqualified self-giving love for others (cf. Phil. 2:6–9).

That Jesus is perfectly human means, therefore, that "his social world is co-extensive with humanity, that he is open to all men and moreover open to all that is in man."[17] In this sense his life can be seen as "the coming of a new humanity, a new kind of community amongst men,"[18] a humanity that is not restricted by any human particularisms such as race, sex, nation, culture, age, historical period, social conditions or religion (cf. Gal. 3:27–28).

To believe reasonably that Jesus is the absolute norm of the *humanum* is to perceive in his historical existence (as presented in and carried by the tradition of the Christian community) the *humanum* that freely, totally and unconditionally locates itself within and embraces the *humanum* in its ultimate context of the entire human race, history-in-progress.

Since the *humanum* or *morale* is primarily the *vita humana*, not the *actus humanus*, contemporary ethics must understand itself, much more than did traditional moral theology, as a science directly concerned with *vita humana,* which can speak legitimately about the *actus humanus* only in this explicit context. The crisis in which moral theology finds itself today should be recognized as nothing less than a crisis of identity. Moral theology can no longer be defined as *"scientia theologica de actibus deliberatis, prout relationem dicunt ad finem ultimum supernaturalem"*[19] or as "that branch of Theology which states and explains the laws of human conduct in reference to man's supernatural destiny."[20] Moral theology must redefine itself today as a science of the Christian life and must transform itself into a new kind of science.

A moral theology that is not immediately or directly but only mediately and secondarily about deliberate acts or laws of human conduct must, of course, continue to discuss human acts. It will discover, however, that it has both more and less to say about them than the classical worldview had. More, in the sense that the meaning of an act will have to be seen explicitly in the context of a personal existence located within history. Less, in the sense that, once seen as only a single and limited expression of the *vita humana,* the *actus humanus* frequently requires considerably less attention than moralists are wont to give. The frequently excessive and even obsessive concern with acts of the classical worldview can be seen, for example, in the notion: "All directly voluntary sexual pleasure is mortally sinful outside of matrimony," "even if the pleasure be ever so brief and insignificant."[21] Such a doctrine can be conceived only through a total failure to recognize that *vita humana,* not *actus humanus,* is the primary locus of the *humanum* and, therefore, of morality.

Vita humana (*vita personalis, vita moralis*) is a reality far greater than acts or the sum-total of acts. *Vita humana* is, for example, a vocation, a profession, a marriage, the "causes" to which one commits oneself, the organizations to which one belongs, a "life-style" and much more. Above all, *vita humana* is a network of personal relationships and a developmental process involving many different stages of personal growth. All this and more is the *vita humana* that must be the focal point of the new moral theology of the future.

To believe that Jesus is the authentic, definitive *humanum* is to accept the difficult truth expressed by his life: "The man who loves his life loses it, while the man who hates his life in this world preserves it to life eternal" (Jn. 12:25). It is to accept the paradox that self-fulfillment is found in history in the sign of the Cross (cf. Gal. 6:14), that self-fulfillment is the agapeic life that empties itself even unto death on a cross in order to be completely for God and others.

The Cross, however, is not only the primary Christian symbol of life and love. It is also the fundamental Christian symbol of sin—the absurd, the mystery of evil, defying rational explanation. Because the Cross is a symbol of the absurd, human reason alone cannot unambiguously recognize its glory, the fulfillment that it represents (cf. 1 Cor. 1:23). Similarly, because the authentic *humanum* in history is under the sign of the Cross, unaided human reason cannot find its way unequivocally to the knowledge that the norm of the *morale* is a life of self-emptying love for others even unto the Cross. Only by reason of the historical contingency of a sin-filled, absurdity-affected world can love mean the Cross and the Cross mean love.

As a creation of God and ontologically good, the human person is a being capable of self-understanding. To the extent, however, that human nature is wounded by sin, the human person is subject to a sin-generated darkness of intellect—that is not simply a natural absence of perfect knowledge, but a darkness participating in absurdity—which impedes self-understanding and an understanding of the norm of self-fulfillment.

Moreover, that Jesus is the norm of the *humanum* is reasonable belief, not purely rational knowledge. If Jesus is this absolute, definitive norm, he is so only in virtue of God's free choice to reveal himself in the historical reality of Jesus. God's free act of self-communication in history, however, cannot be known through purely philosophical knowledge.

For these reasons, then, it is understandable that philosophical ethics or other traditions have often presented as the norm of the *humanum* something other than the life of self-emptying, unrestricted love for others. It is understandable also that the norm of the *humanum* that emerges from traditional moral theology cannot unequivocally be said to be this agapeic life under the sign of the Cross. Traditional moral theology, created within the classical worldview, constructed its morality basically upon the rational necessities that flowed from its understanding of natural law. Only with the dawn of an historical consciousness replacing the classical worldview can it seem even conceivable that ethics is ultimately based on an *historical* reality, the *humanum* that is Jesus. But can ethics ultimately be based on an historical reality?

As noted above, to believe reasonably that Jesus is the absolute norm of the *humanum* or *morale,* one must perceive the quality of absoluteness in his life. In other words, "Jesus is recognized as the Christ because he has brought to fulfillment the deepest moral aspirations of mankind."[22] Of course, interior grace is required for the assent of faith, but this assent is also in virtue of the "natural law" of the deepest moral aspirations of mankind, enabling one to perceive the absoluteness of Jesus' life.

Does this mean that Jesus, the life of Jesus, is ultimately measured by this "natural law"? The law of the deepest moral aspirations of humanity is the law of our concrete nature, not *natura pura,* in the order of salvation. It is the law of a nature intrinsically affected and transformed by the supernatural existential. What the natural law would be for a humanity in the state of *natura pura,* we are unable, in the final analysis, to know with precision and certitude; such a natural law is a remainder-concept, a *Restbegriff.* The law of our concrete nature, however, is a law of humanity's supernatural destiny, the destiny that it has through Christ, the Son of God. Our "natural law," the law of humanity's deepest moral aspirations in history, the law of our concrete, supernaturally affected nature, exists through Christ. He is the measure of our "natural law" (cf. Col. 1:15–17).

A Christian can accept Jesus as the absolute norm of the *humanum* or *morale* in his or her own life only by believing that Jesus is the norm for all, not only Christians. What characterizes Christianity with regard to morality is that the *morale* is the *humanum,* precisely this and nothing more. In the order of salvation, the human being, in virtue of his supernaturally affected nature, is the potentiality for personal self-transcendence in the absolute mystery of the personal God through self-emptying, self-giving love for others. The authentic *vita humana,* a possibility for all through the universal offer of divine grace, is the fulfillment of this potentiality. This is what the God who is incarnated in Jesus Christ means for morality.

Notes

1. Richard A. McCormick, "Notes on Moral Theology," *Theological Studies* 32 (1971), pp. 74–75.

2. Tadeusz Styczen, "Autonome und christliche Ethik als methodologisches Problem," *Theologie und Glaube* 66 (1976), pp. 211–19.

3. H. Noldin-A. Schmitt, *Summa theologiae moralis,* 27th edit. (Innsbruck, 1940), I:78; B. H. Merkelbach, *Summa theologiae moralis* (Bruges, 1956), I:139–40.

4. Charles E. Curran, "Is There a Distinctively Christian Social Ethic?" in *Metropolis: Christian Presence and Responsibility,* Philip D. Morris, ed. (Notre Dame, 1970), pp. 115–16. Emphasis added.

5. Charles E. Curran, "Is There a Catholic and/or Christian Ethic?" *Procedings of the Twenty-Ninth Annual Convention: The Catholic Theological Society of America* 29 (1974), pp. 144–45.

6. *Ibid.,* 146.

7. Louis Monden, *Sin, Liberty and Law* (New York, 1965), p. 31 (*Vernieuwd Geweten,* Bruges 1964).

8. *Ibid.*

9. I have in mind here especially James M. Gustafson, *Can Ethics Be Christian?* (Chicago/London, 1975).

10. Cf. Daniel C. Maguire, "Catholic Ethics with an American Accent," in *America in Theological Perspective,* Thomas M. McFadden, ed. (New York, 1976), pp. 14–15.

11. The index of a traditional moral theology manual, e.g., Noldin-Schmitt, need not list "Jesus," "Christ" or "Lord." Bernard Häring's *The Law of Christ* radically transforms the manualist tradition.

12. Bernard Häring, *The Law of Christ* (Westminister, 1961), I:234 (*Das Gesetz Christi,* Freiburg im Br., 1959).

13. Ia IIae, q. 94, a. 2.

14. L. Monden, *op. cit.,* p. 88.

15. John A. T. Robinson, *Honest to God* (Philadelphia, 1963), p. 76. A better expression of the absoluteness of Jesus would be "the person for others."

16. *Ibid.,* 74, 77.

17. Herbert McCabe, *What Is Ethics All About?* (Washington/Cleveland, 1969), p. 129.

18. *Ibid.*

19. F. Hurth and P. M. Abellan, *De principiis, de virtutibus et praeceptis* (Rome, 1948), I:7.

20. Henry Davis, *Moral and Pastoral Theology* (New York, 1938), I:1.

21. Heribert Jone, *Moral Theology,* trans. by Urban Adelman (Westminster, 1956), p. 146.

22. John Macquarrie, *Three Issues in Ethics* (New York-Evanston-London, 1970), p. 85.

Rethinking Natural Law

John Macquarrie

Let us explore the common ground between Christian and non-Christian morals; and in doing this, we shall at the same time be advancing our consideration of the question of whether, at least under present circumstances, the most appropriate way of doing Christian ethics is the way that sets out from the nature of man, rather than ways that begin from distinctively Christian concepts.

The next step after our discussion of contemporary human nature is to consider the notion of natural law. A recent important symposium, *Christian Ethics and Contemporary Philosophy,* ended with a thoughtful essay by the editor, the Bishop of Durham, on the theme: "Toward a Rehabilitation of Natural Law."[1] Although my own approach will differ from the Bishop's, I agree with him about the need for a rehabilitation of natural law, or, at least, for the recovery of what was of abiding value in the notion of such a law. Indeed, I believe that a viable account of natural law could make a vital contribution toward solving three major problems—the linking of Christian and non-Christian morals, the shape of a contemporary Christian ethic, and the relation between faith and morals.

But natural law—like the corresponding natural theology—is in bad repute nowadays. For a long time it has been under fire from many Protestant moralists, who prefer a christocentric approach. More recently, even some Roman Catholic moral theologians have begun to doubt whether in their tradition too much stress has been laid on natural law and too little on the New Testament. Much of the criticism of natural law has been justified. Any attempt to reformulate it in a better way will be neither an easy nor a popular undertaking. But I believe that such an attempt is urgently required.

A good starting point for our discussion is the assertion, often heard nowadays among theologians who are interested in the relation of Christianity to the secular world, that to be a Christian is simply to be a man. Presumably the expression is an echo of Bonhoeffer: "To be a Christian does not mean to be religious in a particular way, to cultivate some particular form of asceticism (as a sinner, a penitent or a saint) but to be a man."[2] "To be a Christian is to be a man"—what does this mean? Certainly, this statement when made without qualification can be misleading, and it often is. It can be understood as diluting Christianity to the point where it loses all identity; and it can also be understood in the objectionable sense of "annexing" all men to Christianity. Yet, although it can be misunderstood and oversimplified, the statement is, I believe, true in a fundamental way. So far as Christianity offers fulfillment or salvation, it offers a full humanity—or, at least, a fuller humanity.

An illustration of something like this point of view is to be found in the work of Paul Lehmann. In his view of Christian ethics, the policies of the believer should be determined by "what God is doing in the world."[3] If we ask, "Well, what is God supposed to be doing in the world?" Lehmann repeatedly gives this answer: "Making and keeping human life human!" Obviously, this expression is not intended to be a mere tautology, and therefore we must assume that the word "human" is being used in a different (though related) sense on each of its two occurrences. It is in fact fairly clear that God is said to be making and keeping human life "truly human" or "authentically human" or "fully human"; and that there is therefore implied in this assertion a criterion by which a truly human or fully human life may be recognized.

Lehmann does indeed tell us what his standard of such a true humanity is—it is the "mature manhood" of the New Testament, to be tested by being set against the "measure of the stature of the fullness of Christ."[4] The "fullness of Christ" therefore is, for Lehmann, the criterion of the fullness of humanity, and so—although at first sight his idea that the business of Christian morals is to join in the work of making human life authentically human might seem to provide a liberal formula for relating the Christian ethic to general moral principles—he offers a strictly christocentric definition of authentic humanity. Furthermore, he has very few good things to say about secular moral philosophy.

However, I do not think that one must take up a christocentric position. Even if the Christian ethicist holds (as presumably he does) that authentic humanity is to be judged by the standard of Jesus Christ, there is a kind of reciprocity involved in this assertion, so that one might also say that Jesus is recognized as the Christ because he has brought to fulfillment the deepest moral aspirations of mankind. There is a hermeneutic circle here: Christ interprets for the Christian the meaning of authentic humanity or mature manhood, but he is acknowledged as the Christ or the paradigm of humanity because men have interpreted him as such in the light of an idea of authentic humanity that they already bring to him and that they have derived from their own participation in human existence. No doubt the Christian finds that his idea of authentic humanity is enlarged, corrected, and perhaps even revolutionized by the concrete humanity of Christ, yet unless he had some such idea, it is hard to see how Christ could ever become Christ for him.

At this point we may profitably turn to some of the current trends in christology. Among all theological schools there is widespread agreement in placing a new emphasis on the humanity of Christ. The attempt is made to think through from his humanity to his deity, thus following a route opposite to the traditional one, which speculated on how the divine Logos became flesh.

Two examples will provide an illustration of what we have in mind. In the background of them is an understanding of man as a being-on-his-way. Thus Karl Rahner has argued that, from one point of view, christology can be considered as a kind of transcendent anthropology. Christhood is seen as the fulfillment of humanity, the manifestation of what a true humanity ought to be. "Only someone who forgets that the essence of man . . . is to be unbounded . . . can suppose that it is impossible for there to be a man who, precisely by being man in the fullest sense (which we never attain), is God's existence into the world."[5] Our second example is the christological study which David Jenkins undertook in his Bampton Lectures.[6] He begins by inquiring about the meaning of human personhood, and he goes on to interpret Christ as the "glory of man," a phrase suggesting a humanity brought to such a level that it becomes transparent to deity. Of course, neither Rahner nor Jenkins intends to reduce christology to anthropology. Jenkins explicitly says: "The reduction of theology to anthropology was the prelude to reducing anthropology to absurdity."[7] But both of these theologians do believe that a contemporary christology may well take its departure from what we know of the concerns and aspirations of men and show how these reach a fulfillment in Christ; and if human existence has in it the transcendence and mystery which we have seen reason to believe it has, then such a procedure will not fail to do justice to the transcendent dimension of christology. Even the "death of God" theologians recognized in Christ a kind of ultimacy which, if fully analyzed, would go beyond any "merely" anthropological view.

To put the matter in another way, Christ does not contradict but he fulfills our humanity; or, better expressed, he both contradicts it and fulfills it—he contradicts our actual condition but fulfills what we have already recognized deep within us as true human personhood.

These christological considerations are obviously of the highest relevance to our task of trying to relate Christian ethics to the moral aspirations of people who are not Christians. One can agree with Paul Lehmann that the moral criterion for the Christian is Jesus Christ; but if Jesus is recognized by Christians as the Christ because they acknowledge him, in Rahner's phrase, as "man in the fullest sense" or, in Jenkins' way of putting it, as the "glory of man," then the distinctively Christian criterion coincides with the criterion which, even if only implicitly, is already guiding the deepest moral aspirations of all men—the idea, however obscure, of an authentic or full humanity. In traditional theological language, this implicit image toward which man tends in transcending every given state of himself is the *imago Dei.*

In what sense, however, can the Christian believe that Christ does in fact fulfill the potentialities of man, so that his christhood can be considered as a kind of self-transcending humanity which is also the very image of God?[8] What kind of "fullness" or "perfection" can be attributed to him, so that he may be taken as the criterion of "mature manhood"? Of course, it must frankly be acknowledged that there are some humanists and others who find Christ much less than a paradigm for mankind. Yet even today it is remarkable how many non-Christians join with believers in acknowledging the stature of Christ. The usual complaint against Christians is not that they take Christ as the measure of human existence, but that they fail so miserably to do so! But why does the Christian make the claim he does for Christ, in his humanity?

It is quite obvious that Christ was not perfect in the sense of fulfilling all the potentialities of humanity—indeed, the very notion of this kind of perfection would seem to be self-contradictory, for no finite person could realize in himself within a limited life-span all the possibilities of human life. As far as we know, Christ was not a great painter or a great husband or a great philosopher or statesman. One of the most human of all activities is decision. Everyone, in the limited time at his disposal, has to make choices, to take up one vocation rather than another, to marry or to remain single, and so on. To decide (Latin: *de-cidere,* to cut away) is precisely a cutting away of some possibilities for the sake of the one that is chosen. Decision is to be understood as much in terms of what is cut away as in terms of what is chosen. In a finite existence, self-fulfillment is inseparable from self-denial.

Perhaps when we talk of the "fullness" of Christ, we have to look for it in this very matter of decision, so that the fullness is, paradoxically, also a self-emptying, a renunciation of other possibilities for the sake of that which has the greatest claim. We recall the parable of the merchant "who, on finding one pearl of great value, went and sold all that he had and bought it."⁹ Can we say that Christ's fullness or perfection is attributed to him because he gave up all other possibilities for the sake of the most distinctively human possibility of all, and the one that has most claim upon all men, namely, self-giving love? And can we also say that because this love is the most creative thing in human life (for it brings men to freedom and personhood), then Christ manifests the "glory of man" by becoming transparent to the ultimate creative self-giving source of all, to God? And if indeed Christ is understood as the revelation of God, then this surely strengthens the argument for a basic affinity between Christian and non-Christian morals, for what is revealed or made clear in Christ is also implicit in the whole creation. In saying this, I am not "annexing" the whole creation to Christ but rather claiming that what is already present in the whole creation is gathered up in Christ. In other words, I am trying to link Christian and non-Christian moral striving not on the ground of a doctrine of redemption but on the ground of a doctrine of creation.

Christianity, I wish to assert, is not a separate moral system, and its goals and values are not fundamentally different from those that all moral striving has in view. Yet it cannot be denied that there are some ways in which the Christian ethic differs from non-Christian ethics. It seems to me that the differences have to do with the different ways in which the several groups or traditions perceive the goals that are implicit in all moral striving, and the means to these goals; or with the different ways in which they understand and engage in the moral obligations laid upon all; or with the different degrees of explicitness to which the idea of an authentic humanity has emerged in the several traditions.

Of course, there are often differences of prescription between Christian and non-Christian morals. For instance, Christianity prescribes monogamy, while some other traditions do not. But the question of judging between these prescriptions would be settled by still deeper moral convictions shared by the two or more traditions, namely, by asking which prescription best protects and enhances the true humanity of the persons concerned. A distinctive ethical tradition may help its adherents to perceive some aspects of the general moral drive with a special clarity, though equally it may dull their perception of other aspects. For instance, it could be argued that in developing its marriage institutions, the Christian tradition has been more perceptive of what makes for a true humanity than has the Islamic tradition; but one could claim on the other side that Islam has shown itself more perceptive than Christianity in fostering good racial attitudes that put human dignity before color or ethnic background. But fundamental to both traditions is respect for the human person and the desire to enhance human well-being, and this is the implied standard in any comparison of their actual prescriptions and institutions.

We are saying then that what is distinctive in the Christian ethic is not its ultimate goals or its fundamental principles, for these are shared with all serious-minded people in whatever tradition they stand. The distinctive element is the special context within which the moral life is perceived. This special context includes the normative place assigned to Jesus Christ and his teaching—not, indeed, as a paradigm for external imitation, but rather as the criterion and inspiration for a style of life. The context further includes the moral teaching of the Bible, and the ways in which this has been developed and interpreted by the great Christian moralists. There are also the practices of prayer and worship, which are formative for the community and its members. And, not least, there are the many ways in which the moral life is influenced (and, as I hope to show, supported) by Christian faith and hope.

Can we now try to spell out more definitely the nature of that common core which, as I have claimed, underlies and relates all the several moral traditions of mankind? Here we must return to the theme to which a brief allusion was made earlier—to natural law. I said that this proposal would not be very popular in some quarters, and yet, when we inquire why some Christian ethicists object so strongly to the idea of natural law, we find that they give very strange reasons. They seem to be afraid that to allow any weight to natural law would somehow infringe on the uniqueness of the Christian ethic. They seem to be afflicted with an anxiety that Christianity must somehow be distinct and perhaps even have some kind of monopoly of moral wisdom.

For instance, Paul Ramsey in one of his early books asked the question: "By what is Christian ethics to be distinguished from generally valid natural morality, if some theory of natural law becomes an authentic part and, to any degree, the primary foundation of Christian morality?"[10] This question is best answered by a counterquestion: Why should we really want to distinguish Christian ethics from generally valid natural morality? I see nothing threatening in the possibility that the foundations of Christian morality may be the same as the foundations of the moralities associated with other faiths or with nonreligious beliefs. On the contrary, the more common ground Christians can find between their own ethical tradition and what Ramsey calls "generally valid natural morality," the better pleased they ought to be. For this means that there are a great many people who do not profess themselves Christians but who are nevertheless allied with Christians in their moral strivings and ideals. With them the Christian can cooperate with a good conscience—and not just as a tactical matter in some particular situation but because at bottom they share the same moral convictions.

Although Paul Lehmann identifies the end of the Christian with a true or mature humanity, he too attacks the notion of natural law and criticizes the idea of a philosophical ethic.[11] However, he does not enter into details of his objections to natural law, promising to do this in a future book. For the present, therefore, it is impossible to engage in a discussion with him on this matter.

A further objection made to the doctrine of natural law is that it does not take sin with sufficient seriousness. It assumes an innate tendency toward the good, failing to recognize the fallen condition of our human nature. I certainly have no wish to deny the fact of sin, and the question will be fully discussed later.[12] But I do not think of sin as having utterly destroyed the *imago Dei* or as having totally extinguished the drive toward authentic humanity. There is in man original righteousness as well as original sin, a tendency to fulfillment which is often impaired but never quite abolished; for if it were, the very consciousness of sin would be impossible.

Thus, although the idea of natural law is an unpopular one among many writers on Christian ethics today, their objections do not seem to be persuasive. Natural law, in some form, offers good hope of establishing a bridge between Christian ethics and general ethics. Indeed, I shall go further and claim that natural law is foundational to morality. It is the inner drive toward authentic personhood and is presupposed in all particular ethical traditions, including the Christian one.

What is natural law? The expression is ambiguous, and misleading in many ways. Nowadays it might suggest to many people the uniformities of natural phenomena, though in this sense it is more customary to talk about "laws of nature." It is very important to make plain that natural law, as an ethical concept, is quite distinct from any scientific law of nature. It is true that some moral philosophers, especially those belonging to evolutionary and naturalistic schools of thought, try to derive moral laws from biological laws. It has sometimes been argued that in the course of evolution cooperation has proved more successful than competition, and it is inferred that one should therefore be altruistic.[13] But this rests on a confusion between the idea of law as uniformity and law as a norm of conduct which can be accepted and obeyed by a responsible agent. To put the matter in another way, the confusion is between what *is* the case and what *ought to be* the case. One cannot proceed from statements of fact to value judgments, unless indeed one has already smuggled a value-judgment into the alleged statement of fact, as when one says that cooperation is "more successful" than competition. Theodosius Dobzhansky seems to be correct in saying that what can be established biologically is not the content of an ethic but simply "the capacity to ethicize."[14]

We must therefore turn away from biological conceptions of natural law to the strictly ethical sense of the expression. The expression "natural law" refers to a norm of responsible conduct, and suggests a kind of fundamental guideline or criterion that comes before all rules or particular formulations of law. It will be useful to pass in review some of the classic historical statements concerning this idea.

Like natural theology, natural law has its roots in the Greek rather than in the Hebrew contribution to Christian and Western reflection. Perhaps the first trace of the doctrine is to be found in a somewhat obscure saying of Anaximander in which he talks of things "paying the penalty" and "making atonement to each other" for their injustice. Commenting on this saying, Werner Jaeger remarks: "Here is no sober rehearsal of the regular sequence of cause and effect in the outer world, but a world-norm that demands complete allegiance, for it is nothing less than divine justice itself."[15] Incidentally, this comment further clarifies the distinction between "law of nature" in the scientific sense and "natural law" in the ethical sense.

Another early Greek philosopher, Heraclitus, was much more explicit on the subject of a natural law. He tells us that "all human laws are nourished by the one divine law; for this holds sway as far as it will, and suffices for all and prevails in everything." Jaeger's comments[16] are again very illuminating. He points out that Heraclitus seems to have been the first to introduce explicitly the notion of law into philosophical discourse, and, in doing so, he identified "the one divine law" with the *logos,* the primordial word or reason in accordance with which everything occurs. "This theological aspect," claims Jaeger, "makes very clear how profoundly the law of Heraclitus differs from what we mean when we speak of a 'law of nature.' A 'law of nature' is merely a general descriptive formula for referring to some specific complex of observed facts, while Heraclitus' divine law is something genuinely normative. It is the highest norm of the cosmic process, and the thing which gives that process its significance and worth." Jaeger has some further interesting remarks on the reciprocal kind of interpretation done by the Greeks, who used social and human models such as law (*nomos*) to elucidate the cosmos and then in turn sought to throw light on social structures from the order of the cosmos. Such interpretation is not, of course, "merely circular," but can provide some useful reciprocal illumination.

Moving on to Aristotle, we read: "Law is either special [*idios*] or general [*koinos*]. By 'special law' I mean that written law which regulates the life of a particular community; by 'general law,' all those unwritten principles which are supposed to be acknowledged everywhere."[17]

Some of Cicero's remarks on natural law are worth quoting. He provides a more detailed statement than does Aristotle, and especially interesting from our point of view is his theological interpretation of natural law, viewed within the context of Stoic philosophy. He writes: "There is indeed a true law, right reason, agreeing with nature, diffused among all men, unchanging, everlasting. ... It is not allowed to alter this law or to derogate from it, nor can it be repealed. We cannot be released from this law, either by the magistrate or the people, nor is any person required to explain or interpret it. Nor is it one law at Rome and another at Athens, one law today and another hereafter; but the same law, everlasting and unchangeable, will bind all nations at all times; and there will be one common lord and ruler of all men, even God, the framer and proposer of this law."[18]

According to St. Thomas Aquinas, "Among all others, the rational creature is subject to divine providence in a more excellent way, in so far as it itself partakes of a share of providence, by being provident both for itself and others. Therefore it has a share of the eternal reason, whereby it has a natural inclination to its proper act and end; and this participation of the eternal law in the rational creature is called the 'natural law.' "[19]

One last quotation comes from Richard Hooker, in the Anglican tradition. "The general and perpetual voice of men is as the sentence of God himself. For that which all men have at all times learned, Nature herself must needs have taught; and God being the author of Nature, her voice is but his instrument. By her from him we receive whatsoever in such sort we learn. Infinite duties there are, the goodness of which is by this rule sufficiently manifested, although we had no other warrant besides to approve them. The apostle St. Paul, having speech concerning the heathen, saith of them, 'They are a law unto themselves.' His meaning is, that by the force of the light of reason, wherewith God illuminateth everyone which cometh into the world, men being enabled to know truth from falsehood, and good from evil, do thereby learn in many things what the will of God is; which will, himself not revealing by any extraordinary means unto them, but they by natural discourse attaining the knowledge thereof, seem the makers of these laws which indeed are his, and they but only the finders of them out."[20]

A great many ideas are to be found in the passages quoted. The natural law is said to be unwritten; it is not invented by men but discovered by them; it is a kind of tendency rather than a code; it has a constancy or even an immutability. I certainly have no intention of attempting the defense of all the ideas contained in these quotations, even if they could be harmonized among themselves. But I do believe that something can and must be recovered from this pervasive notion of a natural law, and that it can be very relevant to some of our current problems. In the rest of the article, therefore, we shall try to see what is possible by way of reinterpretation and reconstruction.

The discussion will fall into two main parts. In the first, we shall consider the theological or ontological foundations of natural law and endeavor to interpret these in such a way that this law can indeed be seen as a common ground for the different ethical traditions. This discussion will inevitably raise in a provisional way the question of the relation between faith and morals. In the second part of the discussion, we shall consider what can be done toward reinterpreting natural law so that it takes account of the change and development which are characteristic not only of man's images of himself but of his very nature and of the world around him.

1. It is acknowledged as a matter of fact that during most of the course of human history, religion and morals have been closely associated with each other. It is true that there have sometimes been religions with inhuman elements, practicing cruel and degrading rites. It is true also that there have been and are many highly moral persons who have disclaimed any religious convictions. Yet, on the whole, we are bound to say that the bond between religion and morals has been a close one.

How are we to understand this connection? Is it an intrinsic one, or is it merely an external and almost accidental one? Was it, for instance, appropriate that in the earlier stages of human development morals should be protected and inculcated by religion, but that as man becomes increasingly adult, morals should be detached from any connection with religion? This would parallel in the ethical field what has been true in many other fields of human activity, in which arts and sciences that were once pursued under the aegis of religion have become secularized and now flourish in complete autonomy.

Some of the traditional ways of explaining the bond between morality and religion were so inadequate and even repellent that, rather than stay with them, one would prefer to see morality break free from its religious associations. I refer especially to the view that religion provides the sanctions for morality and so the motivation for moral conduct, with its promise of reward for those who do good and its threat of punishment for evildoers. Such beliefs were widespread in ancient societies and persisted right down to the Philosophers of recent centuries. John Locke could write: "The view of heaven and hell will cast a slight upon the short pleasures and pains of this present state, and give attractions and encouragements to virtue, which reason and interest, and the care of ourselves, cannot but allow and prefer. Upon this foundation, and upon this only, morality stands firm and may defy all competition."[21] Few people today believe in heaven and hell in the traditional sense, but they seem to be neither more nor less moral as a result. Even if there was the need for such a doctrine to buttress morality in earlier times, it would seem to have no place in the sophisticated societies of today. But more than this, I think we would say nowadays that to appeal to religion on the ground that it provides the sanctions for morality is to degrade both religion and morals. Religion is reduced to becoming a mere incentive to the moral life, while it is also suggested that men will not be moral apart from a system of ultimate rewards and punishments— surely a very cynical idea.

I believe that there is a connection between religion and morality, and that this connccection is intrinsic and important. However, we must look for a way of interpreting it which will not do violence to the integrity of either religion or morality and that will not impugn the undoubtable achievements of secular morality. It can never be a question of subordinating religion to morality, or the other way around; nor can there be any question of claiming that morality is dependent on religious faith, in view of the plain fact that many non-religious people are highly moral. Let me suggest, however, that natural law provides the link.

Though a religious faith is not to be identified with a metaphysic, it nevertheless always involves its adherents in some vision of the whole, in some fundamental convictions about "the way things are." Natural law too claims to be founded in "the way things are," in ultimate structures that are explicitly contrasted with the human conventions that find expression in our ordinary rules and customs. But natural law need not be given a theological or religious interpretation, and the conception of natural law is by no means incompatible with secular morality, and is indeed implied in some forms of it. Natural law is an ontological ground, common to the various forms of morality, receiving in some of them a religious interpretation, in others a secular. I would say that natural law (or something like it) is implicit wherever an unconditioned moral obligation is recognized. Perhaps this is implicit even in Camus, for in an absurd world it is apparently not absurd to be moral and to pursue the fulfillment of humanity.

That most people do seem to believe in something like natural law may be seen from a simple consideration. There is no human law, not even that promulgated by the highest authority, about which someone may not complain that it is unjust. There seems to be found among most people the conviction that there is a criterion, beyond the rules and conventions of human societies, by which these may be judged.

Every social group or association has some rules. These will normally be founded on the convenience of the members. If someone finds these rules unfair, and is unable to persuade the group to change them, he may have recourse to some superior set of laws to which the group itself is subject. There is always, so to speak, a higher court of appeal, a hierarchy of justice. There may be appeals through a whole series of courts, but even when the highest court of appeal has pronounced its judgment, it still makes sense for someone to say that its ruling was unjust. It is hard to see how this could be the case if justice has a purely empirical origin, explicable in terms of sociology, psychology, biology, and similar sciences.

Some jurists have held that the state is the ultimate source of law, so that what it decrees is *ipso facto* just and right—a theory, incidentally, which is no more arbitrary than the belief that what God decrees is therefore right. Such a positive theory of law, which was grounded in the state, was held in recent times by Nazi jurists in Germany. The state (or nation) was for the Nazi, absolute. But most people would hold that there is an even more ultimate standard than the state, and that the state's laws and decrees can be unjust. According to Vernon J. Bourke, West Germany, Italy, and Japan are countries which have made considerable use of the natural law concept in reconstructing their legal and political institutions in the years following World War II.[22] It is surely significant that the three countries named were precisely lands that had for a time totalitarian rule. The concept of natural law is, among other things, a safeguard against the usurpation by the state of unlimited power.

Sophocles provided a dramatic account of the conflict between the laws of the state and the demands of "natural" justice:

CREON: Now, tell me thou—not in many words, but briefly—knewest thou that an edict had forbidden this?

ANTIGONE: I knew it. Could I help it? It was public.

CREON: And thou didst indeed dare to transgress that law?

ANTIGONE: Yes, for it was not Zeus that had published me that edict; not such are the laws set among men by the Justice who dwells with the gods. Nor deemed I that thy decrees were of such force, that a mortal could override the unwritten and unfailing statutes of heaven. For their life is not of today or yesterday, but from all time, and no man knows when they were first put forth.[23]

This scene from Greek tragedy antedates by some five hundred years a scene in the New Testament in which it is reported: "Then Peter and the other apostles answered and said: 'We must obey God rather than men.' "[24]

Of course, both of these excerpts, like the one quoted from Cicero earlier, are explicitly theological in what they say about the "higher law," and we should clearly understand that a doctrine of natural law does not necessarily commit one to a theistic belief. Governments which allow conscientious objection to military service only on *religious* grounds are acting unjustly. Indeed, one might even argue that to explain natural law or fundamental morality in terms of a divine Lawgiver is the most primitive and mythological way of expressing the idea. In the Old Testament, Moses receives the Decalogue, the basic laws of human conduct, at the hands of Yahweh. Likewise Hammurabi is depicted in Babylonian art as receiving the law from the god Marduk. In more recent times the natural law has sometimes been understood as the "will of God." But in such cases, God has been conceived on the deistic model, as an absolute monarch in the heavens. The natural law is not the "will of God," if this is understood to mean that God's arbitrary decree determines right and wrong. Men have sometimes complained that God has been unjust to them. Their complaints may have been unfounded, but it is interesting that such complaints can even be made, for it indicates that those who make them do not identify justice simply with what God wills. Justice is such an ultimate notion that it cannot depend even on the will of God. This does not mean that it is more ultimate than God, but rather that it is not external or subsequent to God, for it belongs to his very being or nature.

The point has been put so clearly by E. L. Mascall that I can do no better than quote some sentences from him: "To the Scotists, who taught that the formal constituent of God was infinity and that will was essentially superior to intellect, it was natural to say that the moral law rested simply on the arbitrary decree of God and that actions are good because God has commanded them; to the Thomists, on the other hand, it was *being* that was fundamental, with the necessary corollary that the moral law is neither an antecedent prescription to which God is bound by some external necessity to conform, nor a set of precepts promulgated by him in an entirely arbitrary and capricious manner, but something inherently rooted in the nature of man as reflecting in himself, in however limited and finite a mode, the character of the sovereign Good from whom his being is derived. The moral law is thus in its essence neither antecedent nor consequent to God; it is simply the expression of his own self-consistency. To say, therefore, that God is bound by it is merely to say, from one particular angle, that God is God."[25]

In any case, it would be hard to imagine a more abused phrase than "the will of God." People have committed all kinds of wickedness and folly in the belief that they were carrying out the will of God. In milder but no less objectionable ways, they still pressure other people into adopting their policies by representing their own idiosyncrasies as God's will which it would be wrong to disobey—a favorite tactic in ecclesiastical debates. How right Ian Henderson was when he wrote: "To enthrone the will of God in ecclesiastical party politics is to drive out love. For the point in calling your party policy the will of God is just that it enables you to give hell to the man who opposes it. For does that not make him the enemy of God? And what a wonderful opportunity to enable you, Christian that you are, to give vent to all the lovelessness in your nature."[26] Can we be surprised if many decent secular people are suspicious of any attempt to relate morality to any transcendent reality?

Yet we have seen that most people do indeed appeal to a "natural justice" beyond any human court of appeal. The Christian theologian will no doubt seek to link this notion eventually to his concept of God, but he will do so in more sophisticated ways than by the traditional appeal to the will of God. But it is possible to hold a natural law doctrine without giving it a theological formulation, though hardly without some ontological or metaphysical formulation. For the Stoics, the natural law was understood in somewhat pantheistic terms, as the demand of the *logos* dwelling both in man and in the cosmos. Likewise, in Eastern religions, the Hindu *dharma* and the Chinese *tao* are immanent and impersonal principles, not the decrees of a transcendent deity. In modern Western philosophy, one would be more likely to found natural law on a Kantian or neo-Kantian basis of an objectively valid rational order, which grounds moral values just as it does logical values. In each case, the foundations are taken to have an ultimacy and objectivity about them. They are not just "human convention," explicable psychologically, sociologically, and anthropologically. These sciences do explain the actual empirical forms in which morality appears, but not the ultimate demand of morality. Not even the state and not human society as a whole (if this expression refers to anything) can serve as the foundation of morality, but a transhuman order so that, as Hooker expressed it, man is not so much the maker of laws as their discoverer.[27]

Though the acknowledgment of a natural law that judges every human law does not, as we have readily agreed, imply a definitely theistic understanding of the world, nevertheless it points to an ontological interpretation of morality which has at least some kinship with the religious interpretation. For, in both cases, it is supposed that moral values do belong to the very nature of things, so to speak, and are not just superimposed on an amoral reality by the human mind. But surely to recognize that morality has this ontological foundation is already to perceive it in a new depth. Without such a depth, it is hard to see how there could ever be an unconditioned obligation to which one simply could not say no without abandoning one's authentic personhood. There could be only relative obligations, imposed by the conventions of a particular society. Conversely, as has been pointed out by Fritz Buri, where there is no ontological or religious grounding of morality, there is also no sin and "one can speak only of relative but not of unconditioned evil."[28]

The Nazi regime, when man (or superman) decided moral values, should remain as a terrible warning against that complete slide into relativism and subjectivism in which morality has been entirely cut adrift from an ontological basis. The notion of human responsibility and answerability, when explored in its many dimensions, implies an order which man does not create but which rather lays a demand on him.

Although therefore one must nowadays abandon such oversimplified and frequently misleading notions as that the moral law is the will of God or that religion provides sanctions for strengthening the moral law, this does not lead to abandoning all belief in an intrinsic connection between morals and religion; and one can, moreover, see a parallel to such a religious morality in a secular morality which acknowledges a natural law. In both cases, if morality is founded in "the way things are," as natural law doctrine has maintained and as religious faith has maintained, then the moral demand has about it an ultimate character that can hardly fail to let it be experienced with an enhanced seriousness.[29]

2. In the second part of our discussion, we have to take up the question of how far the traditional idea of natural law can be adapted to the thinking of an age whose concepts are dynamic rather than static. So far we have talked of "unconditioned demand" and have sought a stable foundation for morality that could safeguard us from

the vagaries of a thoroughgoing relativism. But it is equally important, in the light of our earlier discussions about man, to try to reinterpret the idea of natural law in a way that allows for flexibility and growth, so that it really does protect and foster the fulfillment of human possibilities. Are we perhaps asking the impossible? Demanding elements of both constancy and stability, while also wanting to acknowledge the pervasiveness of change and to set everything in motion? Or is there a way of embracing both sides?

First of all, I think we should be clear about what we are looking for. We are not looking for some extended system of rules. Just as the substance of faith can never be adequately or precisely formulated in dogmatic propositions, and just as all such propositions have time-conditioned elements that need to be expressed in new and different ways in new historical situations, so the content of the moral life is never exhaustively or adequately formulated in rules and precepts.

The fact that natural law cannot be precisely formulated is already implied in some of the classic definitions and descriptions quoted above. The natural law is "unwritten" (Aristotle). In fact, the very term "law" is misleading, if it is taken to mean some kind of code. The natural law is not another code or system of laws in addition to all the actual systems, but is simply our rather inaccurate way of referring to those most general moral principles against which particular rules or codes have to be measured. It is well known that St. Thomas formulated the first precept of the natural law in extremely general terms: "Good is to be done and promoted, and evil is to be avoided."[30] At first sight, one might be tempted to ask whether this statement says anything or is just a tautology, in the sense that it simply repeats what is already contained in the notions of "good" and "evil." I think, however, we shall find there is more to it than this.

It is assumed that one can go on to elaborate other precepts of the natural law, though these would be of a general kind. Perhaps we could reckon among them the very broad prohibitions which Bishop Robinson accepts as possessing something approaching universal validity.[31] But the really important point in Robinson's statement has to do not with the actual prohibitions which he lists but with the fact that the prohibited activities are all, as he says, "fundamentally destructive of human relationships."

The Decalogue, setting forth the basic demands of the moral life, might be taken as a kind of transcript of the fundamental precepts of natural law, even though the Decalogue itself is supposed to have been "revealed." But simple and basic though the Ten Commandments are, one finds even in them relative and time-conditioned elements. What, for instance, is one to say about the command concerning Sabbath observance?[32] Even with so basic a statement of the fundamental moral laws, there can be disputes as to what really belongs to natural law and what to the historical circumstances under which the statement was formulated. This reinforces our point that the natural law cannot be formulated, and that it is not so much itself a "law" as rather a touchstone for determining the justice or morality of actual laws and rules.

We may consider a more recent example. Sir David Ross lists some half-dozen *prima facie* duties, as he calls them: duties of fidelity (such as promise-keeping and truth-telling), duties of reparation, duties of gratitude, duties of justice, duties of beneficience, duties of self-improvement, and, negatively, the duty of not injuring others. These duties are called *prima facie* to allow for the situational element in morality. In an actual situation, there may be more than one claim on me, and then one has to take precedence over the other. But it is assumed that everyone is aware of the *prima facie* claims and that they are distinct from my fallible personal opinions about more peripheral ethical questions. "The main moral convictions of the plain man," writes Ross, "seem to me to be, not opinions which it is for philosophy to prove or disprove, but knowledge from the start."[33] I am inclined to agree with Ross that there is this kind of fundamental moral knowledge, given with human existence itself. Although he does not use the expression "natural law," I would think it quite appropriate. Furthermore, I would doubt whether the natural law could be particularized much beyond the half-dozen or so general duties which Ross details. And even these are *prime facie* duties, which may be superseded in an actual situation.

We have dwelt at some length on the difficulty of formulating the natural law with any precision and have seen that time-conditioned elements enter into such formulations as there are, and situational elements into its actual application. To this extent, we have already come into conflict with some of the classic descriptions of natural law, especially in their use of such words as "everlasting" and "unchangeable." But we are only at the beginning of our criticism. The notions of change and development have to be taken much more seriously than just allowing that there are changes and development in formulation. The notion of the unchangeableness of natural law was rooted in the idea of an unchanging nature, both in man and in the cosmos.

But if we acknowledge—as we already have done—that man's nature is open, and that he is always going beyond or transcending any given state of himself; and if we acknowledge further that this open nature of man is set in the midst of a cosmos which is likewise on the move and is characterized by an evolving rather than a static order; then we must say that the natural law itself, not just its formulations, is on the move and cannot have the immutability once ascribed to it. But what has perhaps more than anything else discredited the natural law concept is the tacit assumption that there was a kind of original human nature to which everything subsequent is an accretion. This is the confusion of what is natural with what is primitive. One has only to ask the question, "Is it natural to wear clothes?" to see the absurdity of trying to think of man's nature in terms of a primitive given. It is certainly futile to try to erect rules or maintain prohibitions on the basis of a "nature" that has long since been transcended. Man's very nature is to exist, that is to say, to go out of himself, and in the course of this he learns to take over from crude nature and to do in a human (and humane) way what was once accomplished by blind natural forces (both in man and outside of him) working in a rough and ready manner. An obvious example is population control, which need no longer be left to the hazards and diseases of nature without or to the tribal warfares prompted by the aggression of nature within. We have got beyond that kind of nature, and as I claimed in our discussion of man, the pill and the condom are now part of his nature.

But in admitting this, have we not cut away any ground for the other side of our argument concerning natural law? How can natural law provide a kind of criterion for evaluating particular laws? If this natural law is itself variable, can there be any reliable criterion at all? Or is everything reduced to relativism, subjectivism, and pragmatism?

I think we do still have a criterion, but its constancy is not that of a law but of a direction. So again we have to say that the word "law" is not entirely appropriate to describe the kind of thing traditionally meant by "natural law." What is meant is rather a constant tendency, an inbuilt directedness. To think of nature in dynamic terms is not to abandon all structure and reduce everything to flux. Although we talk much nowadays about change—and some people even talk about the "celebration of change"—it need hardly be said that change can be for the worse as well as for the better. The only kind of change we might want to celebrate would be change for the better. Teilhard de Chardin uses the expression "genesis" as a more precise way of saying what is meant. "In Teilhard's mind," writes Christopher Mooney, "we are not simply face to face with 'change' in the world but with 'genesis,' which is something quite different.... The word applies to any form of production involving successive stages oriented toward some goal."[34]

The movement that is envisaged, whether we are thinking of human nature or of cosmic nature, is a movement with direction, an ordered movement. But the movement in the cosmos is very different from the movement in man. The first kind of movement is unconscious evolution; the second has become a conscious moral striving. This corresponds to the difference between "laws of nature" and "natural law" in an ethical sense.[35] We should be quite clear that what we are talking about has nothing to do with the doctrine of an automatic progress of the human race, or with any complacent optimism. As soon as the transition is made from natural evolution to man's responsible self-development, the movement becomes subject to the risks of moral choice and to the actual reversals of sin. It is not like the unfolding of an oak from an acorn. This is something that happens, but in the case of man's development, it is a question about what *ought* to happen. At least in general terms, we know where we *ought* to be going, and we experience guilt when we go in some other direction. We know where we ought to be going because to exist as a human being is to exist with a self-understanding. This is an understanding both of who we are and of who we might become. It involves an image which summons us. To employ theological language for a moment, we might speak of the *imago Dei* both as fundamental endowment and as ultimate goal. Natural law is, as it were, the pointer within us that orients us to the goal of human existence. Actual rules, laws, and prohibitions are judged by this "unwritten law" in accordance with whether they promote or impede the movement toward fuller existence. Natural law changes, in the sense that the precepts we may derive from it change as human nature itself changes, and also in the sense that man's self-understanding changes as he sharpens his image of mature manhood. But through the changes there remains the constancy of direction.

This dynamic understanding of natural law is already implicit in St. Thomas' talk about the rational creature's having "a natural inclination to its proper act and end," while his awareness of the difference between a merely natural development in the world and man's conscious self-development is shown by his acute observation about the difference between a general providence in the world and the creature which has become itself provident.[36]

The directedness of moral striving has a constancy which prevents any lapse into sheer relativism. Even the relativisms of actual historical moral codes have often been exaggerated. Patrick Nowell-Smith claims that the more we study moral codes, the more we find that they do not differ in major principles.[37] All have the same direction, as it were. They aim at the development of a fuller, richer, more personal manhood, and to this extent they are in accord with and give expression to the natural law.

The Christian, we have seen, defines mature manhood in terms of Jesus Christ, and especially his self-giving love. But Christ himself is no static figure, nor are Christians called to imitate him as a static model. Christ is an eschatological figure, always before us; and the doctrine of his coming again "with glory" implies that there are dimensions of christhood not manifest in the historical Jesus and not yet fully grasped by the disciples. Thus discipleship does not restrict human development to some fixed pattern, but summons into freedoms, the full depth of which is unknown, except that they will always be consonant with self-giving love.

But the "natural" understanding of morality leads to conclusions not far from those of the Christian. For if man's nature is to *exist,* then he exists most fully when he *goes out* of himself. Here we strike upon the paradox of the moral life, perceived in many traditions—that the man who would "save" his life, that is to say, preserve it as a static possession, actually loses it, whereas the man who is prepared to venture out beyond himself and even to empty himself attains the truest selfhood.[38]

The discussion of this article, focusing on the concept of natural law, suggests that there is no conflict between the ideals of a Christian ethic and the moral ideals to be found in humanity at large. Rather, there is a fundamental similarity. Christianity does not establish a new or different morality, but it makes concrete, clarifies, and, above all, focuses on a particular person, Jesus Christ, the deepest moral convictions of men. Christ declared he was fulfilling the law, not abolishing it.[39] According to W. D. Davies, even the so-called "antitheses" in the Sermon on the Mount (those passages in which Christ explicitly contrasts his own moral teaching with that of the Mosaic law) do not annul the law but carry it to "its utmost meaning."[40] It is obvious that this view of the matter agrees very closely with the one expounded here. Christian moral teaching is an unfolding of the "natural" morality of all men.

What for want of a better name has usually been called "natural law" is still a very useful concept. We have seen that it provides a firm basis for moral cooperation and community between Christians and non-Christians. We have seen further that natural law, even if it is not explicitly interpreted in theistic terms, nevertheless allows us to see moral obligation in a new depth, as ontologically founded. It safeguards against moral subjectivism and encourages moral seriousness by locating the demand of moral obligation in the very way things are.

Notes

1. *Christian Ethics and Contemporary Philosophy,* ed. Ian T. Ramsey (London: S.C.M. Press, 1966), pp. 382–96.

2. Dietrich Bonhoeffer, *Letters and Papers from Prison,* tr. Reginald H. Fuller (New York: Macmillan, 1962), pp. 222–23.

3. See p. 40.

4. Ephesians 4:13.

5. Karl Rahner, *Theological Investigations,* Vol. I, tr. Cornelius Ernst, O.P. (London: Darton, Longman & Todd; Baltimore: Helicon Press, 1961), p. 184.

6. David Jenkins, *The Glory of Man* (London: S.C.M. Press; New York: Scribner, 1967).

7. *Ibid.*, p. 79

8. Cf. Hebrews 1:3.

9. Matthew 13:45–46.

10. Paul Ramsey, *Basic Christian Ethics* (London: S.C.M. Press, 1953), p. 86.

11. Lehmann, *op cit.*, p. 148.

12. See *Three Issues in Ethics*, pp. 119 ff.

13. Cf. Sir Charles Sherrington, *Man on His Nature* (London: Cambridge University Press, 1940).

14. Theodosius Dobzhansky, *The Biology of Ultimate Concern* (New York: New American Library, 1967), p. 86.

15. Werner Jaeger, *The Theology of the Early Greek Philosophers*, tr. E. S. Robinson (London: Oxford University Press, 1967), p. 36.

16. *Ibid.*, pp. 115–16. Translation of Heraclitus from Jaeger.

17. *Rhetoric*, I, 10. Translation from *The Basic Works of Aristotle*, ed. Richard McKeon (New York: Random House, 1941), p. 1359.

18. Cicero, *De Republica*, III, 22–23. Translation from John Salmond, *Jurisprudence* (London: Sweet & Maxwell, 1930), p. 28.

19. *Summa Theologiae*, II/I, 91, 2. Translation from *Basic Writings of St. Thomas Aquinas*, ed. A. C. Pegis (New York: Random House, 1945), Vol. II, p. 750.

20. Richard Hooker, *Of the Laws of Ecclesiastical Polity*, I, vii, 3 (London: J. M. Dent, Everyman's Library, 1907), Vol. I, pp. 176–77.

21. John Locke, *The Reasonableness of Christianity*, ed. Ian T. Ramsey (London: A. & C. Black, 1958), p. 70.

22. Vernon J. Bourke, "Natural Law," *A Dictionary of Christian Ethics*, ed. John Macquarrie (London: S.C.M. Press; Philadelphia: Westminster Press, 1967), pp. 224–25.

23. Sophocles, *Antigone*, 450–57. Translation from *The Complete Greek Drama*, ed. Whitney J. Oates and Eugene O'Neill (New York: Random House, 1938), Vol I, p. 434.

24. Acts 5:29.

25. E. L. Mascall, *He Who Is* (London: Darton, Longman & Todd, new edition, 1966), p. 122.

26. Ian Henderson, *Power without Glory: A Study in Ecumenical Politics* (London: Hodder & Stoughton, 1967), pp. 94–95.

27. See p. 95.

28. Buri, *op cit.*, p. 14.

29. It may be noted that both Buri and Bultmann in their writing seem to come near to interpreting the meaning of the word "God" as that unconditioned or ultimate element which we experience in the awareness of moral obligation. This seems to reverse the traditional procedure, by deriving an understanding of God from morality rather than morality from an idea of God.

30. *Summa Theologiae,* II/I, 94, 1.

31. See *Three Issues in Ethics,* p. 37.

32. Herbert Richardson has recently claimed that the Sabbath does belong to natural law, because it is related to the creation story and the "rest" of the seventh day. "This explanation of the commandment must be interpreted as implying that the Sabbath is binding not only upon Israel but also upon all other creatures. . . . it is in the same category as the commandment not to murder—it is a universal moral law." *Toward an American Theology* (New York: Harper & Row, 1967), p. 114.

33. David Ross, *The Right and the Good* (Oxford: Clarendon Press, 1930), p. 19.

34. Christopher Mooney, *Teilhard de Chardin and the Mystery of Christ* (London: Collins, 1966), p. 51.

35. See p. 92.

36. See p. 94.

37. Patrick Nowell-Smith, *Ethics* (London: Penguin Books, 1954), p. 18.

38. Cf. Mark 8:35.

39. Matthew 5:17.

40. W. D. Davies, *The Sermon on the Mount* (London and New York: Cambridge University Press, 1966), p. 29.

Can Ethics Be Christian?
Some Conclusions

James M. Gustafson

Can ethics be Christian? The answer is negative if certain restrictive concepts of "ethics" are used. If the concept stipulates that
any reflection on morality that finds justification or warrants for
moral values and principles which are themselves grounded in "private," "historically particularistic," or "nonrational" assumptions is
not ethical reflection, then in principle ethics cannot be Christian. If
a pattern of thought, in order to be ethics, must in each order of moral discourse be exclusively rational, and if Christianity (or any other
religion) is classed as irrational or nonrational, and if particular religious warrants are appealed to in any order of moral discourse,
Christian moral thought is not ethics. For example, if the principle
"you shall love your neighbor as yourself" is justified on the basis
that it is in the Torah and in the Christian scriptures, or that it is a
revelation from God, or that it is an action-guiding principle that is
inferred from the theological assertion that God is love, then on the
basis of the restrictive concept the process is not in the domain of
ethics. If, however, that principle were justified on the grounds
that it is a universalizable principle, and therefore one on which presumably all rational persons can agree, the process would be in the
realm of ethics. Indeed, the biblical language might be interpreted to
mean that one ought to respect each person as an end in himself, or
in some similar way, in order to cleanse it of its particular historical
religious overtones.

Even with a restrictive concept in mind, however, the matter is
more complex than the previous paragraph has indicated. A principle like the love commandment, and most moral principles and val-

ues that guide the actions of Christians, can be generalized, if not applied universally; they can be defended on grounds that do not in the first instance make particular religious or theological appeals. Thus, it might be argued that the morality of the Christian community, or any other religious community, is in the domain of "ethics" insofar as it is "rationally" defensible. It could be excluded from ethics in any order of moral discourse in which the justifying principle was "religious." For example, if a Christian community claimed to obey the love commandment *only* because it was an obligation entailed by its fidelity to Jesus, the commandment would not be "ethical." If the community claimed, in the fashion of many Catholic and Protestant theologians, that the commandment is part of the "natural law" and thus can be known by all reasonable persons, it would be ethical. Insofar as an additional order of discourse was invoked, namely, the more ultimate justification for the natural law, and if Christians then justified adherence to natural law on the basis that it is a gift of God's graciousness in creation, then they would have left the arena of ethics. What was an ethical justification in one order of discourse is further justified in this instance by a nonethical, or theological warrant. If the theological appeal in this order is judged to be incidental or accidental, rather than intrinsic or necessary, to the morality of Christians, it can be asserted that the morality of the Christian community is in the domain of ethics but that Christians are "ethical" for a different general reason than secular rational persons are.

Can ethics be Christian? The answer is affirmative on the basis of two different points of view. They are, first, that ethics must be Christian and *is* Christian in a universally applicable sense because it is in Christ that all things are created, and he is the Lord of all things. The second is that the ethics *of Christians* is and must be exclusively Christian because the community is called to absolute obedience to Jesus as Lord; all of the moral actions of the community must be determined by his lordship.

From the first point of view, Christian ethics and universal human ethics are convertible terms. What is ethically justifiable to do (in a purely rational sense) is the Christian thing to do, and vice versa. This is given theological legitimacy by the doctrine of the Trinity in which Christ, the second person, is the one in and through whom all things are created. From this point of view, in principle there is no distinctive Christian morality, but all morality that is rationally justifiable is Christian. The historical particularity of the source of the life of the church has no particular ethical significance, though its theological significance is tremendous, for Jesus is the revelation of God. Christians have special obligations perhaps, for example, to follow Jesus in lives of self-sacrificial service, but these are not ethical obligations. They are particular religious obligations. Christians have distinctive ideals, but these cannot be called, in a strict sense, moral ideas, for they are not rationally justifiable. If one chooses to call these obligations and ideals "moral," necessarily one has a double ethics, a minimalistic one that is Christian in a grand theological sense, and a more demanding one that is Christian in a special historical sense. With modifications, this point of view can be found in St. Thomas, Luther, and Calvin.[1]

From the second point of view that comes to a strong affirmative answer, not only can ethics be Christian, but the ethics of Christians *must be* Christian. The pattern for this has two distinctive points of orientation. One is that the Christian community has a particular vocation to follow Jesus and the way of life that he exemplified and taught; it is obligated to be fully obedient to his lordship, to be a distinctive people with a distinctive way of life. The second is that while Christ is confessed to be the savior of the world, the sorts of philosophical speculations that give grounds for the convertibility of the Christian and the rational are eschewed. The Christian community has its significant grounding in a historical event, and its history and conduct are to be determined by that historical revelation. This point of view does not imply that every moral act of Christians is distinctively different from the acts of other persons. The honesty of Christians, for example, in their personal or business relations has no visible difference from the honesty of other persons. Indeed, the immediate moral intention of their actions (the intention to be honest) is not distinctive; they would also justify honesty on rational ethical grounds. What is characteristic, however, is that the final justification for honesty would be its consistency with a Christian way of life; a people could not be obedient to the lordship of Jesus and be dishonest. Very important for understanding this point of view is this: Jesus, who is Lord, is known through the gospel accounts of his life and teachings; on the basis of these accounts there are distinctive obligations for his followers and these are of equal authority to the more ordinary moral obligations that also follow from his lordship. "Christian" ethics then is highly distinctive, though not unique in all respects, and to be Christian is to be obliged to follow the distinctive as well as the ordinary morality that is part of a Christian way of life. The ethics of Christians is and must be Christian ethics; all of their moral actions are under Jesus' lordship; since he is Lord, the distinctive aspects of his way of life and teaching are as morally obligatory on those who confess him as Lord as are the ordinary aspects. With some modifications this point of view is present in the early stages of monastic movements (Franciscan morality is one example), in various Anabaptist movements of the sixteenth century, and in "radical" religious movements of the Puritan period (the Quaker movement is one example).

On the basis of a highly restrictive concept of ethics, the latter point of view is not ethics at all; it offers a religious way of life with religious obligations some of which are ethically defensible. The first point of view would, on the basis of a restrictive concept, be ethical throughout until the final justification, the gracious gift of God's creation, is invoked. (Whether "decision is king" only for religious persons at the point of an affirmation or choice either of the "ultimate grounds" of morality or of a definable "way of life" even the philosophers dispute. Certainly it is clear that all moral philosophers, not to mention all rational persons, do not agree on these matters.)

None of these answers to the question, "Can ethics be Christian?" precisely follows from the previous chapters of this book. There is another way to respond to the question "Can ethics be Christian?" This answer, stated in most general terms, is that religion *qualifies* morality, and that ethics can be Christian in the senses (*a*) that the morphology of religious morality can be explicated, and (*b*) that certain action-guiding values and principles can be inferred from religious beliefs as normative for those who share some common Christian experience of the reality of God. The religious qualification of morality can be rather thorough in its consequences, but it does not create an exclusive Christian morality or ethics. This general statement will be developed subsequently; it is important to note that the bases for drawing distinctions used in the answers above are not totally applicable to how my conclusions are drawn. Indeed, the basic question of the title must be refined to. "In what senses is it intelligible to speak of ethics as Christian?"

For the sake of organization and economy of words, attention is given here to three crucial aspects of morality that are qualified by Christian experience and belief, and thus three aspects of ethics. They are (1) the reasons for being moral, (2) the character of the moral agent, and (3) the points of reference used to determine conduct.

It is intelligible to speak of morality, and by derivation of ethics, as Christian in the sense that Christianity offers reasons for morality itself, and reasons for persons to be moral. That morality can be interpreted to have other ultimate grounds than Christian theological ones cannot be gainsaid; social conventions, biological necessity, systems of nontheistic metaphysics, and others have been developed. That persons and communities can have reasons for being moral other than those of the Christian faith and tradition is equally uncontradictable: to be happy, to have peace in society, and other reasons have been given. In Christian experience, however, the religious dimensions have priority over the moral. The existence of God is not posited in order to have an ultimate ground for morality; rather the reality of God is experienced, and this experience requires morality; or, by inference from this experience, the reality of God requires morality. One is not a religious person in order to have reasons of mind and heart to be moral; rather, one is religious as a consequence of experience of the reality of God, and this experience requires that one be moral.

In the religious consciousness of the serious Christian (and I believe also of the devout Jew and Moselm), every moral act is a religiously significant act. To act for the sake of justice for the oppressed is not only a moral act; it is a moral act done for religious as well as moral, indeed for religious-moral reasons, and thus is an act both of fidelity to God and of honor to God. Some Protestant theologians have equivocated on the word "good" to make this point; Luther, for example, believed that an act was truly good only if it was done "in faith." The morally good and the theologically good were collapsed into each other. Such an extreme position does not follow from my analysis. The moral act is qualified by the religious significance it has for the agent in the light of his or her reasons for being moral without collapsing the two references of "good." It is a good act for two distinctive but "overlapping" reasons; it is a morally right or good act because of its consequences or because of the immediate moral principles that governed it. It is also a "good" act for the more ultimate "theological" and "religious" reasons it was done; it was done in fidelity to God, or done to honor God. Since moral intention (for the well-being of creation) is one aspect of the reality of God as experienced, the two distinctive reasons overlap.

If morality is qualified by religion in this sense, then Christian ethics is possible in two aspects. One is making clear the morphology of Christian experience of being moral for "religious" reasons. The second is to develop action-guiding principles and values that can be inferred from these reasons; the ethical task is to answer the question, "If one is moral for these reasons, what sorts of moral action ought one to do?" "What values and principles guide the discernment of what God is enabling and requiring me (us) to do?" Theology does not only provide "ultimate grounds" for morality; the morality that it grounds is qualified by the theological beliefs. Christian religious beliefs do not only ground morality; since the reality of God has compelling clarity through Jesus, the morality that it grounds is qualified by that medium. Thus inferences of principles and values, and the ordering of priority of them, are qualified by him.

It is intelligible to speak of morality and ethics as Christian in a second sense, namely, that the experience of God's reality through the Christian "story" qualifies the characteristics or the "characters" of moral agents. That others than Christians have morally commendable characters cannot be contradicted; they emerge from their life experiences and from their commitment to worthy moral values and principles. In Christian experience, however, the religious dimensions have priority over the moral. An experience of God's reality is not sought to prop up moral character; rather, the reality of God is experienced, and with compelling clarity through Jesus; this experience both engenders and requires characteristics of moral agents that are morally commendable. Persons do not worship God, for example, to shore up weaknesses of moral character; rather, to participate in worship is to express and to evoke an experience of the presence of the ultimate power. This experience has consequences for the moral "sort of person" one is becoming.

In Christian experience of God and its persisting consequences for persons, it is not possible to separate the "religious" characteristics from the "moral" characteristics of persons. Consciousness cannot be *separated* along a line that distinguishes the moral from the religious. That persons who do not share Christian experience can be loving, hopeful, and faithful cannot be gainsaid; to experience the reality of God with special clarity through the Christian story, however, has, and ought to have, the consequences of nourishing (if not creating) loving, hopeful, and faithful dispositions in Christians. There are "readinesses" to act in certain ways, to seek the interests of others rather than one's own for example, that are nourished and sustained not only by actions in accordance with principles that would direct such action but also by participation in the Christian community with its common memories and its central person. To affirm that dispositions, affections, and intentions of a marked Christian sort are the fruits of Christian experience is not to affirm that other "virtues" like courage and justice are not also nourished by it. Indeed they are, for the ultimate power whose reality is experienced wills them as well.

If moral agents are qualified by the religious dimensions of experience in this way, then Christian ethics is possible in its two aspects. First, an intelligible account of these qualifications can be rendered, as I have attempted to do. Second, there are imperatives directed toward the sort of persons Christians ought to become that can be inferred from such an account. The normative, like the analytical, task of ethics includes attention to agents as well as acts. This second aspect of the ethical task is to answer the questions. "If one experiences God's reality, particularly informed by the Christian story, what sort of moral person ought one to become?" "What intentions and dispositions ought to be characteristic of Christians?" Quite reasonably, the answer to these questions is likely to resort to illustrations, by pointing to persons whose own life stories seem to embody those characteristics; this is one basis for the imitation of Christ theme in the history of Christian ethics, and for hagiographies both ancient and modern. The sort of person Christians ought to become is informed and influenced (that is, qualified) by the Christian story.[2]

It is intelligible to speak of morality and ethics as Christian in a third sense, namely, that distinctive points of reference are used to give guidance to moral action. These distinctive points of reference function in two ways in Christian moral reflection. First, religious symbols and theological concepts are used to interpret the moral and religious significance of events and circumstances; they are used in the process of forming a descriptive evaluation, or evaluative description, of the occasions for action. That other symbols and concepts can be used no one can dispute, and that the interpretations forthcoming can be accurate in disclosing the crucial moral issues in political, social, or interpersonal circumstances is equally clear. In the Christian community, however, the authorization for the selection of symbols and concepts is not only their potency in disclosing the moral issues; it is also that the confirmation in experience of the power of these symbols and concepts to articulate the experience of God's reality and of man's life in relation to God authorizes their use. These symbols might be highly specific in a historical sense; the use of the cross is one example. What the cross elucidates can be elucidated by other symbols; again, the use of the symbol of the crucifixion is authorized primarily by the compelling clarity it evokes in Christian experience of God as self-giving and self-sacrificing love.

The second function of distinctive points of reference is to infer and to state action-guiding principles and values that aid the Christian community and its members in discerning what God is enabling and requiring them to be and to do. To find such principles and values is not to guarantee that the actions of Christians are "morally better" than the actions of others whose principles and values are derived from "purely rational" bases. To claim, as the churches seem often to do, that the reason for using Jesus' teachings, or for inferring principles to govern action from theological beliefs, is to develop a "higher" or better morality is a mistake. The prime significance of the Christian experience is its apprehension of God's reality through the Christian story with compelling clarity. A fidelity to God follows which gives distinctive though not exclusive authority to the media through which that experience occurs. Thus there is confidence, though not blind trust, that these historically particular media are a trustworthy basis for finding moral values and principles that are in accord with God's will and reality.

That these values and principles might be distinctive, in the sense that there are claims on the Christian community that appear to be "irrational" and certainly "imprudent" is part of my argument. As we have seen, from a highly restrictive philosophical concept of ethics such claims as that the Christian community ought to be willing to give up its own immediate interests for the sake of others are not moral but religious claims. On the basis of the assumption that certain values and principles have an obligatory character within a "way of life" and that the Christian history and community call for a way of life grounded in the Christian story, it is fitting to call these Christian ethical principles and values. This is clearly not to insist that persons who do not share in that religious way of life must follow those principles or honor those values. While theologically an argument might be made for their universality, the confirmation of their authority is in the history of the Christian community and in personal experience. It is unreasonable to assume that those who do not share the "believing" should be obligated to follow the principles and honor the values that are distinctive to that community. Others may be quite prepared to adhere to these more rigorous demands for other reasons, such as personal ideals or the sustaining ethos of another religious community.[3] But the strength of the claim to engage in such action is qualified by the Christian experience and ethos.

Thus, it is intelligible, and I hope plausible and persuasive, to argue that ethics can be Christian in the senses that have been developed here.[4] If the argument is not persuasive, at least it might locate where the crucial issues are. Its import I believe, is not only for ethical theory but also for the Christian communities and churches. They are deeply concerned about human well-being, prone to make moral judgments on all sorts of events, developing rules of behavior and recommendations for policy, and stimulating moral action among their members. All too frequently, however, they are not very clear and precise about the grounds or reasons for their authorizing all this activity.

Many non-Christians often do what Christians ought to do under similar circumstances. If readers now ask, "If this is the case, then why be religious or Christian?" they have missed the basic point of the book. If one is Christian or religious in order to be moral, just as if one is Christian in order to be happy, the heart of religion is not yet grasped. The heart of religion is the experience of the reality of

God, mediated through all sorts of other experiences. The distinctiveness of the Christian experience of the reality of God is that he is experienced with compelling clarity in Jesus and in the Christian story. The confirmation of this (not an uncritical one) in experience grounds Christian morality. Christian ethics is the intellectual discipline that renders an account of this experience and that draws the normative inferences from it for the conduct of the Christian community and its members. The practical import is to aid the community and its members in discerning what God is enabling and requiring them to be and to do.

Notes

1. The Christology, the ethics, and the relations of the church to the world involved in this point of view are those of Ernst Troeltshch's "Church-type"; those involved in the second are his "sect-type." See Ernst Troeltsch, *The Social Teaching of the Christian Churches* (Glencoe, Ill.: Free Press, 1949), I, pp. 331–43.

2. See James M. Gustafson, "The Relation of the Gospels to Moral Life," in Donald G. Miller and D. Y. Hadidian, eds., *Jesus and Man's Hope* (Pittsburgh: Pittsburgh Theological Seminary, 1971), 2: 103–17.

3. See, for example, L. Jacobs, "Greater Love Hath No Man . . . The Jewish Point of View on Self-Sacrifice," *Judaism* 6 (1957): 41–47.

4. I believe the formal pattern of my analysis will bear the weight of a more inclusive range of materials. Thus, ethics can be "religious" in this way, when religion refers to generalizations based either on the characteristics of various historical religions or on some "generic" or functional concept of religion. Further, the formal pattern might function as a basis for "comparative" religious ethics. My own research has concentrated on Catholic and Protestant ethics, with Jewish ethics and law increasingly in view; I am not competent to make a range beyond these. Other scholars, happily among them are former students and colleagues of mine, are gaining the competence to do such work. See, for example, David Little, "Comparative Religious Ethics," in Paul Ramsey and John F. Wilson, eds., *The Study of Religion in Colleges and Universities* (Princeton: Princeton University Press, 1970), pp. 216–45.

Does Religious Faith Add to Ethical Perception?

Richard A. McCormick, S. J.

Thus far this volume has studied value perception and decision-making from several points of view. The task of the remaining essays is to focus explicitly on religious faith (and its source, revelation) and its relation to decision-making—and again, from several perspectives. The particular question I want to raise can be posed in any number of ways. Let me try just a few. How does religious faith affect decision-making in government—or in any other area for that matter (e.g., the practice of medicine, the profession of law)? Does one's faith add to one's ethical perceptions, and if it does, what does it add? Is not a morally wrong judgment morally wrong independent of religious belief? Is not a right decision right whether one is a believer or not?

Theologians have been deeply concerned with this question in recent years. They formulate the question variously. For example is there a specifically Christian ethics? Does Christian faith add material content to what is in principle knowable by reason? Is Christian morality autonomous? Is Christ the norm for the morally good and right, and in what sense? These questions may appear academic, at the margin of real life. Actually, the proper answer to them is of great importance.

For instance, if Christian faith, rooted in God's revelation, tells us things about right and wrong in human affairs that we would not otherwise know, then it is clear that decision-making in government risks integrity unless it is Christianly informed and inspired. Furthermore, the answer to the question raised affects public policy. Public policy, while not identical with sound morality, draws upon and builds upon moral conviction. If Christian faith adds new material (concrete, behavioral) content to morality, then public policy is even more complex than it seems. For example, if Christians precisely as Christians know something about abortion that others cannot know unless they believe it as Christians, then in a pluralistic society there will be problems with discussion and decision in the public forum.

Moreover, the answer to these questions affects the churches' competence to teach morality authoritatively, and how this is to be conceived and implemented. Thus, if Christian faith and revelation add material content to what is knowable in principle by reason, then the churches conceivably could teach moral positions and conclusions independently of the reasons and analyses that recommend these conclusions. This could lend great support to a highly juridical and obediential notion of Christian morality. The very processes we use, or do not use, to judge the moral rightness or wrongness of many concrete projects (e.g., donor insemination, in vitro fertilization, warfare, poverty programs, apartheid) would be profoundly affected. The question, then, is of enormous importance.

I
FAITH AND ETHICS

Before entering the discussion of this question, some precision must be given to the terms "faith" and "ethics". By faith, I refer to *explicit*, Christian faith, not a faith that remains implicit or nonthematic. I say this because there is a sense in which even explicit nonbelievers can be said to encounter the grace of Christ, be touched by it and therefore be living the life of faith even though it remains unrecognized as such.

Next a word on the term "ethics" (as it is used in the question: does faith add to one's ethical perceptions?). There are four levels at which the term can be understood where rightness or wrongness of conduct is concerned. Only one level is of special concern, at least in terms of the discussion as we find it in recent theological literature.

(1) First, there is what we might call an *essential* ethic.[1] By this term we mean those norms that are regarded as applicable to all persons, where one's behavior is but an instance of a general, essential

moral norm. Here we could use as examples the rightness or wrongness of killing actions, of contracts, of promises and all those actions whose demands are rooted in the dignity of the person.

(2) Second, there is an *existential* ethic. This refers to the choice of a good that the individual as individual should realize, the experience of an absolute ethical demand addressed to the individual. Obviously, at this level not all persons of good will can and do arrive at the same ethical decisions in concrete matters. For instance, an individual might conclude that his/her own moral-spiritual life cannot grow and thrive in government work, hence that this work ought to be abandoned. Or, because of background, inclination, talent (etc.) an individual might choose to concentrate time and energy on a particular issue rather than on others.

(3) Third, there is *essential Christian* ethics. By this we refer to those ethical decisions a Christian must make precisely because he/she belongs to a community to which the non-Christian does not belong. These are moral demands made upon the Christian *as Christian*. For instance, to regard fellow workers as brothers and sisters in Christ (not just as autonomous, to-be-respected persons), to provide a Christian education for one's children, to belong to a particular worshipping community. These are important ethical decisions that emerge only within the context of a Christian community's understanding of itself in relation to other people. Thus, to the extent that Christianity is a Church in the above sense and has preordained structures and symbols, to this extent there can be and must be a distinctively Christian ethic, an essential ethics of Christianity which adds to the ordinary essential ethics of persons as members of the universal human community the ethics of persons as members of the Church-community.

(4) Fourth, there is *existential Christian* ethics—those ethical decisions that the Christian *as individual* must make, e.g., the choice to concentrate on certain political issues not only because these seem best suited to one's talent, but above all because they seem more in accord with the gospel perspectives.

II
CHRISTIAN FAITH AND ESSENTIAL ETHICS

The problem that has above all concerned theologians involves ethics in the first sense only, i.e. *essential* ethics. In light of the foregoing precisions, the question could be worded as follows: does explicit Christian faith add to one's ethical (*essential* ethics) perceptions of obligation new content at the material or concrete level? This is the more precise form of the question now agitating theologians under a different formulation: sc., is there a specifically Christian ethics? But this latter formulation I judge to be too vague and sprawling, and one that allows discussants to seem to disagree with each other, when in reality they are not addressing the same question. More concretely, it should be readily granted that revelation and our personal faith do influence ethical decisions at the latter three levels (existential, essential Christian, existential Christian). One's choice of issues, and the dispositions and motivations he/she brings to these issues can be profoundly affected by one's personal appropriation of revealed truth, by one's prayer life, and by the community in which these develop. It is this level and these modalities that are highlighted in most literature when it refers (cf. below) to a "style of life" and "intentionality," a "new dynamism and power," a "special context."

A few statements of opinion on this question will help give the flavor of the discussion. John Macquarrie, the well known Anglican theologian, states that the Christian ethic is not distinctive in its ultimate goals or its fundamental principles. These are shared with all serious minded people of all traditions. Therefore the distinctiveness is not to be found in the concrete moral obligations derived from an authentic humanity but in the degree of explicitness surrounding the notion of authentic humanity. "The distinctive element is the special context within which the moral life is perceived. This special context includes the normative place assigned to Jesus Christ and his teaching—not, indeed, as a paradigm for external imitation, but rather as the criterion and inspiration for a style of life."[2]

J.M. Aubert prepares the way for his own answer by studying the question in St. Thomas.[3] Thomas' point of view is gathered from his treatment of the relation of human virtues to Christian virtues, and from his discussion of the relation between the law of Christ and human morality. With regard to the virtues, Aubert maintains that Thomas clarified a long patristic heritage by explaining the autonomy and value of human virtue. An earlier Augustinian concern to avoid Pelagianism tended to smother the human with the overwhelming gratuity and supremacy of the theological virtues. Thomas recovered this human aspect with no compromise on the supremacy of the theological order. For him charity was the form of the virtues, suffusing and dynamizing them, but leaving them intact as the genuinely human expressions or ways of charity.

With regard to law, Thomas taught that the law of Christ should animate and transfigure all of human life. This implies that human life already has a moral content to which charity will give a new sense. But Thomas insisted that the law of Christ adds of itself no new particular moral prescriptions. It introduces a new dynamism and power. The resultant new life is essentially a more total and divinized way of leading a human life, a human life having its own proper demands which man perceives by reason and conscience.

On the basis of his study Aubert concludes that it is faith which is the truly distinguishing (or formal) cause of the specificity of Christian morality. But this must be properly understood. Since there is only one destiny possible to all men, there is existentially only one morality common to Christians and non-Christians. That means that there is a material identity between Christian moral demands and those perceivable by reason. However, faith operates a distinctiveness in the manner and intentionality of living these common moral demands. That is, it renders explicit the presence of charity. The Christian builds a life style on this explicitness. Therefore the specificity of Christian morality is found essentially in the very style of life, the manner of comporting oneself and of accomplishing the moral tasks which the Christian has in common with other men—a manner more dynamic, more assured, more joyous, more capable of following the example of Christ dying for other men. For it is ultimately the law of the cross which remains the essentially Christian model of the manner of practicing the moral law. . . .

In several valuable studies Joseph Fuchs, S.J., pursues in depth the notion of "Christian intentionality" mentioned by Aubert.[4] It is Fuch's thesis that prescinding from this intentionality Christian morality is, in its materiality and concreteness, human morality. Therefore both Christians and non-Christians must seek the answers to moral questions by determining what is genuinely human. It is the intentionality brought to the authentically human which specifies Christian morality.

How are we to understand this intentionality? To explain it, Fuchs recalls that in the moral act there are two aspects: the specific act itself and through it one's self-realization with reference to an Absolute. This self-realization in relation to an Absolute is the decisive element in morality, even though we are not reflexly conscious of it. Thus there is "a certain intentionality which transcends and fulfills the individual moral act." Now the Christian does not relate himself to God only as the Absolute, but to God as Father, to God who gave us His love in the person of Christ, and who is in His Christ our salvation. It is this deep-seated stamp on our consciousness which is distinctive of Christian morality. Or, as Fuchs puts it: "This Christian intentionality is what makes the moral behavior of the Christian truly and specifically Christian, at every moment and in every aspect, even when it appears at first to be simply conduct conforming to human morality."[5] Everything the Christian does is an expression of this personal, conscious, and freely willed relation to the Father of Jesus Christ. This intentionality is present to us without explicit and systematic reflection on our part.

III
FAITH AND ITS INFLUENCE ON MORALITY

While Christian intentionality is the decisive element in Christian morality, there is another important aspect which Fuchs underlines. The Christian knows in faith and acknowledges certain realities which he alone can acknowledge: the person of Christ, the Holy Spirit at work in us, the message of salvation, the Church, the Christian community, the sacraments, teaching authority. Our relationship to these realities belongs to our being and must be realized in our conduct. It will do so at the level of a deeper and richer motivation.

Franz Böckle (University of Bonn) pursues the line taken by

Fuchs and lists three ways in which faith exercises an influence on morality.[6] First, faith in God's redemptive act in Jesus Christ gives to the radical act of self-determination (fundamental option) its basic ground and sense. This basic decision (*metanoia*) is the basis of the moral life and stamps all our activity, as Fuchs notes. Secondly, faith deepens and renders secure the insights important for individual acts. Here Böckle distinguishes "morally relevant insights" from "moral judgments." Faith has a direct influence only on the insights, not on the moral judgments themselves. Finally, Böckle argues that faith forbids the absolutizing of any created good.

The English Jesuit philosopher Gerard J. Hughes approaches the question by exploring the Christian justification for moral beliefs.[7] Does the Christian, he asks, base his moral beliefs upon grounds not available to the non-Christian? Hughes rejects the opinion that derives the substantive content of our moral knowledge from specifically Christian sources. The teaching and example of Christ provide, rather, a stimulus, a context and a motivation. For instance, we cannot read the New Testament seriously without being forced to re-examine our current moral values and beliefs. Here Hughes is close to Böckle's distinction between morally relevant insights and moral judgments. The Christian revelation continues to inject a divine discontent into our secular moral thinking and to throw light on the status of the moral life as a whole, though the implications of this discontent must be sought by the ordinary methods of ethical reflection.

Karl Rahner is one of the great theologians of this century. Rahner's thought on this problem can be summarized as follows. Since Christian ethics is the objectifcation in Jesus Christ of what every man experiences of himself in his subjectivity, "it does not and cannot add to human ethical self-understanding as such any material content that is, in principle, 'strange' or 'foreign' to man as he exists and experiences himself in this world."[8] However, a person within the Christian community has access to a privileged articulation, in objective form, of this experience of subjectivity. Precisely because the resources of Scripture, dogma, and Christian life are the fullest available "objectifications" of the common human experience, "the articulation of man's image of his moral good that is possible within historical Christian communities remains privileged in its access to enlarged perspectives on man."

These are but a few statements by contemporary thinkers of a positon that is traditional within the Catholic community, at least since the time of Aquinas.[9] The Roman theologians F. Hürth and P. M. Abellan summarized it as follows: "All moral commands of the 'New Law' are also commands of the natural moral law. Christ did not add any single moral prescription of a positive kind to the natural moral law ... That holds also for the command of love ... The ethical demand to love God and one's neighbor for God's sake is a demand of the natural moral law."[10]

This tradition must be carefully understood. It refers above all to the intelligibility of moral norms and asserts that while there can be mysteries of faith, there can be no mysterious ethical norms which are simply closed off to human insight. Thus "human insight and reasoning" must be understood in its broadest sense. That broad sense would include two clarifications. First, it does not exclude the fact that the individual values that generate a norm can experience a special grounding and ratification in revelation. Quite the contrary. Thus our faith that God loves each individual and calls each to salvation deepens our insight into the worth of the individual.

Secondly this broad sense of "human insight and reasoning" suggests that there are factors at work in moral convictions that are reasonable but not always reducible to the clear and distinct ideas that the term "human reason" can mistakenly suggest. When all these factors are combined, they suggest that the term "moral reasoning" is defined most aptly by negation: "reasonable" means not ultimately mysterious.

This portion is found in Suarez, Vermeersch, H. Küng, A. Auer, B. Schüller and a host of other Catholic theologians. It is also broadly shared by Protestant authors like Bultmann, Cullmann, E. Troeltsch.[11] Recently, however, there has been a small reaction against this analysis. It is found particularly in the writings of B. Stoeckle, J. Ratzinger and Hans Urs von Balthasar.[12] They put great emphasis on the idea that for the Christian, Christ "makes himself present as the only norm in every situation" (von Balthasar), that his word is "the ultimate decisive moral norm" (Schurmann). These statements are not false, of course, but they do not raise the issue as to *how* one originally knows God's will, whether through faith alone as a distinct manner of knowing or through human insight and reasoning. Jesus' word is the "ultimate decisive norm" even when one accepts the fact that Christ simply recalled and renewed with his authority natural moral demands—sc., those available in principle to human reasoning processes.

Thus far some current statements. I should now like to develop a possible understanding of the matter in the hope that it may provide a structure within which the relation of religious belief to decision-making in government can be enlightened. I shall proceed in two steps: the origin of moral judgments and the relation of Christian perspectives to these judgments.

Origins of Moral Judgments

The first thing to be said is that moral convictions do not originate from rational analyses and arguments. Let me take slavery as an example. We do not hold that slavery is humanly demeaning and immoral chiefly because we have argued to this rationally. Rather, first our sensitivities are sharpened to the meaning and value of human persons and certainly religious faith can play an important part in the sharpening. As Böckle notes, it can influence our insights. We then *experience* the out-of-jointness, inequality and injustice of slavery. We then *judge* it to be wrong. At this point we develop "arguments" to criticize, modify, and above all communicate this judgment. Reflective analysis is an attempt to reinforce rationally, communicably, and from other sources what we grasp at a different level. Discursive reflection does not *discover* the right and good, but only *analyzes* it. The good that reason seems to discover is the good that was already hidden in the original intuition.

This needs more explanation. How do we arrive at definite moral obligations, prescriptions, and proscriptions? How does the general thrust of our persons toward good and away from evil become concrete, even as concrete as a code of do's and don't's, and caveats? It happens somewhat as follows—and in this I am following closely the school of J. de Finance, G. de Broglie, G. Grisez, John Finnis, and others who are heavily reliant on the Thomistic notion of "natural inclinations" in explaining the origin of basic moral obligation. We proceed by asking what are the goods or values man can seek, the values that define his human opportunity, his flourishing? We can answer this by examining man's basic tendencies. For it is impossible to act without having an interest in the object, and it is impossible to be attracted by, to have interest in something without some inclination already present. What then are the basic inclinations?

With no pretense at being exhaustive, we could list some of the following as basic inclinations present prior to acculturation: the tendency to preserve life; the tendency to mate and raise children; the tendency to explore and question; the tendency to seek out other men and obtain their approval—friendship; the tendency to establish good relations with unknown higher powers; the tendency to use intelligence in guiding action; the tendency to develop skills and exercise them in play and the fine arts. In these inclinations our intelligence spontaneously and without reflection grasps the possibilities to which they point, and prescribes them. Thus we form naturally and without reflection the basic principles of practical or moral reasoning. Or as philosopher John Finnis renders it:

> What is spontaneously understood when one turns from contemplation to action is not a set of Kantian or neoscholastic "moral principles" identifying this as right and that as wrong, but a set of values which can be expressed in the form of principles as "life is a good-to-be-pursued and realized and what threatens it is to be avoided."[13]

We have not yet arrived at a determination of what concrete actions are morally right or wrong; but we have laid the basis. Since these basic values are equally basic and irreducibly attractive, the morality of our conduct is determined by the adequacy of our openness to these values. For each of these values has its self-evident appeal as a participation in the unconditioned Good we call God. The realization of these values in intersubjective life is the only adequate way to love and attain God.

Further reflection by practical reason tells us what it means to remain open and to pursue these basic human values. First we must take them into account in our conduct. Simple disregard of one or other shows we have set our mind against this good. Second, when we can do so as easily as not, we should avoid acting in ways that inhibit these values, and prefer ways that realize them. Third, we must make an effort on their behalf when their realization in another is in extreme peril. If we fail to do so, we show that the value in question is not the object of our efficacious love and concern. Finally, we must never choose against a basic good in the sense of spurning it. What is to count as "turning against a basic good" is, of course, the crucial moral question. Certainly it does not mean that there are never situations of conflicted values where it is necessary to cause harm as we go about doing good. Thus there are times when it is necessary to take life in the very defense of life, in our very adhering to this basic value. That means that taking life need not always involve one in "turning against a basic good." Somewhat similarly, one does not necessarily turn against the basic good of procreation (what Pius XII called a "sin against the very meaning of conjugal life") by avoiding child-bearing. Such avoidance is only reproachable when *unjustified.* And the many conflicts (medical, economic, social, eugenic) that justify such avoidance were acknowledged by Pius XII. Suppressing a value, or preferring one to another in one's choice cannot be simply identified with turning against a basic good. My only point here is that particular moral judgments are incarnations of these more basic normative positons, which have their roots in spontaneous, prereflective inclinations.

Even though these inclinations can be identified as prior to acculturation, still they exist as culturally conditioned. We tend toward values as perceived. And the culture in which we live shades our perception of values. Philip Rieff in *The Triumph of the Therapeutic* notes that a culture survives by the power of institutions to influence conduct with "reasons" that have sunk so deeply into the self that they are implicitly understood.[14] In other words, decisions are made, policies set not chiefly by articulated norms, codes, regulations, and philosophies, but by "reasons" that lie below the surface. This is the dynamic aspect of a culture, and in this sense many of our major moral problems are cultural. Our way of perceiving the basic human values and relating to them is shaped by our whole way of looking at the world.

Let me take an example from another area of concern, that of bioethics. In relating to the basic human values several images of man are possible, as Callahan has observed.[15] First there is a power-plasticity model. In this model, nature is alien, independent of man, possessing no inherent value. It is capable of being used, dominated, and shaped by man. Man sees himself as possessing an unrestricted right to manipulate in the service of his goals. Death is something to be overcome, outwitted. Second, there is the sacral-symbiotic model. In its religious forms, nature is seen as God's creation, to be respected and heeded. Man is not the master; he is the steward and nature is a trust. In secular forms, man is seen as a part of nature. If man is to be respected, so is nature. We should live in harmony and balance with nature. Nature is a teacher, showing us how to live with it. Death is one of the rhythms of nature, to be gracefully accepted.

The model which seems to have "sunk deep" and shaped our moral imagination and feelings—shaped our perception of basic values—is the power-plasticity model. We are, corporately *homo technologicus.* The best solution to the dilemmas created by technology is more technology. We tend to eliminate the maladapted condition (defectives, retardates, and so on) rather than adjust the environment to it. Even our language is sanitized and shades from view our relationship to basic human values. We speak of "surgical air strikes" and "terminating a pregnancy", ways of blunting the moral imagination from the shape of our conduct. My only point here is that certain cultural "reasons" qualify or shape our perception of and our grasp on the basic human values. Thus these reasons are the cultural soil of our moral convictions and have a good deal to say about where we come out on particular moral judgments.

Once the basic values are identified along with their cultural tints and trappings, theologians and philosophers attempt to develop "middle axioms" or mediating principles. These relate the basic values to concrete choice. The major problem any professional ethic faces is to reinterpret the concrete demands of the basic values in new circumstances without forfeiting its grasp on these values.

IV

THE CHRISTIAN PERSPECTIVE AND MORAL JUDGMENTS

There may be many ways to explain the influences of Christian faith on the moral norms that guide decision-making. For instance, the very notion one entertains of the Supreme Being can influence normative statements. If one thinks of God above all as the creator and conserver of order, then this yields a certain attitude toward human interventions into the givenness of the world. If, however, one also believes God is the enabler of our potentialities, then a quite different normative stance becomes feasible, as James Gustafson has pointed out.[16] (Cf. Haughey.)

My own view on the relation of Christian belief to *essential* ethics would be developed as follows. Since there is only one destiny possible to all men, there is existentially only one *essential* morality common to all men, Christians and non-Christians alike. Whatever is distinctive about Christian morality is found essentially in the style of life, the manner of accomplishing the moral tasks common to all persons, not in the tasks themselves. Christian morality is, in its concreteness and materiality, *human* morality. The theological study of morality accepts the human in all its fullness as its starting point. It is the *human* which is then illumined by the person, teaching and achievement of Jesus Christ. The experience of Jesus is regarded as normative because he is believed to have experienced what is to be human in the fullest way and at the deepest level.

The Second Vatican Council stated something similar to this when it asserted that "faith throws a new light on everything, manifests God's design for man's total vocation, and thus directs the mind to solutions which are *fully human.*"[17] It further stated "But only God, who created man to His own image and ransoms him from sin, provides a fully adequate answer to these questions. This he does through what he has revealed in Christ His Son, who became man. Whoever follows after Christ, the perfect man, *becomes himself more of a man.*"[18]

Traditionally, theologians referred to moral knowledge as originating in "reason *informed* by faith." The word "inform" is important. It does not mean *replaced* by faith. It is in explaining the term "inform" that we may hope to see more precisely how faith influences moral judgments at the *essential* level.

I have noted that our concrete moral judgments are applications originating in insights into our inclinations toward basic human values or goods. I have also suggested that our reasoning processes about these basic values can be distorted by cultural biases.

Let us take an example. It can be persuasively argued that the peculair temptation of a technologically advanced culture such as ours is to view and.treat persons functionally. Our treatment of the aged is perhaps the sorriest symptom of this. The elderly are probably the most alienated members of our society. More and more of them spend their declining years in homes for senior citizens, in chronic hospitals, in nursing homes. We have shunted them aside. Their protest is eloquent because it is helplessly muted and silent. But it is a protest against a basically functional assessment of their persons. "Maladaptation" is the term used to describe *them* rather than the environment. This represents a terribly distorted judgment of the human person.

Love of and loyalty to Jesus Christ, the perfect man, sensitizes us to the meaning of persons. The Christian tradition is anchored in faith in the meaning and decisive significance of God's covenant with men, especially as manifested in the saving incarnation of Jesus Christ, his eschatological kingdom which is here aborning but will finally only be given. Faith in these events, love of and loyalty to this central figure, yields a decisive way of viewing and intending the world, of interpreting its meaning, of hierarchizing its values. In this sense the Christian tradition only illumines human values, supports them, provides a context for their reading at given points in history. It aids us in staying human by underlining the truly human against all cultural attempts to distort the human. It is by steadying our gaze on the basic human values that are the parents of more concrete norms and rules that faith influences moral judgment and decision-making. That is how I understand "reason informed by faith."

In summary, then, Christian emphases do not immediately yield moral norms and rules for decision-making. But they affect them. The stories and symbols that relate the origin of Christianity and nourish the faith of the individual, affect one's perspectives. They sharpen and intensify our focus on the human goods definitive of our flourishing. It is persons so informed, persons with such "reasons" sunk deep in their being, who face new situations, new dilemmas, and reason together as to what is the best policy, the best protocol for the service of all the values. They do not find concrete answers in their tradition, but they bring a world-view that informs their reasoning—especially by allowing the basic human goods to retain their attractiveness and not be tainted by cultural distortions. This worldview is a continuing check on and challenge to our tendency to make choices in light of cultural enthusiasms which sink into and take possession of our unwitting, pre-ethical selves. Such enthusiasms can reduce the good life to mere adjustment in a triumph of the therapeutic; collapse an individual into his functionability; exalt his uniqueness into a lonely individualism or crush it into a suffocating collectivism. In this sense I believe it is true to say that the Christian tradition is much more a value-raiser than an answer-giver. And it affects our values at the spontaneous, prethematic level. One of the values inherent in its incarnational ethos is an affirmation of the goodness of man and all about him—including his reasoning and thought processes. The Christian tradition refuses to bypass or supplant human deliberation and hard work in developing ethical protocols within a profession. For that would be blasphemous of the Word of God become human. On the contrary, it asserts their need, but constantly reminds men that what God did and intends for man is an affirmation of the human and therefore must remain the measure of what man may reasonably decide to do to and for himself.

V

THE INFLUENCE OF FAITH

If this is a satisfactory account of the relation of Christian faith to decision-making (at the *essential* level), it means that faith informs reason because the reasoner has been transformed. This transformation means practically: (1) a *view* of persons and their meaning; (2) a *motivation* in the following of Christ; (3) a *style* of performing the moral tasks common to persons (communitarian, sacramental, cross of Christ, Holy Spirit). I think it quite possible that persons with such a view, motivation, style, might come to some different practical conclusions on moral matters, as indeed the historical Christian churches have. But these conclusions will not be in principle unavailable to human insight and reasoning in the broadest sense. That is what is meant, I believe, by the two assertions we find in Catholic Christian tradition. The first admits that our reasoning processes are "obscured by the sin of our first parent" and that revelation is necessary so we can know "expeditiously, with firm security and without error those things that are not in principle impervious to human reasons." (DB 1286) Second, notwithstanding this realism about our sinful (even if redeemed) condition, this tradition refuses to bypass or supplant human deliberation and hard work in normative ethics.

What does all this have to do with decision-making in government work? In private seminar-discussions, our collaborators from the government sector repeatedly have indicated that their faith does have an influence on their decision-making and conduct; yet, secondly, all found it hard to isolate this.

Here we see in combination the strong conviction that religious faith does influence decision-making, yet the inability on the part of very articulate and experienced people to show very specifically what this influence is. This is, I believe, to be expected and for several reasons. First, religious faith does not originate new moral claims at the essential level. At this level, the relation of faith and concrete ethics is one of informing reason, or what is the same, transforming the reasoner, not eliminating or replacing him. It does this at a very profound level, what I have called the prethematic level, or the level of insight associated with our spontaneous inclinations. Thus, faith and reason are closely intermingled and it is difficult to sort out their independent influence.

Secondly, the levels at which religious faith does have a profound and original impact (essential Christian, existential Christian) are different for different individuals, and are experienced differently. That is because the claims originated by faith at these levels relate to individual talent, capacity, training, spiritual growth, etc. This means that it is difficult to generalize on the relation of faith to decision-making.

Finally, many deliberations and decisions in government work are concerned not directly with basic human goods, but with alternative strategies and perceived differences of means to achieve these goods. Such strategies—and differences in strategy—are probably best illumined and explained by disciplines and studies not directly related to faith.

On a December 1977 visit to London, Governor Edmund Brown, Jr., was asked how his belief in Catholicism affected his politics. He replied: "I do think one's values determine decision-making.

And very simply, theological assumptions affect the shape and direction of government decisions." The first statement is correct and obvious. As for the second, Governor Brown did not specify how theological assumptions affect one's values. Had he tried he might have had a great deal of trouble. Or better, where our common moral tasks are concerned (and is not that preeminently the work of government—the common good?), he might have found himself speaking of a view of man and the world, a motivation, and a style of approach and performance. Indeed, he did precisely that. When asked about his own frugality, he remarked: "The closer leaders can be to the life-style and the ways of the population they serve, the better the democracy." Jesus said some remarkably similar things. Brown's statement is profoundly biblical—and utterly reasonsable. We should expect such a conjunction after the Incarnation.

In sum, one need not be a Christian to be concerned with the poor, with health, with the food problem, with justice and rights. But if one is a Christian and is not so conerned, something is wrong with that Christianity. It has ceased to be Christian because it has ceased to be what its founder was—human.

NOTES

1. I borrow this usage from Norbert Rigali, S.J., "On Christian Ethics" *Chicago Studies* 10 (1971) 227–247.
2. John Macquarrie, *Three Issues in Ethics* (New York: Harper and Row, 1970) 89.
3. J.-M. Aubert, "La Spécificité de la morale Chrétienne selon Saint Thomas," *Supplément* 92 (1970) 55–73.
4. Joseph Fuchs, S.J., "Gibt es eine specifisch Christliche Moral?" *Stimmen der Zeit* 185 (1970) 99–112; "Human, Humanist and Christian Morality" in *Human Values and Christian Morality* (Dublin: Gill and Macmillan, 1970) 112–147.
5. "Human, Humanist and Christian Morality," p. 124.
6. Franz Böckle, "Glaube and Handeln" *Concilium,* 120 (1976) 641–647. Very similar to Böckle's distinction between insights and judgments is Helmut Weber's notion of a biblically inspired understanding of man and the world. Cf. "Um das Proprium Christlicher Ethik" *Triertheologische Zeitschrift* 81 (1972) 257–275.
7. Gerard J. Hughes, S.J., "A Christian Basis for Ethics," *Heythrop Journal* 13 (1972) 27–43.

8. James F. Bresnahan, S.J., "Rahner's Christian Ethics" *America* 123 (1970) 351–354.

9. For further literature cf. Richard A. McCormick, S.J., *Theological Studies* 32 (1971) 71–78; 34 (1973) 58–60; 38 (1977) 58–70.

10. F. Hürth, P.M. Abellan, *De Principiis, de virtutibus et praeceptis,* 1 (Rome: Gregorian University, 1948) 43.

11. Cf. Bruno Schüller, S.J., "Zur Diskussion über das Proprium einer Christlichen Ethik" *Theologie und Philosophie* 51 (1976) 331.

12. Cf. *Theological Studies* 38 (1977) 65.

13. John M. Finnis "Natural Law and Unnatural Acts" *Heythrop Journal* 11 (1970) 365–387.

14. Philip Rieff, *The Triumph of the Therapeutic* (New York: Harper & Row, 1966).

15. Daniel Callahan "Living with the New Biology" *Center Magazine,* 5 (July–Aug. 1972) 4–12.

16. James Gustafson, *The Contributions of Theology to Medical Ethics,* (Milwaukee: Marquette University, 1975).

17. *The Documents of Vatican II* (New York: America Press, 1966) p. 209.

18. *Ibid.,* p. 240.

Magisterium of the Church, Faith, Morality

Joseph Ratzinger

SURVEY OF THE PROBLEM

The crisis of faith, which is making itself increasingly felt in Christendom, is more and more clearly seen to be also a crisis in awareness of the fundamental values of human life. On the one hand it is nourished by the moral crisis of mankind and on the other hand it has repercussions on the latter, making it more acute. When the attempt is made to survey the panorama of the present discussions on this matter, strange contradictions are met with, which, however, are closely connected with one another. On the one hand, particularly since the meeting of the World Council of Churches at Upsala, there is an increasingly clear tendency to define Christianity primarily as "orthopraxis" and not as "orthodoxy." There are various reasons for this. Reference should perhaps be made to the seriousness of the racial problem for American Christian communities. Their religion has not succeeded in breaking down the barriers of separation and therefore the validity of faith itself seems to be questioned, since it has not been able to bring to life the love that is the root of the Gospel. In this way a practical question becomes the touchstone of the intrinsic value of doctrine, the proof of what is Christian: where "orthopraxis" is so glaringly absent, "orthodoxy" seems questionable.

Another origin of the trend towards "praxis" lies in the various movements of "political theology," which on their side have different motives. Common to them all is great perplexity due to the questions raised by Marxism. The concept of "truth" is regarded here with suspicion or at least as being without value. To this extent this theory is identified with the fundamental feeling that gives rise to positivism.

Truth is considered unattainable and its proclamation only an alibi for group interests, which are thus consolidated. Only praxis can decide (still according to this view) the value or lack of value of theories. So if Christianity wishes to make some contribution to the construction of a better world, it should create a better praxis—not seek truth as a theory, but reestablish it as a reality.

The claim that Christianity should become "orthopraxis" of joint activities for a more human future and leave orthodoxy aside as unfruitful or harmful, takes on here a far more fundamental character than in the case of the pragmatic standpoint described above. It is clear at the same time that both positions tend to unite and strengthen each other. In both cases there remains little room for a magisterium, although if these principles were applied consistently it should appear again in a different form. Certainly, a magisterium that wished to formulate a preconstituted truth with regard to correct human praxis and wished to measure praxis by this truth, would fall on the negative side of reality as an obstacle to creative, forward-looking praxis. It would appear as the expression of interests concealed under the label of "orthodoxy" and opposed to the advance of the history of freedom. On the other hand it is admitted that praxis needs reflection and well thought out tactics, for which reason the tie between Marxist practice and the "magisterium" of the party is perfectly logical.

The movement that would like to define and realize Christianity as orthopraxis is opposed at the other end (and in fact often passes into it suddenly) by the position that maintains there is no specific Christian morality; on the contrary Christianity must take its norms of behavior every time from the anthropological knowledge of its own age. Faith does not offer any independent principle of moral norms but on this point refers strictly to reason; anything that is not guaranteed by reason would not be supported by faith. This assertion is justified with the statement that, even in its historical sources, the faith did not develop any morality of its own but followed the practical reason of contemporaries in the different periods.[1] This can be seen already in the Old Testament, where value concepts from the time of the patriarchs to sapiential literature were in continual change, conditioned by contact with the development of the moral concepts of collateral cultures. Nowhere can there be found, they say, a moral sentence limited only to the Old Testament, of which it could be said that it is the result exclusively of faith in Jehovah; in the moral field everthing was borrowed elsewhere. According to this theory, this applies also to the New Testament: the virtues and vices listed in the Pauline epistles reflect Stoic morality and in this way are the acceptance of the rational canons of human behavior at that time. For this reason their value lies not in the content, but in their structure: as a reference to reason as the only source of moral norms.

It need hardly be said that also with this point of departure there is no room for an ecclesiastical Magisterium in the moral field. For norms essentially based on the tradition of faith would, according to this thesis, spring from the misunderstanding that the teachings of the Bible are absolute and perennial indications while they are only a reference to the positions reached at different moments by the knowledge attained by reason.

It is clear that, in both cases, it is a question of fundamental problems of Christianity, which cannot be dealt with sufficiently in a few pages. In the first case, when the interpretation of Christianity as "orthopraxis" is made not only on the pragmatic plane but also on the plane of principles, the problem in discussion is truth and above all the fundamental question of what reality is. With the problem of being it is a question, in the last analysis, of the first article of the faith, even though people are not always specifically aware of the fact and positions are seldom pushed to their radical extremes. In the second case it seems to be a question above all of a particular historical problem, the historical origin of certain biblical teaching. A closer examination shows that the problem is a more fundamental one, namely how to determine what is specifically Christian in view of the changing historical forms of Christianity. At the same time there is at stake the problem of the interpretation of the relationships between faith and reason and between faith and man in general; and finally, in particular, the question of the possibility and limits of reason as compared with faith.[2]

II
FIRST COUNTER-DEDUCTIONS

Let us begin with the most obvious and simplest things and then go on to the specific question, that is, the problem of the historical origin of biblical teaching in the moral field. In the first place it is necessary to examine a general methodological question. The hypothesis that what is received can never become one's own, is quite simply false. We know this from our own life. The theological principle "What hast thou that thou hast not received?" (1 Cor. 4, 7) is evident even on the purely human plane; but we know it also from the whole history of culture: the dimension of a culture is shown by its capacity of communication, its capacity to give and take, yes, take, receive and assimilate. The originality of Christianity in the moral field does not lie in the sum of principles which have no parallels elsewhere (if there are any such principles, which is very problematic). It is not possible to distill what is specifically Christian in this field by taking away everything that was borrowed from others. Christian originality consists rather in the new overall conception into which man's quest and aspiration was directed by faith in the God of Abraham, in the God of Jesus Christ. The reference of morality to pure reason is in no way proved by the fact that the moral teaching of the Bible has its origin in other cultures or philosophical thought. Such an assertion would represent a short circuit of thought that can no longer be tolerated. What is decisive is not the fact that these principles can be found elsewhere, but only the problem of the place they do or do not occupy in the spiritual structure of Christianity. It is this point, therefore, that must be studied next.

Here, too, let us begin with a very simple observation. It is incorrect from the historical point of view to say that Christianity took over at all periods the morality of its contemporary environment, that is, the degree of moral knowledge reached by reason. For "the environment" as such and a unitarian "morality" all ready to be taken over, did not exist. We see rather that, amid tensions that were often highly dramatic, the elements of the juridico-moral tradition of the surrounding world were divided into those which, corresponding to the figure of Jahweh, could be assimilated by Israel and those which, on the basis of its representation of God, had to be rejected. The battle of the prophets is in the last analysis connected with this problem. Whether we think of Nathan, who forbids David to take on the form of a despotic Oriental potentate, free to take his neighbor's wife if he likes; or of Elijah, who, defending Naboth's right, defends the right guaranteed by the God of Israel, against the absolutism of kings; or of Amos, who in his battle for fair wages for workers and dependents, is mainly defending the image of the God of Israel—it is the same thing. Even the whole conflict between Jahweh and Baal cannot be reduced to a pure "dogmatic" question but is connected with the inseparable unity of faith and life, which is at stake here: the option for one God or for the gods is in every case a life decision.

III

THREE EXAMPLES OF THE UNION OF FAITH AND MORALITY

The Ten Commandments

With these arguments we have now reached the heart of the matter, which we will now try to clarify with three characteristic examples. Let us cast a glance first of all at the Ten Commandments (Ex. 20, 1–17; Dt. 5, 6–21), one of the central formulations of Jahweh's will regarding Israel, by which the morality of Israel and of the Church has always been renewed. It can be shown without any doubt that these Commandments have models both in the Egyptian lists of crimes that must not be committed and in the lists of questions of Babylonian exorcism. Even the introductory formula: "I am the Lord thy God," is not completely new. Yet it gives the "ten laws" a new significance: they are connected with faith in the God of Israel, the God of the Covenant and his will. The "Ten Commandments" indicate what is the essence of faith in God, of acceptance of the covenant with Jahweh. At the same time they define the image of God himself, whose essence is manifested in his will. This fact connects the Ten Commandments with the fundamental revelation of God in Exodus 3, since here, too, the manifestation of God is expressed concretely in the manifestation of his will in ethical matters: He has heard the groans of the oppressed and has come to liberate them. With these words the introduction to the Ten Commandments is connected both with the version in Exodus 20 and with its repetition in Deuteronomy: Jahweh presents himself as the God who has brought Israel out of Egypt, the house of bondage. This means that the Ten Commandments are, in Israel, part of the very conception of God. They do not take their place alongside the faith, alongside the alliance; they show who the God is with whom Israel is in alliance.[3]

Connected with this is the particular development of the conception of "holy" in biblical religion. From the standpoint of the history of religion, "holy" indicates in the first place the "being-quite-different" of divinity, its specific atmosphere, from which the particular rules for relations with divinity are drawn. In Israel, too, this was so to begin with as a large number of biblical passages show. But when Jahweh presents his particularity, his "being-quite-different," in the Ten Commandments, it becomes clear (and the prophets make people more and more aware of it) that the "being-quite-different" of Jahweh, his holiness, is a moral greatness to which man's moral action must correspond, according to the Ten Commandments. The conception of holiness, as the specific category of the divine, merges, even in those ancient strata of tradition to which the Ten Commandments belong, with the conception of morality, and this is precisely the novelty, the singularity of this God and his holiness. But here, too, lies the new value that morality acquires, which determines the criterion of choice in the dialogue with the ethics of peoples, until there arises that lofty concept of holiness which, in the Old Testament anticipates the divine figure of Jesus: "I will not execute my fierce anger . . . for I am God and not man, the Holy One in your midst . . ." (Hosea, 11, 9). "There can be no doubt that with the proclamation of the Ten Commandments in Israel, there takes place the election of Israel, says Gerhard v. Rad in his *Theology of the Old Testament.* He also presents the consequences of this correlation on the liturgical life of Israel.[4] All this does not mean, of course, that right from the beginning the Ten Commandments were understood in all their deep significance and that mere enunciation at once brings with it essential moral knowledge. The history of the interpretation of the Ten Commandments from the earliest times to their reformulation in Jesus' Sermon on the Mount, shows rather that they could and were obliged to bring about an even deeper understanding of the divine will and thereby also of God and man himself. What has been said makes it clear that though individual parts of the Ten Commandments come from an environment outside Israel, this does not prove that they do not belong to the faith of the covenant. After all, this assertion could be made only by starting from the premise that the reason of peoples and the revelation of God are paradoxical, unconnected by any analogy, that is, starting out from a precise position about the relationship between revelation and reason, which the biblical texts do not show to be true, but on the contrary clearly show to be false.

The Name "Christian"

Let us choose a second example, this time in the field of early Christianity, in which it is again a question, as for Israel in the Ten Commandments, of a central issue: the meaning of the words "Christian" and "Christianity" at the time when the Church was coming into being.[5] From Acts 11, 26 we know that this name was given to the community of believers in Antioch for the first time. Although the origin and initial meaning of the denomination are still debatable in the present state of the sources, it is nevertheless clear that it at once took on an ironical meaning and that it became in Roman law the designation of a crime liable to punishment: Christians are members of Christ's conspiring sect. From Hadrian onwards, therefore, to bear the name "Christian" is expressly declared a penal offense. Peterson has shown that the accusations against the Christians, as found in Suetonius and Tacitus, are part of the political propaganda "carried on against real or presumed conspirators."[6] Yet already in the time of Ignatius of Antioch we see the Christians taking over this dangerous word to designate themselves, proud to bear it and to prove themselves worthy of it. What happens when this insulting name, liable to penal penalties, is consciously assumed and borne?

There are two possible answers. In the first place there is in St. Ignatius a marked theology of martyrdom, which leads to assumption of the name which itself involves martyrdom. Communion with Jesus Christ, which for him is faith, means in the eyes of the world participation in a conspiracy for which the punishment is death. This is for the bishop of Antioch an outside view, which gets a glimpse of what there is inside, but in a form completely different from the reality: communion with Jesus is, in fact, participation in his death and only in this way also in his life.[7] This means: the conception of the common conspiracy of Christians with Christ contains this element of truth, that Christians do not take over just a theory from Jesus, but participate in his choice of life and death and repeat it in their own way. "Since we have become his disciples, we must learn to live in a Christian way."[8] In this sense, for the Syrian martyr bishop Christianity is completely "orthopraxis," it means imitating Jesus' way of life. But what is this way of life? This question leads to a second consideration. For the pagan the word "Christian" means a conspirator, who is represented according to the patterns of political propaganda as guilty of terrible crimes ("flagitia"), in particular, "hatred of mankind" and dissoluteness "stuprum").[9] Against this view Ignatius uses a play on words which was used for a long time in Christian apologetics. In Greek phonetics the word "chrestos" (good) was (and is) pronounced with the "i": christos. Ignatius takes advantage of this when he precedes the sentence "let us learn to live in accordance with Christianity" with the words "let us not be insensitive to its goodness (chrestotes, pronounced christotes)."[10] The conspiracy of the Christian is a conspiracy to be "chrestos," a conspiracy to do good. One hundred years later Tertullian still says: "The word Christian is taken from the expression to be good."[11] The connection between conception of God and moral idea, which we found in the Ten Commandments, is repeated here in Christianity in a highly sublime and demanding way. The name "Christian" means communion with Christ, but for that very reason, the willingness to accept the martyrdom of good. Christianity is a conspiracy to do good. The theological and moral qualities are inseparably bound up with the name and, even deeper, with the essential concepts of Christianity.[12]

Apostolic Teaching

But with this Ignatius and the early Christian theology that follows him are strictly on the plane of apostolic preaching, which we will now take as our third example. The close connection between faith and "imitation" of the Apostle, which is "imitation" of Jesus Christ, is characteristic of St. Paul's preaching. The first Epistle to the Thessalonians is particularly precise in this respect: " . . . we gave you a pattern of how you ought to live . . . live by that pattern. You have not forgotten the instructions we gave you by the command of the Lord Jesus" (1 Thess. 4; 1 ff.). The "live" belongs to tradition, the order does not come from just anywhere, but from the Lord Jesus; the specifications that follow are taken from the Ten Commandments and explain them in a Christian way, adapted to the special situation of the Thessalonians.

At this point it might be objected that here the main question concerns only the formal intention of "good," which is beyond all doubt characteristic of Christianity. But the essential problem: "in what does this good consist?" is not answered by theological sources, but decided on each occasion by reason and time. And then reference can be made to a text that seems to confirm this, such as Phil 4, 8: "Finally, brothers, fill your minds with everything that is true, everything that is noble, everything that is good and pure, everything that we love and honor, and everything that can be thought virtuous or worthy of praise." These, it is said, are concepts of popular philosophy, in which accepted standards of good are clearly proposed to Christians as their standards. But it could at once be answered that the text goes on to say: "Keep doing all the things that you learnt from me and have been taught by me and have heard or seen that I do" (4, 9). It could be added that after all this passage is a commentary on 2, 5: "In your minds you must be the same as Christ Jesus" where we find the same necessary connection between Jesus' way of thinking and Christian existence as we came across it in Ignatius.

But on the historical and objective plane it is necessary to go deeper. It is certainly true that Paul, here as elsewhere, refers to that moral knowledge that awakened the conscience of the pagans, and it is true that he identifies this knowledge with God's true law, according to the principles set forth in Rom. 2, 15. But that does not mean that the *Kerygma* is reduced here to a generic exhortation to adhere to what is considered good by reason in each individual case. Two facts contradict this view: 1) historically speaking, this "reason of time" has never existed and never will. What Paul found was not a precise position of research on good, which he could just take over, but a confusion of contradictory positions of which Epicurus and Seneca are only two examples. This being so, it was not possible to proceed by accepting these positions. It was necessary, on the contrary, to make a decisive and critical separation, in which the Christian faith formed its new options in accordance with the Old Testament standards and with the "way of thinking of Jesus Christ."

These options were condemned by the outside world as "conspiracy," but were only all the more resolutely considered as the real "good" by Christians themselves.

Contrary to the above-mentioned opinion is, secondly, the fact that for Paul conscience and reason are not two changeable standards, which say one thing today and another tomorrow. Conscience proves it is what it is precisely by saying the same things as God said in the covenant with the Jews; as conscience, it reveals what is abiding and thus leads necessarily to the way of thinking of Jesus Christ. The real thought of the apostle Paul is seen most clearly, perhaps, in the first chapter of the Epistle to the Romans, where that connection of morality with the conception of God, which we found to be a characteristic of the Old Testament, is repeated. Lack of the notion of God brings about the moral deficiency of the pagan world; conversion to God in Jesus Christ coincides with conversion to imitation of Jesus Christ. Paul had already developed the same thought in 1 Thessalonians: the non-holiness of pagans is due to the fact that they do not know God; God's will is "sanctification," which is received, in the moral sense, directly in the message of grace. Anyone who reads Paul's epistles carefully will easily see that apostolic preaching is not a moralizing appendage the contents of which could be changed, but is the concrete designation of what faith is and is therefore linked indissolubly with its central point. In this the Apostle is only following the example of Jesus who, in the introduction and conclusion of his teaching on the kingdom of God had connected indissolubly this central subject of his preaching with the fundamental moral decisions that come from the image of God and are closely linked with him.[13]

IV
FAITH—MORALITY—MAGISTERIUM

The reference to apostolic teaching with the connection between faith and morality brings up the matter of the Magisterium. For the apostolic epistles are an exercise of the teaching authority. In them Paul takes up a position "magisterially" also on the moral aspect of faith. The same applies to all the epistles in the New Testament and to the Gospels, which are full of moral instructions, and also to the Apocalypse. In his teaching, Paul does not theorize about human rationality, but sets forth the inner necessity of grace, as H. Schlier has pointed out forcibly in his fine article on the originality of Christian teaching.[14] Actually, although the apostle is convinced he has the authority (2 Cor. 8, 8), he does not use the form of explicit command too often (1 Thess. 4, 10 f.; other texts in Schlier, p. 342). He does not want to correct the Christian communities with reproofs and the rod, as teachers corrected children in ancient times—he prefers fatherly persuasion in the Christian family. But precisely by doing so he makes it clearly understood that behind his words is the mercy of God himself calling. In his exhortation it is grace that exhorts, it is God that exhorts; it is not a variable accessory to the Gospel, but is guaranteed by the authority of the Lord, even when it is not presented in the form of a command or doctrinal decision.[15] The same can be said when the central themes of his doctrine are considered: salvation in Christ, baptism, the communion of the Body of Christ, the last judgment.[16] The line of demarcation drawn by grace in regard to the life of those who do not know God is quite clear: it is abstention from wantonness, greed, envy and quarrelsomeness; inclination to obedience, patience, truth, trust and joy: in these attitudes the fundamental command of love is unfolded.[17]

What we see in Paul is continued in the writings of the successors of the apostles, in which the apostolic doctrine is explained in a way suited to the situation.[18] This means that, for the New Testament, the ecclesiastical Magisterium does not end with the time of the Apostles. The Church therefore remains apostolic also in the post-apostolic era, and it is her permanent task to see to it that the legitimate successors of the apostles defend the unchangeability of the apostolic doctrine. Luke sets this forth expressly in the crisis of transition, taking as the model of the Church of all times the original community of Jerusalem, which "remained faithful to the teaching of the apostles" (Acts 2, 42), and indicating the elders as overseers of this faithfulness (Acts 20, 17–38).[19]

It is not necessary to develop in this connection a detailed theory of the ecclesiastic Magisterium and its centralization in the Magisterium of Peter's successor, although it would not be hard to present the lines that run in this direction in the New Testament: on the one hand the concept of tradition and succession that is made increasingly clear and on the other hand the theology of Peter. It is evident that the fundamental value of the apostolic succession consists precisely in the authority to preserve the apostolic faith, and that the consequent magisterial authority essentially comprises also the duty to show concretely the moral necessity of grace and specify it in the different periods.[20]

With this the circle of our thought returns to the beginning again. The practice of faith belongs, in fact, to Christian faith. Orthodoxy without orthopraxis loses the essence of Christianity: the love that comes from grace. At the same time, however, it is admitted that Christian practice is nourished by Christian faith: by the grace that appeared in Christ and was attributed to the *sacramentum Ecclesiae*. The practice of faith depends on the truth of faith, in which man's truth is made visible through God's truth and is raised one step higher. It therefore radically contradicts a practice that seeks first to produce facts and through them establish the truth; against this complete manipulation of reality it defends God's creation. Man's fundamental values, which it gets to know from the example of Jesus Christ, are withdrawn by it from all manipulation. Defending the creation, it protects man. It is the irrevocable task of the successors of the apostles to keep the apostolic teaching present in this way. Since grace is in relation to the creation and the creator, the apostolic doctrine (as continuation of the teaching of the Old Testament) has to do with reason. Both flight into pure orthopraxis and the withdrawal of objective morality from the field of faith (and the Magisterium belonging to the faith) are equivalent, despite first appearances, to an accusation of heresy made against reason. In the one case reason is denied the capacity of knowing truth, and renunciation of truth is raised to a method; in the other case, faith is excluded from the field of reason and the rational is not admitted as a possible content of the world of faith. Thereby either faith is declared nonrational or reason non-believing or both. At the same time, on the one hand reason is taken as being univocal with its own time, which is not the case, and on the other hand its testimonies tally to such an extent with the standards of the time that truth disappears in time and the rational differs according to time, so that when all is said and done we end up by accepting the pure dominion of practical reason.

The faith of the Apostle, as is seen from Rom. 1 and 2, has a higher concept of reason. St. Paul is convinced that reason is capable of truth and that therefore the faith cannot be constructed outside the rules of reason, but finds its way of expressing itself by communicating with the reason of peoples, accepting and refusing. This means that both the process of assimilation and the process of negation and criticism must start from the fundamental decisions of faith and has its firm points of reference in the latter. Reason's capacity of truth means at the same time the objective constancy of truth, which agrees with the constancy of faith.

The task of the Magisterium of the Church in the moral field follows from what has been said. Faith comprises, as we have seen, fundamental objective decisions in the moral field. The task of the Magisterium is first and foremost to continue apostolic teaching and defend these fundamental principles should reason yield to time or capitulate before the omnipotence of practice. The value of these principles is that they correspond to the fundamental knowledge of human reason, purified, deepened and amplified in contact with the life of faith. The positive-critical dialogue with reason must, as has been said, be extended to all times. On the one hand it is never completely clear what is really reason and what is only apparently "rational"; on the other hand there exist at all times both phenomena, the apparently rational and the appearance of truth through reason. In the process of assimilating what is really rational and rejecting what only seems to be rational, the whole Church has to play a part. This process cannot be carried out in every detail by an isolated Magisterium, with oracular infallibility. The life and suffering of Christians who profess their faith in the midst of their times has just as important a part to play as the thinking and questioning of the learned, which would have a very hollow ring without the backing of Christian existence, which learns to discern spirits in the travail of everyday life. The whole Church's experience of faith, thinkers' researches and questionings, are two factors; the watchful observation, listening and decision of the Magisterium is the third. That correct doctrine is not exercised automatically but requires the "exhortation and reprimanding" of the responsible pastors of the Church, was experienced by the Church in the first century, and for that very reason she formed the office of those who, with prayer and the laying on of hands, are called to the succession of the apostles. For the Church this office is indispensable today, too, and where her competence is challenged as regards essential decisions for or against an interpretation of morality following upon grace, the fundamental form of apostolic tradition itself is shaken.

Notes

1. Thus lastly, after others, H. Küng; *On Being a Christian,* trsl. by Edward Quinn (Doubleday & Co., New York 1974): "The *distinguishing features* even of the *Old Testament ethics* did not consist in the individual precepts of prohibitions, but in the Yahweh faith . . ." The directives of the "second tablet" for interpersonal relationships go back to the moral and legal traditions of the pre-Israelite semi-nomadic tribes and have numerous analogies in the Near East. . . . "These fundamental minimal requirements then are not specifically Israelite. . . . All that is specifically Israelite is the fact that these requirements are subordinated to the authority of Yahweh, the God of the Covenant" (p. 542). Counter question: Did, for instance, Israel's image of God come into being without borrowings from and parallels to the world around her? Were not moral and legal requirements in the rest of the Orient linked to the authority of the respective deity? Similar questions intrude, when Küng, in relation to the New Testament asserts: "The ethical requirements of the New Testament . . . did not fall from heaven either in content or form" (p. 543). Did the rest of the New Testament fall from heaven? It should be obvious that an argumentation of this sort is inadmissable.

2. The question is carefully discussed—to be sure in a wholly different direction—in B. Schüller, "Die Bedeutung des naturlichen Sittengesetzes für den Christen," in G. Teichtweier and W. Draier, *Herausforderung und Kritik der Moraltheologie* (Wurzburg, 1971) pp. 105–130. The balance of the individual aspects that he tries to achieve can probably best be seen in the summary expressed in the sentence: "In view of the fundamental rational comprehensibility of all moral requirements, the ethical principles of the New Testament must be viewed as a maieutic mediation of moral insight" (p. 118). Here everything hinges on how one interprets "fundamental rational comprehensibility" and with what qualification one accordingly understands "maieutic" mediation. I cannot wholly avoid the impression that Schüller employs the concept "reason" somewhat too unproblematically. I refer especially to p. 111: "Granted that with Rom 1 it is pre-supposed that man . . . is conscious of himself as a moral being. Under this presupposition the commandment to love God and one's neighbor most surely illumines reason." It is clear that this pre-supposition is fundamental for that which

follows; at the same time there is missing here the realistic context of experience with which Paul elaborates on it and restricts it.

3. Cf. II Cazelles, *Dekalog,* in: II *Haag, Bibel-Lexikon* (Benziger 1968²) pp. 319–23 (Lit.); G. von Rad, *Theologie des Alten Testaments* I (Munich 1958) pp. 188–230.

4. *Op. cit.,* p. 193.

5. Cf. in addition especially E. Peterson, *Christianus,* in: (same author), *Frühkirche, Judentum und Gnosis* (Freiburg 1959) pp. 64–87. I am indebted to the still unpublished Regensburg dissertation by K. Bommes, *Das Verständnis des Martyriums bei Ignatius von Antiochien* (1974) for valuable suggestions in regard to the question.

6. Peterson, p. 80.

7. Magn. 5, 1.

8. Magn. 10, i *(ebenda* 168).

9. Peterson p. 77ff.

10. Magn. 10, 1.

11. Apol. III *(C CHR* I 92: *Ad Nat* 1 3, 8f *(C CHR* I 14): *Christianum vero nomen . . . de unctione interpretatur. Etiam cum corrupte a vobis Chrestiani pronuntiamur . . . sic quoque de suavitate vel bonitate modulantum est.* Cf. Peterson, p. 85.

12. The coordination of teaching and life in the Christian baptismal catechesis as in the baptismal ritual, in which the articulation of refusal and acceptance combines a moral confession (and vow) with the profession of faith, is in keeping with this. This unity is not only fundamental for the whole patristic tradition from Justin (for example, *Apol.* 1 61, I) up to Basilius *(De Spiritu Sanctu* 15, 35 PG 32, p. 130f, where the whole exegisis of the central baptismal event rests on this combination): it applies to the New Testament itself, where moral human rationality in the letters clearly refers to the baptismal catechesis and commitment, so that one could read the preaching of John the Baptist as a Christian pre-baptismal catechesis. Cf. the exegsis of Lk 3, 1–20 in H. Schürmann, *Das Lukasevangelium* I (Freiburg 1969) pp. 148–187.

13. These assertions intentionally do not deal directly with the technical discussion of present-day moral theology on "deontological" or mere "teleological" norming of moral action. A penetrating and fundamental orientation on this topic is provided by B. Schüller, *Neuere Beiträge zum Thema "Begründung sittlicher Normen,"* in: I. Pfammatter and F. Furger, *Theologische Berichte* IV (Einsiedeln 1974) pp. 109–181. To the extent that we are concerned with a conceptual formulation and the elaboration of a thought-system, the appropriate answer must be sought in technical discussion and cannot be clearly concluded from preconceptions of the basic biblical data. Despite this necessary methological limitation there are indications which I feel have not been sufficiently taken into account in the discussion up to now. Thus, take the following as an example of the insufficiency of "abbreviated formulas" of teleological thought-patterns on the subject of

norms: "Every action that is *objectively*—secundum rectam rationem—not justified in the concrete human situation is 'intrinsece malum' and therefore absolutely to be avoided." (J. Fuchs, *Der Absolutheitscharakter sittlicher Handlungsnormen,* in: *Testimonium Veritatis,* Frankfurt 1971, pp. 211–240, citation 236). Here one might ask what "concrete human reality" and "recta ratio" are. Both terms remain formal in such statements and in the last resort are meaningless, even when one, with Schüller (*op. cit.,* p. 173) tries to fill them out and concretize them along the lines of Kant's categorical imperative. Even if the problem of concept-formulation and systemization is left open, it must still be asked whether the clear substantial constants which matured in the course of the biblical history of faith and have been formulated in the baptismal catechesis, do not make a deontological grounding of norms unavoidable. This entire problem, it seems to me, (as already alluded to in footnote 2) lies in the abstract neutrality of the concept of reason, which actually presides over the discussion in too unreflected a way. A further and a specially concentrated discussion on this point is a must.

14. H. Schlier, *Besinnung auf das Neue Testament* (Freiburg 1964).

15. Schlier pp. 141–144.

16. *Ibid.,* pp. 344–352. Paul acknowledges here the "teleological" motive (the future judgment and reward) quite as much as he argues "deontologically" in terms of the implications of being a member of the body of Christ.

17. *Ibid.,* p. 352ff, especially p. 355.

18. P. 343: "The disciples of the apostles and the other Christians, however, all warn on the basis of the apostolic admonition and, indeed, in such a way that they unfold and apply it as the appropriate tradition for their situation." This seems to be a fundamental statement as regards the abiding substantial grounding of Christian ethics as well as for its very substance—the unfolding of the apostolic admonition as a standard-setting tradition adapted to the situation.

19. Cf. in this connection F. Mussner, *Die UNA SANCTA nach Apg 2, 42,* in: (same author), *Praesentia salutis* (Düsseldorf 1967) pp. 212–222.

20. Cf. L. Bouyer, *L'Eglise de Dieu. Corps du Christ et temple de l'Esprit* (Paris 1970) pp. 401–447; Y. Congar, *Ministères et communion ecclesiale* (Paris 1971) pp. 51–94.

Nine Theses
in Christian Ethics

Hans Urs von Balthasar

The Christian who lives by faith has the right to base his moral activity on his faith. Since the content of his faith, namely Jesus Christ, who revealed to us God's trinitarian love, assumed not only the form and the guilt of the first Adam but also the limitations, anxieties and decisions of his existence, there is no danger that the Christian will fail to find the first Adam in the Second Adam and along with him his own moral dilemma. Even Jesus had to choose between his Father and his family: "My child, why have you done this to us?" (Luke 2:48). Thus the Christian will make the basic decisions of his life from Christ's perspective, that is, from his faith. One cannot properly designate an ethics, which proceeds from the fulness of revelation and then works back to the defective preparatory stages, as a "descending" ethics (in contrast to a so-called "ascending" ethics which proceeds from anthropological data as its primary foundation).

Nor should one qualify this ethics as non-historical just because it gives priority to the New Testament over the Old. One must remember that the road is determined and illumined by the destination—a point which applies even to this unique road of salvation which attains its goal only in the dialectic between discontinuity and superabundance (stressed by Paul), and inner fulfillment (stressed by Matthew and James). It is undoubtedly correct to say that from the historical and chronological point of view theses 5 and 6 should have come before the Christological theses, and that theses 7 and 9 should have preceded all of them. However, it is a fact that the Christian lives in the specifically "eschatological age." He must constantly

strive to overcome in himself those tendencies that belong to the preparatory stages so that he can pass on to what belongs to the final
stage of human existence. Rather than excluding, this includes the
fact that Christ too lived his obedience to the Father not only in a
prophetic, as it were immediate vision of him, but also by keeping the
Old Law and by believing in the promise. The Christian follows him
in that too.

Our theses are given only in outline form and many essential
points have been omitted. For instance, the text speaks of the Church
only indirectly. Nothing is said about the Sacraments nor about their
relationship to the authority of the Church. Nothing is said about
various opinions of far-reaching consequences which confront the
Church today and which she must face eventually. We only wanted
to consider Christian ethics as it comes forth from and depends on
the mystery of Christ, which is the center of the history of salvation
as well as of the history of man.

I
THE FULFILLMENT OF MORAL LIFE IN CHRIST

1. *Christ as the Concrete Norm*

*THESIS 1: Christian ethics must be elaborated in such a way
that its starting point is Jesus Christ, since he, as the Son of the Father,
fulfilled the complete will of the Father (= everything that must be
done) in this world. He did this "for us" so that we might gain our
freedom from him, the concrete and plenary norm of all moral action,
to accomplish God's will and to live up to our vocation to be free children of the Father.*

1. Jesus Christ is the concrete categorical imperative, in the
sense that he is not only a formal, universal norm of moral life,
which can be applied to everyone, but also a concrete and personal
norm. By virtue of his suffering for us and the eucharistic giving up
of his life for us as well as his handing it on to us *(per ipsum et cum
ipso),* he has given us the interior strength to do the will of the Father
with him (cum ipso).

Thus his imperative is based on the "indicative" (cf. Rom. 6:7ff.; 2 Cor. 5:15). The will of the Father, however, is twofold: 1) to love his children in him and with him (1 John 5:1f.), and 2) adoration in spirit and in truth (John 4:23). Christ's life is at the same time action *and* cult. This unity is the perfect norm for the Christian. It is only with an attitude of deep respect (Phil. 7:12) that we can cooperate in the saving work of God. His absolute love infinitely surpasses us, being more unlike our love than like it *(in maiori dissimilitudine)*. Liturgy therefore cannot be separated from moral life.

2. The Christian Imperative places us beyond the question of autonomy vs. heteronomy:

a) Because the Son of God, begotten by the Father, is "another" *(heteros)* but not something other than *(heteron)* the Father. As God he is autonomously equal to the Father (his Person coincides with his procession and thus with his mission). On the other hand, as man he possesses in himself the divine will and his own affirmation of it as the very foundation of his existence (Heb. 10:5f.; Phil. 2:6f.) and as the inner source of his personal activity (John 4:34ff.). This also holds true for those cases in which he wishes to experience in suffering the resistance of sinners to God.

At this point please note: When the divinity of Christ is not acknowledged he appears necessarily only as a human model, and so Christian ethics once again becomes *heteronomous* on the supposition that the Christ-norm is considered simply binding on my moral activity. Or, it becomes *autonomous* when his example is still interpreted as the perfect way for the human moral subject to determine himself.

b) As created beings we remain *"heteron,"* but we are also given the capacity to unfold our personal and free activity by virtue of God's strength (the "drink" becomes in us a "spring" or "well" [John 4:13ff; 7:38]). This strength comes to us from the Eucharist of his Son through our being reborn with him from the Father and through the gift of their Spirit. Since God in bestowing his grace works gratuitously and since we likewise should act gratuitously when we love (Matt. 10:8; Luke 14:12–14), the "great reward in heaven" (Luke 6:23) can therefore be nothing else but Love itself. Thus in God's eternal plan (Eph. 1:10) the last end coincides with the first movement of our freedom *(interior intimo meo;* cf. Rom. 8:15ff.26ff.)

By virtue of the reality of our divine filiation all truly Christian actions are performed in freedom. To be more precise: for Christ the total burden of the saving task laid upon him *(dei)*—which will take him to Calvary—flows forth from his privilege of revealing in full liberty the saving will of God. For us sinners, however, the freedom of the children of God often becomes a heavy cross both with regard to our personal decisions and in the framework of community life. Even if it is true that the purpose of the rules of the Church is to free the believer from the alienation of sin and to lead him to his true identity and freedom, they may and indeed often must seem to be harsh and legalistic to the imperfect believer, just as the will of the Father appeared harsh to Christ hanging on the cross.

2. *The Universality of the Concrete Norm*

THESIS 2: The norm of the concrete existence of Christ is both personal and universal, because in him the Father's love for the world is realized in a comprehensive and unsurpassable way. This norm, therefore, embraces all men in their different ethical situations and unites all persons (with their uniqueness and freedom) in his Person. As the Holy Spirit of freedom it also hovers over all men in order to bring them to the kingdom of the Father.

1. The concrete existence of Christ—his life, suffering, death and bodily resurrection—takes up in itself, supplants and abrogates all other ethical systems. In the last analysis, a Christian has to give an account of his moral life only to this norm which proposes the prototype (Jesus) of perfect obedience to God the Father. Christ abolishes in his own being the difference that separates those "who are subject to the Law" (Jews) from those "without the Law" (Gentiles) (1 Cor. 9:20ff.), slaves from their masters, men from women (Gal. 3:28), etc. In Christ all have received the same freedom of the children of God and strive for the same goal. The "new" commandment of Jesus (John 13:34) as realized in Christ is more than the principal command of the Old Law (Deut. 6:4ff.). It is also more than just the sum of the commandments of the Decalogue and their particular applications. The perfect fulfillment of the will of the Fa-

ther in the Person of Christ is an eschatological, unsurpassable synthesis. Hence it is itself an apriori, universal norm.

2. Since Christ is the incarnate Word and the Son of God, he abolishes in himself the separating duality of the Old Testament Covenant. More even than a mediator (who intervenes between opposed groups), he is a personified encounter and for this reason he is a "unifier": "an intermediary implies more than one; but God is one" (Gal. 3:20). The Church of Christ is nothing else but the plenitude of this one Person. She is his "body" to which he gives life (Eph. 1:22f). She is his "bride" insofar as he forms "one flesh" (Eph. 5:29) or "one Spirit" (1 Cor. 6:17) with her. Even as "the people of God" she is no longer many, but "you are all one in Christ Jesus" (Gal. 3:28). To the extent that Jesus' work of salvation was accomplished "for all," life in his community is at the same time both personalizing and socializing.

3. That our destiny was already determined by Jesus' death on the cross ("one has died for all; therefore all have died . . . that those who live might live no longer for themselves," 2 Cor. 5:14–15), that we have been inserted "into Christ," does not constitute our alienation. Rather, it constitutes our being "transplanted" out of the "darkness" of our sinful and alienated being into the truth and freedom of divine sonship. It is for this that God created us (Eph. 1:4ff.). By the power of the cross we have been given the Holy Spirit of Christ and of the Father (Rom. 8:9. 11). In that Spirit the Person of Christ and his work are made present in all ages and are also at work in us. The same Spirit also makes us continuously present to Christ.

This mutual inclusion has a markedly ecclesial dimension for the believer. For, love for one another, which is the object of the new command that Jesus gave us to fulfill, is poured out into the hearts of the faithful (Rom. 5:5) antecedently in a more profound way through the outpouring of the Holy Spirit of the Father and of the Son as the divine "We." On the personal level of the Church, actual membership in "one body" includes the conferring of a personal consciousness of one another among the members. The moral task of the Christian is to accomplish this in a vigorous way. In this way the Church is open to the world, just as Christ is open to the Father and his all-embracing Kingdom (1 Cor. 15:24), and both "mediate" only in immediacy. Such personal immediacy characterizes, therefore, all Church structures and activities—even to the most particular ones.

3. *The Christian Meaning of the Golden Rule*

> *THESIS 3: On Jesus' lips and in the context of the Sermon on the Mount, the "Golden Rule" (Matt. 7:12; Luke 6:31) can be described as the sum total of the Law and the Prophets only because it firmly roots in Christ all that Christians mean to each other and give to each other. This rule, therefore, goes beyond mere human fraternity and includes the interpersonal exchange of the divine life.*

1. The "Golden Rule" occurs in Matthew—and even more directly in Luke—in the context of the Beatitudes, of a forsaking of claims of distributive justice, of the love of one's enemies, of the demand to be "perfect" and "merciful" as the heavenly Father is. For this reason, gifts received from the Father are precisely what a Christian may expect from his neighbor and what he should give to his neighbor. This confirms once again that both the "Law" and universal "brotherly love" have their "end" (Rom. 10:4) in Christ.

2. The "Law" itself was not just an expression of brotherly love. Rather, it revealed the faithfulness of God our Savior who wanted to enter into a covenant with his people (cf. Thesis 6). The prophets, however, spoke of a fulfillment of the Law that would not be possible until God should abolish all heteronomy and place the law of his Spirit in the hearts of men (Jer. 31:33; Ezek. 36: 26f.).

3. From the Christian point of view no social ethics or ethics of the person can abstract from the fact that God is addressing himself to us. In order to be morally correct dialogue between men presupposes, as the very condition of its possibility, a dialogue between God and man, whether human beings are explicitly aware of it or not. Man's new relationship with God, however, has a direct relationship to the dialogue between Jew and Gentile, master and servant, man and woman, parents and children, rich and poor, etc. But this dialogue must now be conducted on a new level.

Thus Christian ethics takes on the form of the cross: though both vertical and horizontal, this "form" can never be isolated from its concrete content, that is, from Jesus who was crucified and lifted up between God and men. He makes himself present as the only norm in every situation. "All things are lawful for me" (1 Cor. 6:12; cf. Rom. 14–15), if I only remember that I owe my liberty to my belonging to Christ (1 Cor. 6:19; ch. 3:21–23).

4. Sin

THESIS 4: Only where God in his love has gone to the very end does human guilt appear as sin, and the attitude behind it as proceeding from a spirit positively hostile to God himself.

1. The unique and concrete character of the personal moral norm (= Jesus) implies, regardless of whether one admits it or not that all moral guilt refers to Christ, is accountable to him and was carried by him on the cross. The nearness of the morally functioning Christian to the source of divine holiness, which vivifies him because he is a member of Christ, turns guilt with regard to a mere "law" (according to the Jewish view) or with regard to a mere "idea" (according to the Greek view) into sin. The holiness of the Holy Spirit in Christ-and-Church convinces the world of its sinfulness (John 16:8–11)—a world to which we also belong ("if we say we have not sinned, we make him a liar," 1 John 1:10).

2. The presence in the world of God's absolute love increases man's guilt so that it becomes a demonic No, more negative than man realizes; indeed, it tries to lure him into the anti-Christian camp (cf. what the Book of Revelation says about the beast, what St. Paul says about the powers of this world; cf. also 1 John). The individual, as a part of the battle of Christ-and-Church against these powers, must also fight with the "armor of God" (Eph. 6:11). The work of the devil shows itself above all in a proud gnosis without love, which pretends to be coextensive with the agape that is submissive to God, but actually "puffs up" (1 Cor. 8:1). Because this gnosis does not want to acknowledge the concrete personal norm (Jesus), it depicts sin as mere guilt—as a transgression of a law or as opposition to an idea—and it will try to exculpate the guilt by appeals to psychology, sociology, etc.

3. The full impact of anti-Christian sin strikes the very center of the personal norm: it pierces the heart of the Crucified who concretely represents in this world the trinitarian love of God. That Jesus on the cross took upon himself our sins remains a mystery of faith—one that cannot be shown by philosophy to be "necessary" or "impossible." Hence judgment over sin is reserved to the crucified Son of Man to whom "all judgment" has been given (John 5:22). "Do not judge" (Matt. 7:1).

II
THE OLD TESTAMENT ELEMENTS OF THE FUTURE SYNTHESIS

5. *The Promise (Abraham)*

THESIS 5: The moral subject (Abraham) is constituted by God's call and by obedience to this call (Heb. 11:8).

1. After Abraham had made his act of obedience, the deeper meaning of his call as an unforseeable, universal promise becomes clear (for "all peoples" but brought together in one individual: "semini tuo" Gal. 3:16). The name of the obedient one is the same as the name of his mission (Gen. 17:1–8); since the promise and its fulfillment stem from God, Abraham is given a supernatural fertility.

2. Obedience is faith in God and thereby a valid response (Gen. 15:6) which takes possession not only of the mind but also of the body (Gen 17:13). Obedience, therefore, requires that one must be prepared to return the freely given gift (Gen. 22).

3. Abraham lives in a spirit of obedience which, in view of the unreachable stars above, waits for the promise.

Concerning 1: All biblical ethics is based on the call of a personal God and on man's answer to it in faith. God shows himself in his call as the One who is faithful, truthful, just, merciful, etc. From the name of God the name of the one who answers (i.e., his unique personality) is derived and fixed. The divine call sets the human subject apart for the encounter with God (Abraham must leave his tribe and land). By answering the call ("Here I am," Gen. 22:1) he receives his mission which then becomes for him an obligatory norm of behavior. In his dialogues with God Abraham becomes, as a result of his mission, the founder of a community. In the perspective of the Bible all relations within this community depend on the vertical relationship of the founder or mediator with God, or on God's intervention which establishes the community (Exod. 22:20; 23:9; Deut. 5:14ff.; 15:12–18; 16:11ff.; 27:17ff.). This divine intervention is the grace which God offers and over which man has no power, but which is the norm of all his actions (cf. the Parable of the Unforgiving Debtor in Matt. 18:21ff.). In the Old Testament the actual openendness of Abraham's blessing is gradually and more clearly understood as having a messianic fulfillment. Thus the "opening up" to "the Gentiles" (Gal. 3:14) is effected in the gathering together of Jesus' followers and the bestowing on them of the Holy Spirit (through faith in him).

Concerning 2: The moral subject is affected in all his dimensions by the "covenant" (Gen. 15:18ff.) which is based on God's call and man's response: it concerns the challenge of faith and also his body and possessions ("my covenant shall be in your flesh an everlasting covenant," Gen. 17:13). In order that Isaac, who was conceived and born by God's power, might be protected against all subsequent human self-will, Abraham is ordered to give him back to God. If the faith of the childless Abraham was already faith in God, "who gives life to the dead and calls into existence the things that do not exist" (Rom. 4:17), then the faith of the father, who returns the son God promised to him, is indeed a firm faith in the resurrection. "He considered that God was able to raise men even from the dead" (Heb. 11:19).

Concerning 3: Abraham's life (and with it the period of the whole Old Covenant, including the period of the Law) can only be a clinging to God in faith, without the possibility of changing God's promise into his fulfillment. The people of the Old Testament could only "look forward" (Heb. 11:10) in a type of "seeking" (*ibid.* 14) which cannot be more than a "having seen it and greeted it from afar" and a recognition of the fact that they remain "strangers and exiles" in this world (*ibid.* 13–14). Precisely because the fathers of old were not able to attain the goal—but still persevered—were they worthy of praise (Heb. 11:39). This point is important for what follows.

6. The Law

THESIS 6: *The Law proclaimed at Sinai goes beyond the promise made to Abraham to the extent that it explicitly reveals—even if provisionally from outside and from above—the mind of God. The purpose of this new revelation is to make possible a more intense re-*

sponse from those living under the covenant: "I am holy; therefore you also must be holy." This "must," which has its foundation in God's innermost being, is directed at man's inner attitude. That man can respond to this "must" follows from the absolute truthfulness of God who offers man the covenant (Rom. 7:12). However, this truthfulness of God does not yet find its counterpart in a similar absolute truthfulness of man. Such truthfulness resides only in the promise made to Abraham, which is later repeated in a new and more precise way in the sayings of the prophets.

1. The Law is given in addition to the promise and does not abrogate the promise (Rom. 7; Gal. 3). For this reason it is intended to be only a more precise determination of a faith that waits. From different directions it throws light on the conduct of the man who is "just in the eyes of God." Of course, this conduct agrees with the fundamental structures of man's existence (natural law) because God the author of grace is also the Creator. However, the motive of this correct conduct is not man but the more profound revelation of God's holiness as found in his fidelity to his Covenant. Hence, there is no question here of an imitation of God's essence in the Greek sense, but of a response to his conduct as manifested in his "mighty deeds" towards Israel. But since the one perfect response (Jesus) remains the object of the promise, the Law retains its dialectical character in the way St. Paul understands it: in itself good, it still increases transgressions. To that extent it is both a positive and a negative "taskmaster" that eventually leads to Christ.

2. Looked at from God's point of view, the "must" of the Law is an offer to live a holy life before God in the security of the Covenant. Yet this gracious offer is only the first act of God's saving activity that will be perfected only in Christ. For the time being this activity reveals, not only the positive attitude of man, but also his (negative) incapacity to respond fully—a perfect response remaining as before the object of the promise. The discrepancy between man's response as demanded by the Law and the insufficiency of his actual response is felt by man to be unbearable. One can sustain it only with the patience which faith and hope give. In two ways man seeks to get around this problem:

a. He tries to make the Law (Torah) an absolute which takes

the place of the living God. By trying to fulfill literally the letter of the law the Pharisee thinks that he can give a perfect response (something that is actually impossible). Many different ethical systems have been derived from this attitude which makes an abstract and formal "must" the fundamental norm. For example, one may point to neo-kantian ethics which postulates a realm of "absolute values," to structuralistic and to phenomenological ethics (Scheler). All of these systems tend to establish the human subject as his own legislator, as an idealized, autonomous subject who imposes limitations on himself in order to reach perfection. The germs of these types of ethical systems lie in the ethical formalism of Kant.

b. A second way to overcome this tension is to consider the Law a foreign element and then replace it with Promise and Hope. It is argued that a law which is imposed from outside and declares us guilty in our hearts (e.g., Kafka) cannot proceed from a faithful and merciful God, but only from a tyrannical demiurge (this point of view explains E. Bloch's alliance with gnosticism; compare also Freud's super-ego). As an illusion of former generations this "demiurge" must be overcome by hope in the future—a hope which proceeds from man's own autonomous resources.

c. Both escapes come together in dialectical materialism which identifies the Law with the dialectical movement of history and in this way eliminates the Law. Marx knows that it is not the negative abolition of the Law (namely, communism) which will bring about the desired reconciliation, but only a positive humanism which allows the Law to be absorbed into the spontaneity of freedom. We are dealing here with an atheistic counterpart to Jeremiah 31 and Ezekiel 34. Corresponding to the provisional character of Old Testament ethics, transcendental reconciliation in the Old Testament (as in its modern imitations) remains primarily a political "liberation." Its subject is primarily the people as a whole and not the person whose unique worth comes to light only in Christ.

3. When Christian faith in the fulfilled promise of Christ dies out, it is not the extra-biblical ethical systems which dominate the history of mankind; rather, it is the Old Testament forms which are related to the Christian ones. Because an awareness of the fulfillment brought by Christ lingers on, Old Testament ethics return as a most grotesque absolutism: absolute law and absolute prophecy.

III
FRAGMENTS OF EXTRA-BIBLICAL ETHICS

7. *Conscience*

THESIS 7: 1. Extra-biblical man is awakened to theoretico-practical self-awareness as the result of a free, loving call from his fellow men. When answering this call he experiences (in his "cogito ergo sum") both the intelligibility of reality as such (as true and good) which reveals itself and thereby constitutes man in freedom, and the fact that his freedom is marked by a relationship to other human beings.

2. Man's entire being has a natural inclination ("necessitate naturalis inclinationis," De veritate 22,5) to the transcendental good. This inclination to the known good takes the form of first moral principles (synderesis or basic conscience). There also exist tendencies to the good in the sensible part of man's being since the whole is permeated by his spirit.

Neither the self-discovery involved in the first insight, nor the strong attraction of particular temporal goods, nor the fact that sin often obscures man's awareness that the good is a gift—none of these can destroy the innate orientation of man to the good. Thus St. Paul could say that the pagans are judged "by Jesus Christ according to my gospel" (Rom. 2:16).

3. Abstract formulae which state man's inclination to the good as the result of "natural law"—for example, the statement that human fellowship is a "categorical imperative"—have been derived from this basic conscience and actually refer back to it.

Concerning 1: In the act of being called or loved by his fellow man, man awakens in his *"cogito ergo sum"* to an awareness of the identity between intelligibility and reality. He also experiences this identity, which is a created reality, as not absolute, simply because it appears to him as a gift. In this transcendental disclosure of reality three things are given simultaneously:

a. Man is confronted with the absolute identity of spirit and being, and thus with a most perfect self-possession in full freedom. This Absolute lets things share in itself (we call this Absolute, God, *"qui interius docet inquantum huiusmodi lumen animae infundit,"* St. Thomas, *De Anima* 5 ad 6).

b. When man is awakened to God who gives himself, he becomes aware of the difference between absolute freedom and given freedom. In seeing this difference he becomes aware of the invitation to respond in freedom to this absolute gift.

c. At first there is no sharp distinction between the call from the Absolute and that coming from one's fellow men. Experience will show that the other is "merely" one who has also been awakened. However, this experience shows that the original unity of both invitations (i.e., from men and God) cannot be dissolved.

Concerning 2: Just as, in the original identity of being and intelligibility (as true, good and beautiful), freedom as autonomy and grace as gift *("diffusivum sui")* are together, so also in the created being freedom and inclination towards the good are inseparable. The active drawing power of the absolute good confers on the act of the free response an element of "passivity" that does not violate its freedom (*S. Th.* I, 80, 2; 105, 4; *De veritate* 25, 1;22, 13, 4).

This tendency to let oneself be determined and conducted by what is good in itself is present in man's entire being. Of course, if one abstracts from man's totality, then it is clear that man's sensible nature by itself cannot attain a knowledge of the absolute good but must stop at the level of particular goods. Man's true moral task is to render his entire bodily and spiritual life ethical *(ethizesthai)*. The result of this process is called "virtue." This is also necessary because the call of his fellow men obliges him to let his freedom be determined by other free, bodily persons. It also obliges him to determine the freedom of others. This must take place under the influence of the good, but each time it requires the intellectual illumination of the matter which mediates the process.

The insight into the good itself, once attained in the *"cogito ergo sum"* (in other words, the transparency of the *"imago Dei"* which enables man to see its sources in God), does not remain actualized. Nevertheless, it perdures in the memory *"tamquam nota artificis operi suo impressa"* (Descartes, *Med.* III, Adam-Tannery VII, 51). Since this insight has co-determined the first awakening of the mind, it cannot be totally forgotten, even when one turns away—either consciously or habitually—from the light of the good in order to pursue particular goods which are either pleasurable or useful. More-over, the insight is at least a transcendental preknowledge of revelation; it constitutes as it were the *place* from which the "posi-tive" revelation of the Old and New Testament has always been ad-dressed to all men. However, when this revelation proceeds from concrete historical events, then we should not forget that the call of our fellow men (which is both transcendental and dialectical) is just as original as the call of the good itself *(bonum in communi)*.

Only the *Magister Interior* can measure the intensity and clarity that such a "positive" revelation might have outside of the Old and New Testaments. But according to St. Paul, the *Magister Interior* judges the hearts even of the pagans according to the norm, which is now sufficiently explicit, of God's gift of himself in Jesus Christ.

Concerning 3: The original radiancy of the good as grace and love expects a free answer of loving gratitude. When this light of the good itself has grown dim, a warning sign appears. Its purpose is not to take the place of one's better self, nor to represent it, but only to call it back into mind. Insofar as the warning sign concerns the main situations of an incarnate and socially constituted mind, it reveals it-self as the "natural law." This natural law should not be divinized; rather, it must retain its essentially relative character of referring to the good. In this way natural law will not become stifled, but will be able to point to the liveliness and self-giving nature of the good. Kant's categorical imperative has not escaped the danger of unbend-ing harshness, for his formalism made him place abstract "duty" over against the natural "inclination" of the sensible part of our be-ing. What true ethics should do, however, is to give to the person's inclination to the Absolute Good priority and dominion over con-trary particular inclinations. Thus the inclinations man fully accepts and makes his own in view of the absolute norm, coincide with sur-rendering himself to the divine good and with giving himself to his fellow men.

8. *Pre-Biblical Natural Order*

THESIS 8: Wherever a self-revelation of the sovereignly free and personal God is absent, man tries to find the bearings for his moral life in the order of the world around him. Since man owes his existence to a multiplicity of cosmic laws, it is quite natural that he both fuse and confuse his origin from God with his origin from nature. However, such a theocosmological ethics disintegrates wherever biblical revelation comes in contact with a particular culture.

1. Pre-biblical ethics, which finds its norms in nature, can ask about the good that is proper to human nature *(bonum honestum)* by setting up an analogy with the good that is proper to infra-human existing things. This human good, however, will be contained within the limits of the surrounding natural order. Insofar as this natural order has an absolute (i.e., divine) aspect, it opens up a certain area for orderly moral behavior; but insofar as it contains a this-worldly, finite aspect, it does not allow man's personal freedom to reach its full perfection. The result is that the goals of human activity remain partly political (within a micropolis or a macropolis), partly individualistic and partly intellectualistic, since pure knowledge of the constant laws of the universe appears to be the most noble thing man can strive for.

2. When biblical revelation enters on the scene, the supremely free God, who is radically different from created nature, invites man to share in a type of freedom which is not modeled on anything found in infra-human nature. But wherever man refuses to acknowledge, in a Christian way, that this freedom is really a gift from God, logically he can locate the source of his freedom only in himself and so understand moral behavior as a type of legislation for himself. In its first stages this may take the form of a return to the pre-biblical mythical understanding of the universe (cf. Spinoza, Goethe, Hegel), but later even this will be abandoned (cf. Feuerbach, Nietzsche).

3. Once this development has begun, it is irreversible. It is true that there exists a tendency (cf. above 6, 3) to reduce Christian ethics to what was, in the Old Testament, a stage of preparation. Yet we can also notice a certain influence of the light of Christianity on non-Christian religious and ethical thought (e.g., the Christian influence on Indian social thinking: Tagore, Gandhi). Besides an explicitly dogmatic knowledge of God there is also an existential knowledge; this reminds us of the warning, "Do not judge."

9. *Post-Christian Anthropological Ethics*

THESIS 9: A possible basis for a post- but non-Christian ethics can now be sought only in a dialogue relationship with other men (e.g., I—Thou; I—We). Since gratitude to God for one's life, expressed in divine worship, is now no longer the permanent, fundamental act of the free human person, mutual gratitude between human subjects can have no more than secondary, purely relative value. The limitations placed on one another by free persons who experience their own unlimited transcendence appears to be imposed on them from outside. A synthesis between the fulfillment of the individual and that of the community is not possible.

1. In a post-Christian age, what remains of the "nature" or "structure" of human existence is the reciprocity of two finite freedoms. Only by means of a call from another person do both of them become aware of themselves and of their ability to respond and to call others. In this way it seems that the "Golden Rule" is attained once again. However, since the one who is addressed by another does not simply receive his freedom from that other (if he did, he would necessarily be "heteronomous"), and since God's call—which is the real foundation of both freedoms—is excluded, the mutual self-surrender of both persons remains limited and calculating. Intersubjectivity will either be understood as a secondary and basically unintelligible quality of the subject, or the two human subjects remain monads with no influence on one another.

2. The so-called "human sciences" can contribute valuable knowledge about particular aspects of the phenomenon of man, but they cannot offer a solution to this fundamental problem of interhuman relations.

3. The anthropological problem reaches its climax at the point where the death of the individual person renders the synthesis between his personal perfection and his social integration simply impossible. The meaningful elements in both of these aspects remain disconnected. Therefore, they even make the development of an obvious this-worldly ethics impossible. However, in face of the meaninglessness of death—and thus of his life which is always moving towards death—man can refuse to acknowledge any ethical norms.

Personal and social fulfillment are harmonized only in the resurrection of Christ who is the guarantee not only for the fulfillment of the individual but also for the Church community and through her for the whole world so that God, without eliminating the reality of the world, can be "all in all."

The Debate on the Specific Character of a Christian Ethics: Some Remarks

Bruno Schüller, S.J.

What is it precisely that makes a Christian ethics Christian? To this question Catholic moral theologians have been devoting a good deal of thought for over a decade now. So important is the question considered to be that the International Theological Commission chose it for the subject of its meeting in December 1974.[1] Yet this concentrated collaborative effort has as yet failed, it seems, to produce the satisfactory explanation it has been seeking. At least it cannot be said that any consensus is forming; in fact, the contrary is rather the case: the variety of positions on the subject is increasing.

In his day G. E. Moore was of the opinion that the difficulties and contradictory views of which ethics shows such a plenty are chiefly due to a very simple cause: People attempt to answer questions before having accurately ascertained *what kind of a question* it is they are attempting to answer. Often enough, too, the reason why it seems impossible to answer a specific question with a Yes or a No is that we are dealing not with a single question but with a whole set of questions.[2]

Even in Moore's day, of course, this diagnosis of a discussion that produces no agreement was not original. This fact is unimportant, however, provided that the diagnosis is correct. The unmistakable lack of detachment that marks the various positions on the Christian character of Christian ethics may not be conducive to a careful analysis of the questions raised and of the language in which the questions are formulated. A moral theologian, moreover, may have the idea that he should not involve himself in this kind of analysis lest he find himself abandoning his own proper field and wandering off into the realm of logic.[3] In any case, only if the necessary distinctions are made and their material significance is demonstrated can it be decided whether or not Moore's diagnosis is accurate in a specific instance, that is, whether or not questions that ought to be clearly distinguished in the discussion are in fact being partially or wholly confused and treated as though they were a single question.

In my opinion there are two distinctions especially that could be profitable in the current discussion of the specific character of a Christian ethics. These are the distinctions (1) between exhortation and normative ethics, and (2) between the genesis and the truth-value (validity) of moral or morally significant insights. I am not claiming that these two distinctions, if consistently applied, will show clearly what precisely it is that makes a Christian ethics Christian. But at least they will be helpful in the examination and analysis of certain questions.

I.
EXHORTATION AND NORMATIVE ETHICS

It appears at first sight that Christian ethics has a foundation which is peculiarly its own. The sequence of gospel and law, divine indicative and divine imperative, seems to show this. The sequence is clearly expressed in Eph 5:1–2: "Therefore be imitators of God as beloved children. And walk in love, as Christ loved us and gave himself up for us." The moral imperative, "Walk in love," is said to have for its standard or measure the love which God and Christ have for us human beings. At the same time, moveover, this love of God and Christ is viewed as the reason why Christians must walk in love. The verses cited are also to be read as saying: "Be imitators of God *because* you are children whom he loves!" and "Walk in love *because* Christ has loved us."[4] In short, the love of God and Christ is both motive and standard for the love Christians are required to have. The same kind of nexus is just as clearly expressed in what might be called the foundational Christian formulation of the commandment regarding love of neighbor: "A new commandment I give you, that

you love one another; even as I have loved you, that you also love
one another" (Jn 13:34).[5]

As everyone knows, the New Testament and especially the Pauline corpus contain many passages in which the demands of morality
are linked with the gospel as the message of God's action for the salvation of the human race.[6] We need only remind the reader of two
texts: As men and women reconciled with God, be reconciled with
him! (2 Cor 5:19–20); as men and women dead to sin, sin no more!
(Rom 6:8–13; cf. also 1 Cor. 5:7; Gal 5:24–25; likewise Rom 12:1
and Eph 4:1 which mark the transition from the kerygmatic section
of the letters to the exhortatory section). The appeal to the gospel as
normative for moral imperatives frequently takes the form of repeating in an "ought" statement what the gospel sets forth in an "is"
statement: We are people who already live in the Spirit; therefore we
must walk in the Spirit (Gal 5:25)!

It is also said of Old Testament law that it has its foundation in
Yahweh's deeds for the salvation of Israel.[7] The New Testament relationship between gospel and law is clearly recognizable in the Old
Testament in the relationship between covenant and torah. Before
Yahweh expresses his will for the moral order in the ten commandments, he reminds Israel that he has freed it from slavery in Egypt
and thus proved himself its redeemer. Consequently, the linking of
moral exigencies with God's saving action is characteristic of biblical
ethics in its entirety. Since, however, the good news conveyed in the
New Testament is doubtless to be distinguished from that of the Old
Testament, it is to be expected that this new or further good news
will set a specific imprint on morality.

All this has been expounded often enough and sheds some light
on our problem. Yet we may feel obliged to inquire more closely into
what it is precisely in the relationship between gospel and law, covenant and torah, that is illuminating. As a first text for this examination we may take Dt 15:12–15. Here regulations are set down for the
manumission of slaves. If a slave is a Hebrew, he is to be set free after
six years of service as a slave, and when this moment comes he is to
be provided with all the necessities of life. Once this principle has
been enunciated, a reason for it is given: "You shall remember that
you were a slave in the land of Egypt, and the Lord your God redeemed you: therefore I command you this today." The relationship

between Old Testament gospel and law, as expressed in this text can evidently be restated in a short sentence: Just as you were a slave and were set free, so you must free your slaves.

It takes no great acumen to recognize in this short sentence an application of the golden rule. We may take as the basic formulation of the golden rule the statement: Treat others as you wish others to treat you. The presupposition, of course, is that everyone wants others to treat him or her *well.* Next, we can reformulate this golden rule in two ways, depending on whether the good treatment by others is something that has already happened or something still to be looked for: (1) Others have done good to you; you should likewise do good to others; (2) Do good to others, and others will do good to you (variant: in order that others may do good to you). It is only a short step to including God (Yahweh, Christ) among the "others." Then the relationship between gospel and law (covenant and torah) seems to be simply the golden rule as reexpressed in the first of our two formulations: God has done good to you; you should likewise do good to others.

At this point we begin to suspect that the relationship between gospel and law is not an example of normative ethics. The golden rule, as interpreted in Mt 7:12 and Lk 6:31, defines the moral good. But the moral good is only a necessary and not an adequate determinant of what is morally right.[8] Moreover, the relationship between gospel and law does not really amount to an analysis and grounding of the golden rule; rather it calls the golden rule to mind and makes use of it in an urgent exhortation. The requirement: "Do good to others as God has done good to you" means, at bottom, "Act as the golden rule bids you to act," and this in turn amounts to saying: "Act in a morally good way." If you speak thus to others, you are undoubtedly exhorting them. The legal prescription set down in Dt 15:12 that no one is to keep a fellow countryman in slavery for more than six years certainly cannot be proved to be a morally right precept by a reference to the fact that Yahweh had liberated Israel from slavery in Egypt. The moral rightness of this legal prescription is evidently presumed, and the reminder of Yahweh's redemptive action is meant to incite the addressee to observe the law: "Free a slave when the law makes it a duty for you to free him."[9]

In any case, the hortatory character of the Decalogue is already clear from the fact that its commands and prohibitions are consistently in the logical form of foregone conclusions. The normative character of God's saving action can indeed be glimpsed if we interpret the content of the gospel in the light of the first and second tables of the Decalogue: (1) Yahweh freed you from enslavement to foreign gods; therefore you must have no foreign gods alongside Yahweh! (2) Yahweh acted justly toward you; therefore you must act justly toward others. But it should be quite clear that the division of the Decalogue in terms of content cannot be derived (solely) from the redemptive action of Yahweh.

In Eph 5:3ff. the moral imperative, "Walk in love," is given detailed explication in a series of analytically evident commands and prohibitions: no immorality, impurity, covetousness, silly talk or thoughtless foolery, no idolatry; but rather thanksgiving, goodness and righteousness. The way in which love (agape) is negatively defined by listing vices strongly suggests that it is by now taken for granted that love forms the substance of all moral imperatives, so that the term "love" serves formally as an expression of moral value, just as "goodness" and "righteousness" do.[10] We must bear in mind, of course, the kind of love on the part of God and Christ of which the New Testament gospel is speaking. It is the love of him who reconciles the human race to himself, frees it from its sins, makes it upright, and enlists it in the service of righteousness. It is thus a love that looks to man as a moral being and that therefore is to be regarded as moral by its nature. The gospel is a statement about the moral goodness of God and how this goodness makes itself known to human beings who, when judged by the demands of morality, prove themselves sinners. To this extent the gospel itself already uses the language of morality.

When formulated, gospel and law admittedly yield different types of ethical proposition. Law is articulated in ought-statements such as: You shall love your neighbor as yourself; it is morally good and required that every person love his neighbor as himself. The gospel, on the other hand, finds expression in such statements as: God forgives you your sins; you have died to sin and become the servant of righteousness. These are admittedly indicative sentences. They say something about what God has actually done and about man's actual condition. At the same time, however, they assess this action and this condition from a moral standpoint. They are ethical propositions in the same sense as: Peter is just because he treats likes alike. This last statement assumes the validity and acceptance of the ethical rule that a person is just if he treats likes alike. The statement is directly concerned with Peter's freely adopted attitude to this ethical rule: Peter acts in fact as the ethical rule requires.

All this is to say that the gospel deals with ethical goodness as *something real.* Insofar as the gospel is embodied in the action of Jesus Christ, it proclaims a moral goodness that has become a reality through perfect obedience. And insofar as it is addressed to Christians, the gospel again has in view a moral goodness that becomes a reality through obedience: Christians have died to sin as is required of them, and have become the servants of righteousness as is required of them. As a proclamation of the action of Jesus Christ and of Christian existence, the gospel is dealing with requirements that *have been fulfilled,* while the law is dealing with moral requirements that are still *to be fulfilled.* Thus it becomes clear, once again, that in the relationship of gospel and law there can be no question of normative ethics, that is, of determining and articulating the content of the requirements of morality.

If we assume that a person is righteous and that he proves this by his thinking and acting, he thereby becomes a *model* for all those who acknowledge that they too are called to righteousness. If I acknowledge that Peter has dealt justly with me, I am by that very fact being exhorted: "As Peter has dealt with you, so you should deal with him and everyone else." This brings us back to the golden rule. The Christian acknowledges that God has shown him nothing but (moral) goodness and love. In virtue of this acknowledgment he is challenged to imitate God as his model and, like God, to show goodness (as far as he can) to everyone. The golden rule, as rephrased in our first formulation, makes of the person at whose hands we have experienced goodness, the model for our own moral behavior: As Christ has loved us, so we should love one another; as God has forgiven us in Christ, so we should forgive one another (Eph 4:32). The normative character of the gospel as the message of God's action and Christ's action for the salvation of the human race is thus the normative character of a model.

A model as such, however, is a *norma normata.* This becomes immediately evident when the exemplarity of the model must be described in terms of the model's fulfillment of the requirements of morality through obedience. Then the requirements of morality are the *norma normans,* while the model in question is a *norma normata* in relation to these requirements. This is true even of Jesus Christ as exemplar, whenever the New Testament represents his life and death as the exercise of obedience or the fulfillment of the Father's will.

And yet certain difficulties arise when we think of God's exemplary action as a *norma normata.* Such a view is possible only if we look in human terms at the purely noetic structure of our insight into God's exemplarity. Only if we suppose that human persons already experience themselves as called to be morally good, can God appear to them as a model to be unconditionally imitated, once they have recognized him as the absolute embodiment of moral goodness. Were we to think of the action of God or the action of Christ as constituting the concept of moral goodness we would fall into a theonomous and Christonomous moral positivism. We would then be implicitly claiming that "to act in a morally good way" is the same as "to act like God" and "to act like Christ," with neither the word "God" nor the word "Christ" containing "to be morally good" as a distinctive element in its meaning. But, like every moral positivism, a theonomous and Christonomous moral positivism does away with all authentic morality. In fact, the exemplarity of God and the exemplarity of Christ are not the standard for the *meaning* of "to be morally good" but for the *exercise* of moral goodness. This is why reference is made to them when there is question of the fulfillment of the demands of morality, that is to say, in the context of exhortation.

If we were to conclude from God's action for man's salvation, as from an ultimate logical premise, to the behavior that is morally binding on human beings in relation to one another, we would immediately be faced with the difficulty of determining in what respect the action of man, though like God's action, must at the same time be profoundly unlike it. Only God can forgive sin. What is meant, then, by saying that human beings are to forgive one another? God effects the salvation of the human race. Human beings, on the other hand, can at best actively work for the well-being of others. How can we determine, from the concept of man's "salvation," in what the well-being of man consists? The human person is a finite being, and narrow boundaries are antecedently set for him when it comes to translating the attitude of love into works of love. Finally, in this determination of similarity and dissimilarity, we may not forget that we human beings can conceive and speak of God's action only by taking concepts and representations originally derived from our human world and applying them in analogy and metaphor to the divine action.

When the Bible speaks of imitating God it runs into none of these difficulties because it is talking the language of exhortation. The point of comparison is given in an expression that conveys the essence of moral goodness. The same holds for the exemplarity exercised by Christ. "The behavior of Jesus" is "example and model of love that serves and that sacrifices itself."[11] Yes, but what kind of love would it be that was unwilling to serve and sacrifice itself? Whatever else it might be it could at least not be taken as summing up in itself all the requirements of morality. The word "serve" functions precisely to show that the love in question is a moral quality. And if the requirements of morality are to be characterized by their unconditionality, how else are they to be embraced if not "with all your heart and all your soul"? If we allow moral goodness its unconditional character, it can in certain situations of conflict require even the surrender of our life. Finally, love of enemies is the definitive criterion of love's authenticity. "For even sinners love those who love them" (Lk 6:32).[12] Thus, whatever action we point to as characterizing the behavior of Jesus, it serves to show that Jesus fulfilled the requirements of morality in the form of his Father's will, and did so to the ultimate degree. But since the requirements of morality bind all, all who believe in Jesus Christ are also bound by the commandment: "Walk in love, as Christ loved us and gave himself up for us, a fragrant offering and sacrifice to God" (Eph 5:2).

The authoritative nature of the action of God and Christ could easily suggest that the relationship between gospel and law contains the answer to the fundamental question of a normative ethics. But insofar as this authority is that of a model to be imitated, it is clear that the real context of this linking of law with gospel is exhortation.

Of course, to say this is hardly to express the deepest meaning of an exhortation, since the latter appeals to the gospel not simply as a standard but also and primarily as the motive for the fulfillment of the requirements of morality. If the gospel, as addressed to human beings, is already a fulfillment of the requirements of morality, and if God has already reconciled the world to himself, and if, consequently, human beings already *are* reconciled to God, then it is hard to see why there is still need of exhorting people to let themselves be reconciled to God. We seem to have here a dilemma in the original sense of the term. Either the indicative of the gospel is true, and then the imperative of the law seems meaningless, because superfluous, or the imperative of the law is meaningful, but then the indicative of the gospel cannot, it seems, be true.

In the final analysis, the debate between Augustine and Pelagius had this dilemma at its center, as did the conflict between the Reformers and Catholic theology, and the dispute on grace within the Catholic Church between the Dominicans and the Jesuits. The solution of the dilemma seems to be this: An exhortation which appeals to the gospel for its basis suggests that although the fulfillment of the requirements of morality is the free and responsible act of the human beings to whom these requirements are addressed, yet it is antecedently and concomitantly a fulfillment which is a gift of God in Christ.

Exhortation that does not start from the gospel could be the fruit of a Pelagian misunderstanding of the requirements of morality and could in turn elicit or foster a similar misunderstanding in others. It could be taken as a call to justification by works and could by that very fact impede what it expressly aims to bring about, namely, the fulfillment of the imperatives of morality. The case is quite different with exhortation that appeals to the gospel. Such exhortation leaves room for God's grace. It takes the paradoxical forms of Phil 2:12–13: "Work out your own salvation with fear and trembling; for God is at work in you, both to will and to work for his good pleasure." If we keep this paradox in mind, it may be possible to understand better why gospel and law are interrelated in the way described.

Gospel and law both aim at man's salvation: the gospel insofar as this salvation is wholly a sovereign act of grace on God's part; the imperatives of morality insofar as this same salvation can be awarded to man only if man through free obedience allows it to be given to him as a reward. Exhortation that appeals to the gospel does not for that reason cease to find expression in genuine imperatives. It must therefore pass over into a second kind of exhortation: that which looks to the coming judgment and to retribution according to deeds.

This kind of exhortation, too, can be reduced to the golden rule, and specifically to the second formulation of the restated rule: "Judge not, and you will not be judged; condemn not, and you will not be condemned; forgive, and you will be forgiven.... For the measure you give will be the measure you get back" (Lk 6:37–38). The Lord's Prayer connects the petition for God's forgiveness with the protestation that the petitioners forgive one another. The parable of the merciless servant (Mt 18:23–35) shows how exhortation that appeals to the gospel and exhortation that takes the judgment as its point of reference are interconnected. After the servant has had a debt of ten thousand talents cancelled for him by the king, he meets a fellow servant who owes him a hundred denarii. In this situation two forms of exhortation are addressed to the first servant: You have been forgiven; therefore, forgive your fellow servant, or else you will not be forgiven!

We catch a glimpse here of the broad range of problems which dogmatic theology deals with in the treatises on grace and justification. In our present context we need not go into these. The important thing is the insight that when, in the Old Testament and the New Testament, the requirements of morality are brought up in connection with the gospel and the future judgment, we have exhortation, not normative ethics.

As we have already pointed out several times, exhortation finds expression in ethical statements the truth of which is taken as self-evident. It would be wrong to conclude from this that exhortation is something which need not be taken entirely seriously. Admittedly, exhortation of itself does not convey any new moral insights. But it does have or is intended to have the result that the person addressed allows its moral insights to touch him personally and that he hears them as a challenge to be converted, do penance, change his life, and act as he knows he ought to act. Exhortation is to be evaluated not primarily in terms of its truth-value but in terms of its effect-value, that is, according to whether it is effective or ineffective, whether it succeeds or fails. We would form a very inadequate idea of exhortation if we looked for it only in catalogues of virtues and vices or in lists of commands and prohibitions such as the Decalogue and the rules for households. No, exhortation may also be given through stories, parables, metaphors and narratives.[13] Exhortation seems to be most effective when it takes the form of "simple good example." M. Scheler says in this regard: "There is nothing in this world that so inherently, directly and necessarily *leads a person to become good* as the simple perception—provided it be insightful and adequate to its object—of a good person *in* his or her goodness."[14]

From another point of view, the individual has experience of effective exhortation in his own conscience, insofar as the latter here and now challenges, admonishes, cautions, condemns or absolves him. Any exhortation people give one another in words or silently can attain its goal only if it is accepted by the conscience of those addressed and thus becomes an exhortation of the conscience to itself. To the extent that the individual's conscience urges him to do good and condemns him for doing evil, it mediates the original exhortation that comes from God. In Reformation theology this divine exhortation is depicted in the doctrine of the *usus legis.* This doctrine of its nature has nothing to do with normative ethics. It treats of how God brings his moral will to bear on the sinner through accusation and a verdict of guilt, and on the just through exhortation. The sequence gospel—law is characteristic of bibilical exhortation and especially of Christian exhortation (cf. Jn 13:24).

In contrast to what we have been saying about exhortation, there is a very old thesis of normative ethics that is widely accepted in the various churches. As stated by F. Hürth and P. M. Abellán it runs: "All the moral precepts of the 'new law' are also precepts of the natural moral law. Christ did not add to the natural moral law even a single moral precept of a purely positive kind. . . . This holds even for the commandment of love. . . . The moral requirement of love for God and of love for man on account of God is a requirement of the natural moral law."[15] R. Bultmann formulates the thesis as follows: "If we look at the content of the moral imperatives, there is no specifically Christian ethics; and if one would characterize, say, the commandment of love as a specifically Christian commandment one should remember that St. Paul said that all the commandments of the Law were comprehended in the commandment of love (Rom. 13:9). These commandments, however, can be known to every man before he has heard the Christian message. Every man has a conscience, and can know what is good and what is evil. True Christian preaching does not have special demands to make with respect to ethics."[16]

This thesis deals with normative ethics inasmuch as it takes a position on the question of how the Christian comes to know the requirements of morality. The position is that in principle he does it in the same way that every human being does, namely, through his conscience or natural reason. The natural moral law, as understood in Catholic theology, has natural reason as the subjective power by which it is known. We shall not discuss here the ways in which justification for this thesis has been sought. Suárez, Butler, Newman, Rashdall and many others were philosophers as well as theologians; they probably thought of themselves as in a position to prove philosophically the validity of all the moral requirements that applied to them as Christians.

This thesis, which still today—or today once again—is defended by many moral theologians has, strange to say, been suspect for some time now not only of being a novelty but also of having its origin in a rationalistic outlook. There are those who seem to identify exhortation and normative ethics and who therefore think that this thesis denies the special character of biblical and Christian exhortation and consequently everything that would distinguish a Christian ethics. This misunderstanding in turn explains the effort to demonstrate from scripture the Christian character of Christian exhortation, for the purpose of thereby disproving the supposedly rationalistic thesis in normative ethics.

Now, of course the Christian is called to follow Christ and imitate him. The "behavior of Jesus" is "example and model of love that serves and that sacrifices itself." His word is the "ultimate moral norm."[17] Of course, "Christ is the categorical imperative in concrete form, insofar as ... by his suffering ... he empowers us interiorly to do the Father's will along with him *(cum ipso)*."[18] But these statements of Christian belief are completely irrelevant to the question of *how*, intellectually, we originally know the moral will of God: whether only through faith as a specific form of knowledge or already through reason. The word of Jesus continues to be an "ultimate moral norm" even if we suppose that "Christ reconfirmed these [natural] precepts with his authority and made them even more binding."[19]

A striking aspect of the statements we have just been quoting is that they use a vocabulary which we would expect to find rather in normative ethics. For example: that Christ is "the categorical imperative in concrete form." This sounds as though Kant's various formulations of the categorical imperative should be replaced by an exhortation such as: "Act at all times as Christ acted!" But if we were to give this last statement the same logical status that Kant ascribed to the formulations of the categorical imperative, we would be involved in a Christonomous moral positivism. On the other hand, neither does the statement mean that Christ is an "imperative" to the extent that he "does the Father's will," for then "the Father's will" or "God's will" would be the real categorical imperative.

The non-identity of Christian exhortation and normative ethics will not long escape anyone who does not neglect to go into such questions as the "important casuistic decisions that face the contemporary Church."[20] On this point it is instructive to read Karl Barth who at one time made an effort to develop a normative ethics in terms of Jesus Christ. After the venturesome analogical conclusions drawn in "Christengemeinde und Bürgergemeinde" [Christian Community and Civic Community],[21] we are finally told in "Politische Entscheidung in der Einheit des Glaubens" [Political Decision within the Unity of Faith] that in taking a position on political and legal questions the Christian too is called upon to "use his own mind."[22]

Biblical ethics is very largely exhortation. This explains why exegetes can write extensive and excellent books on New Testament ethics without feeling obliged at some point along the line to formulate explicitly the specific questions and problems of a normative ethics.[23] True enough, since exhortation is a call to conversion and a challenge to decide in favor of what is morally good, it is impossible to talk about the exhortatory parts of scripture without analyzing the distinction between good and evil. Consequently, exegetical works on New Testament ethics give a great deal of space to such themes as justification by works, morality as distinguished from mere legality, the unconditional character (or radical nature) of the moral law, the doing of good for the sake of a promised "reward," and so on. The broad area of moral right and wrong is often described in New Testament exhortation with the help of words naming virtues and vices. This area, too, is frequently discussed by the exegetes. To all of this as such there can be no objection. But when a position is taken in exegesis on a question of normative ethics, there is frequently a begging of the question, that is, the very mistake that is inevitable when one passes off an exhortation for an argument in normative ethics. Thus, for example, the indissolubility of marriage is seen as based on the moral requirement of unconditional fidelity, whereas in fact the content of marital fidelity depends entirely on whether marriage is rightly to be regarded as indissoluble.[24]

The theologian whom the Bible renders familiar primarily with exhortations frequently does not seem to find it easy to come to grips with normative ethics. For example, he may come upon the two rival theories regarding the source of ethical norms—the teleological and the deontological—and form the judgment: "Paul is acquainted . . . with 'teleological' motivation (future judgment and retribution) just as he also argues 'deontologically' from the implications of membership in the body of Christ."[25] But to use the future judgment as an "argument" is to engage in judgment-based exhortation and not to deal with normative ethics. The *lex praemians* [law that rewards] and the *lex poenalis* [law that punishes] presuppose the *lex moralis (praecipiens vel prohibens)* [moral law that commands or prohibits] to be already known. Only when it is already established that a certain type of action is morally reprehensible can one meaningfully urge that "anyone who acts thus will not inherit the kingdom of heaven." Furthermore, one is a member of Christ in virtue of the gospel. To "argue" from the implications of membership in Christ means therefore to exhort by appealing to the gospel.

All this makes it clear that in determining the specific characteristics of a Christian ethics it would be profitable to distinguish between exhortation and normative ethics. Moreover, we need only read what Hürth and Abellán write in their chapters "The Final End," "The Theological Virtues," "Acts That Are Voluntary and Morally Good," and "The New Law," and we will no longer doubt that their thesis in normative ethics in no way implies that Christian ethics lacks a distinct and specific character of its own.

Objection can indeed be raised against the view that the commandment of love as the sum and substance of the moral law is in principle (*per se*) accessible to natural moral reason. The objection does not, however, directly deny the thesis but seeks rather to limit it substantially. Recall all the errors and confusions to which, as experience shows, people succumb who are forced to rely on natural reason alone for their grasp of the moral law. Paul offers a striking picture of such people in the first chapter of Romans. Others endeavor to confirm Paul's judgment with all sorts of evidence, for example, by comparing the moral philosophies of Aristotle, Epicurus, the Stoics, Kant, Scheler and others with Christian ethics. All these historical variations on philosophical ethics are meant to show by their lacunae and errors what the real state of human reason is. The conclusion drawn: Rely on faith, not on reason.

In order to test this objection, it will be worth our while to distinguish between the genesis and the truth-value of moral insight.

II
GENESIS AND TRUTH-VALUE (VALIDITY) OF MORAL INSIGHT

"Christian ethics" is frequently taken to mean the imperatives of morality as Jesus lived and preached them. To the believer in Jesus this is a normative concept in ethics. The person of Jesus assures him of the vaildity or truth of this understanding of morality.

It must then be asked whether the writing and preaching of a Martin Luther, a John Calvin, or an Alphonsus Liguori on ethics can be called "Christian ethics." The answer evidently depends on whether and to what degree these men in their interpretation convey what they intend to convey, namely, the imperatives of morality as lived and preached by Jesus. Only with substantial reservations would Luther have agreed that Liguori was presenting a Christian ethics, and vice versa. In justification of his criticism each would have referred the reader not to his own writings but the New Testament or certain writings in the New Testament. And as a matter of fact anyone who wishes to form a judgment about Christian ethics in the sense given the term here must undertake the task of determining from the New Testament writings just how Jesus understood and explained the requirements of morality. The student may perhaps look to a Luther or a Calvin or a Liguori as a commentator, but he will endorse what they say only insofar as it helps him grasp the original moral teaching of Jesus.

For purposes of comparison a Christian ethics should be set

over against the understanding of the requirements of morality that is inherently accessible to natural reason. This understanding may be called "natural ethics" or "philosophical ethics." How does one elaborate this natural ethics? It might be thought that in working out such an ethics we should follow the philosophers: Aristotle, the Stoics, Kant, and so on. But then the question of truth-value immediately arises: Kant, relying solely on his own powers of reasoning, interprets the requirements of morality thus and so, but is his interpretation correct? This question is unavoidable if for no other reason that Aristotle, the Stoics, and Kant are, to say the least, not fully in agreement on the correct understanding of the demands of morality. Clearly, then, these philosophers stand in the same relation to a correct (true) natural ethics that Luther, Calvin and Liguori do to a Christian ethics understood as normative. All these philosophers are determined to make a proper use of their reasoning powers and to interpret correctly the requirements of morality, but their mere determination is no proof that they are successful. If the reader wants to find out whether or not they are successful, he has no alternative but to start philosophizing himself and to decide which understanding of the demands of morality reason judges to be correct. If he is judicious, he will also become a student of Aristotle, Kant and others. But he may not settle for any "swearing by what the teacher says." He must pursue a systematic study of philosophical ethics, and this study is not reducible to a study of the history of philosophical ethics.

In addition to the normative concept of Christian and natural-philosophical ethics, of which we have just been speaking, there is another concept of ethics; it may be described as the "historico-genetic." It is quite usual when speaking of the ethics presented by Luther, Calvin or Liguori to say without any reservation that it is a Christian ethics. But how is the adjective "Christian" to be understood in this context? It serves to characterize the ethics in terms of its "begetters" and of the manner in which it was "begotten." Luther, Calvin and Liguori were Christians and theologians. Their declared purpose was to understand and explain the ethics of Jesus. They make this clear by the fact that in their argumentation they appeal to the New Testament as their ultimate authority. This is reason enough to call them "Christian ethicians" and their ethics a "Christian ethics." To do so is to leave open the question of how far their ethics agrees with the ethics Jesus himself lived by and preached.

This historico-genetic understanding of the term "ethics" is the one usually applied to "natural ethics" and especially to "philosophical ethics." Thus no one has the slightest hesitation about applying the adjective "philosophical" to the ethics both of a G. E. Moore and an H. A. Prichard, although these two men interpret the requirements of morality in ways that contradict one another to a great extent, so that both cannot have presented the correct (true) natural ethics.

When theologians, be they exegetes or systematic theologians, compare Christian ethics and natural ethics, they think and write of Christian ethics in a completely normative sense. They do not appeal to an Augustine, a Thomas Aquinas, or a Luther as though these were their ultimate authority, from which no appeal could be made to a higher tribunal. And yet these same theologians usually take natural ethics in a historico-genetic sense. This is perfectly legitimate when, as is frequently the case with exegetes, the intention is primarily a historical study. "In order to bring out the specific character of the primitive Christian ethos" the latter is contrasted "first with the Jewish, then with the pagan ethics" current in the world in which primitive Christianity found itself.[26] However, in elaborating such a contrast the student must bear in mind that possible differences between the primitive Christian ethos and Stoic ethics need not also be a distinction between Christian ethics and a normatively understood natural ethics.

It is said, for example, that the concept of *tapeinophrosyne* is to be found "in pagan Greek usage only in a bad sense." In fact, among the Stoics it can even be found in the lists of vices.[27] But this does not justify the conclusion that the moral attitude called *tapeinophrosyne* in the New Testament is alien to a normatively understood natural ethics. It might well be that in dealing with this particular area the Stoics did not make a right use of their reasoning powers, just as a Christian and theologian can err in his understanding of the faith. As the example given may indicate, even a comparison intended solely as historical requires some familiarity with systematic ethics as well. If the term *tapeinophrosyne* occurs in the Stoic lists of vices while the New Testament regards it as a basic attitude required by morality, the only conclusion that immediately follows is that the Stoics and the New Testament attach contrary moral valuations to the *word tapeinophrosyne*. The Stoics and the New Testament would be expressing opposed moral judgments of a specific interior attitude only if at a moment logically prior to their moral judgment they were to offer identical descriptions of the attitude in all its significant traits.

It seems nonetheless to be often the case that theologians concerned with system building intend to compare Christian ethics *as such* with natural ethics *as such*. They proceed by presenting as natural ethics the ethics of one or other philosopher: the ethics of Epictetus or Kant or Scheler or Bloch; or frequently they are content with very sketchy references to the history of philosophy or with references to whatever ethics is currently popular. In doing so, the theologians seem to think that genuine philosophical ethics is to be identified with the ethics which the "others," i.e., non-Christians, cultivate.[28]

It is clear that such a procedure leads inevitably to a distorted (and unfair) comparison. For example, in the resultant comparison the *one* Christian ethics, inherently true and certain, is set over against the seemingly bewildering multiplicity of philosophical opinions from Plato down to the modern positivists and analytical philosophers. The superiority of a Christian ethics that is presented in *this* manner is really to be explained simply by logical sleight-of-hand. After all, one need only take "Christian ethics" in a historico-genetic sense, and one would have no great difficulty in producing a picture of it that is no less bewildering than the picture of philosophical ethics understood in a historico-genetic sense.

If we correlate Christian ethics with faith and natural ethics with reason, the same defect shows up in the way in which faith (*fides*) and reason (*ratio*) are often compared. People take "faith" in a normative sense, so that "faith" is equivalent to "true faith." This identification is rendered all the easier inasmuch as in the language of theology "faith" very often means "truth of faith" (*fides quae creditur*). The term "reason," on the other hand, is understood in a genetic sense, so that one may without inconsistency attribute to reason every manner of self-deception and error. Once again, this identification is made easier because when people speak of "reason" they are usually thinking of a faculty or *power* of knowing. Now it is immediately evident that, given these assumptions, faith must exercise toward reason the functions of a critical guardian, since truth exposes errors as such.

But it takes no great ingenuity to conceive the relation between faith and reason in such a way that they automatically exchange their roles. One need only use the word "faith" in a genetic sense so that it includes erroneous beliefs and superstitions. Then one takes "reason" in a normative sense so that only "true reason" (="reason that knows the truth") is meant. At this point reason becomes the critical guard in relation to faith. Then what a theologian claims is a mystery of faith may prove in fact to be a logical absurdity.[29]

Therefore, if we want to compare faith and reason from a gnoseological point of view, we must compare true knowledge through faith with true knowledge through reason, or truths of faith with truths of reason. Then the relation between the two turns out to be that *fides supponit rationem et transcendit eam* [faith supposes reason and goes beyond it].

Similarly, the comparison should be made between the demands of morality as Jesus lived and preached them and the demands of morality as these present themselves in the form of truths grasped by reason. Since the Christian believes in Jesus Christ, he is certain that Jesus perfectly fulfilled the requirements of morality in his life and authentically interpreted them in his preaching. Consequently, the Christian has every reason for relying unconditionally on Jesus as an infallible authority in matters of morality. But it by no means follows from this that the demands of morality as lived and interpreted by Jesus take us beyond the realm of knowledge accessible to reason. From the theological viewpoint the requirements of morality, insofar as they are accessible in principle to natural reason, are commandments of the Creator. If we keep this in mind it is not clear how anyone can show that Jesus did not intend simply to revalidate the commandments of the Creator against possible misunderstandings.

But even if we prescind from this point, the question of whether and to what extent the requirements of morality as lived and interpreted by Jesus are accessible to rational insight must be answered in principle by undertaking the task of making the moral message of Jesus intelligible in terms of reason. Even as a Christian theologian the student must at this point engage in philosophizing. It cannot be objected that since the Christian already believes, he is unfitted for such philosophizing; that he will be inclined to claim as a truth of reason what in the last analysis he owes solely to his Christian faith. Such a tendency to rationalism does occur. But the opposite tendency, to fideism, also occurs among theologians: that is, the tendency to restrict the possibilities of reason as much as possible, in order to extend the sphere of faith that much the more. To the fideist philosophical skepticism and philosophical positivism are the most endearing of all the historical forms philosophy has taken. Yet how else is anyone to err who attempts to define gnoseologically the realms of faith and reason except by falling into either rationalism or fideism? But if the Christian is to be ill-fitted for philosophizing simply because he can err, then everyone else is equally unfit for philosophizing because everyone else too is capable of erring.

Whether the person who systematically studies philosophical ethics is a Christian or a non-Christian is relevant only to the genesis and not to the truth-value of his ethics. It seems advisable to keep in mind a very simple example of the extent to which questions of the genesis and questions of the truth-value of a (real or supposed) moral insight must be kept separate. A pupil does his sums and writes: $2 + 2 = 5$. We may ask whether this arithmetical computation is true or false, and by what right we claim it to be erroneous. Then we are dealing with the truth-value of an arithmetical computation. But we can also ask how the pupil came to make such a mistake: whether he was distracted or was absent when the rules of addition were explained. Then we are asking for a genetic explanation of an erroneous arithmetical computation. One may not object that the example is badly chosen because there is a fundamental difference between an arithmetical computation and a moral value-judgment. The difference need not be challenged, but, provided we recognize that moral propositions too are *truth-related,* i.e., that they can be true or false, then it is evident that in their regard too we must distinguish carefully between genesis and truth-value or validity.[30]

The genesis especially of existentially significant insights and errors is to all appearances connected with the moral condition of the person. One who gives himself to a life of selfishness may in consequence become so insensitive to the requirements of morality that in fact he does not comprehend them. According to the church's teaching man's reason has been "darkened by the sin of the first man."[31] The encyclical *Humani generis* adds an explanation: the truths of morality are of a kind that challenges the person to a life of selflessness; as a result of original sin, however, the person is under the influence of self-centered desires. In matters of morality, therefore, he readily persuades himself that what he wishes not to be true must be false or at least doubtful. This explains why he often finds it so difficult to achieve correct moral insights.[32] In this connection, the First Vatican Council points to the need of the Judeo-Christian revelation if human beings in their present state are to know "readily, with firm certitude, and without any admixture of error" truths "relating to God which in themselves are not beyond the power of reason to attain."[33] Since, on the other hand, faith is also a form of obedience and a transformation "through the renewal of the mind," it brings an existential openness to "what is the will of God, what is good and acceptable and perfect" (Rom 12:2; see also Phil 1:9–10).

All these statements have to do with the *genesis* of moral insights and errors. They are not relevant to a gnoseological distinction of the sphere of possible knowledge through reason from the sphere of knowledge through faith. Neither the person's "blindness to values" nor his existential openness change the status of a moral value-judgment from the viewpoint of the theory of knowledge.

(Justifying) faith in the Pauline sense of the word is not only a specific type of knowledge; it also includes obedience to the moral law, the renunciation of sin, and the determination to live a life in the service of righteousness. This may explain why the obedience of faith as an existential openness to moral imperatives, and the knowledge of faith insofar as it is to be distinguished from knowledge through reason, have at times been lumped together without distinction. (Traditional Catholic theology, however, does have the concept of *fides informis,* that is, a faith which is possible even for sinners, and thus does not include a basic obedience to the moral law.) On the other hand, faith as moral obedience must also bring about an existential openness to the demands of morality insofar as these are truths of reason.

Now, the genesis of correct insights and of errors is an extremely complex process in which a large number of varied factors may play a part. Among these factors the moral condition of the person is only one, even if possibly a very important one. Thus despite their honest and upright obedience of faith the Christians of the primitive community saw nothing morally suspect in certain forms of slavery. It is therefore possible to say only that, all other things being equal, the person who has been transformed "through the renewal of his mind" will have superior moral insight. But—again, all other things being equal—he would also have to become thereby the better philosophical ethician.

"Faith" in the sense of "obedience" is a positive, (religio-)moral value-term just as are "fidelity" and "righteousness." As such it has "unbelief" (= "disobedience") for its contrary, just as "fidelity" and "righteousness" have "infidelity" and "unrighteousness" for their contraries. The situation is different when "faith" refers to a specific type of knowledge. Knowledge through reason is different from knowledge through faith, but the two are not opposed as contraries, any more than sense knowledge is contrary to intellectual knowledge. If we look at knowledge as a value in itself, we can place the various types of knowledge on a hierarchic scale, according, for example, to the existential importance of the truths that relate primarily to one or other specific type of knowledge. Even then, however, no contrarieties are discernible between these various types of knowledge.

Then too, the word "reason" is likewise used at times as a positive, practical valuational term, somewhat as the Christian term "faith" is. For example, it can be said that reason commands this or that behavior. As a practical valuational term "reason" has, as is to be expected, its contrary, namely, "unreason." According to the context a command of reason will have to do with behavior that is utilitarian and meaningful or perhaps also morally good and right.

Now if we permit the gnoseological fields of meaning of "faith" and "reason" to overlap with their fields of meaning as religio-moral and practical values, bewildering consequences ensue. Faith, because it is not reason, becomes unreason; reason, because it is not faith, becomes unbelief. This seems to reduce to an absurdity the thesis that even for the Christian the requirements of morality are, with logical priority, the object of reason and not of faith. "The removal of the content of morality from the realm of faith . . . means that reason has become heretical." For, as a result, "faith has been removed from the sphere of reason, and what is rational is not admitted to be a possible content of the world of faith as well. Consequently, either faith is regarded as unreasonable or reason is regarded as unbelieving, or both positions are maintained."[34]

The argument is as remarkable as the transformation it contains of a simple non-identity into an opposition of contraries, of a statement intended as gnoseological into a religio-moral value-judgment. The transformation is effected via the following series of terms: (a) non-faith (non-believing), disbelief; (b) non-reason (non-rational), irrational. Now if we take "faith" in the Pauline sense of "the obedience of faith," then it is analytically evident that faith and morality are inseparable. Then faith *means* a "resolute determination against sin and for righteousness." The entire hortatory content of the Pauline letters could be entered in evidence of this statement. But this tells us nothing about whether faith as a specific type of knowledge gives, with logical priority, the insight into good and evil, sin and righteousness.

Because we like to use the imposing word "decision" in characterizing faith, and therefore speak of "the decision of faith," we obscure the distinction between faith as obedience and faith as a type of knowledge. For we use the term "decide" in both a cognitive and a volitive sense: (a) he cannot decide (=cannot judge, cannot make out) whether this manner of acting is right or wrong; (b) he cannot decide (= cannot resolve, cannot bring himself) to do what he knows he ought to do. While it is quite uncontested and incontestable that (justifying) faith as obedience is a decision on the side of morality, it is on the contrary a disputed question whether or not through his faith as a mode of knowledge the Christian decides (= forms a judgment concerning) in what the distinction between good and evil, morally right and morally wrong consists.

The distinction between the genesis and the truth-value of moral insights should serve to make clear the precise meaning of the traditional thesis that even for the Christian the knowledge of the requirements of morality is, with logical priority, the object of his reason and not of his faith. The thesis is concerned only with the gnoseological status of judgments about moral imperatives, only with the question of whether these judgments can be shown to be true or false in *logical* independence of the knowledge which comes through the Judeo-Christian faith. The thesis takes no position on the genesis of the knowledge of moral imperatives. It is therefore fully compatible with all that scripture, tradition, and experience tell us of the influence of the person's moral state on his moral insights and errors. As a matter of fact, many of the theologians who defend the thesis insist emphatically that it is difficult to over-estimate the importance of Judeo-Christian revelation for the genesis of correct insight into the requirements of morality.[35]

The distinctions between exhortation and normative ethics and between the genesis and the validity of moral insights can help clarify only partially the question of the specific character of Christian ethics as this is being discussed today. By way of conclusion let us recall a problem that has lately been formulated in this context. The problem may be said to be of a metaethical kind. If the assumption is made that only through the Judeo-Christian faith do human beings become conscious of their relationship to God as their Creator, then the question of the specific character of a Christian ethics is being identified with the question of the specific character of a theistic ethics. Then the thesis that the requirements of morality as Jesus preached them are inherently accessible to natural reason is implicitly understood as meaning that the moral requirements voiced by Jesus can be shown to be valid even in the supposition of some form of atheism.

This clearly amounts to a shifting of the problem. In saying this I do not, of course, mean to deny that it is well worthwhile reflecting on how far people can get with natural ethics if atheism is presumed true. It seems that the metaethical theory of decisionism, which is a form of non-cognitivism, permits instructive considerations on this subject. The point remains, however, that then the subject being discussed is no longer the specific character of a Christian ethics. It must be acknowledged at least of Judaism and Islam that they share with Christianity the substance of the first article of the creed.

Notes

1. In *Prinzipien christlicher Moral* (Einsiedeln, 1975), J. Ratzinger edits three essays connected with the Theological Commission's study: (1) H.

Schürmann, "Die Frage nach der Verbindlichkeit der neutestamentlichen Wertungen und Weisungen"; (2) J. Ratzinger, "Kirchliches Lehramt—Glaube—Moral"; (3) H. Urs von Balthasar, "Neue Sätze zur christlichen Ethik." We shall be making frequent reference to these essays.

2. G. E. Moore, *Principia Ethica* (Cambridge, 1903[1]), Preface.

3. Cf. H. Rotter, *Grundlagen der Moral* (Zürich, 1975), p. 8.

4. H. Schlier, *Der Brief an die Epheser* (4th ed.; Düsseldorf, 1963), pp. 230 and 255: "The *kathōs* includes . . . both a comparison and a motive. In the parallel passage, 5:2, the motivational aspect of the conjunctive is even primary." Cf. also H. D. Wendland, *Ethik des Neuen Testaments* (Göttingen, 1970), pp. 92 and 95.

5. Cf. R. Bultmann, *The Gospel of John: A Commentary,* tr. by G. R. Beasley-Murray, R. W. N. Hoare, and J. K. Riches (Philadelphia, 1971), p. 525: "*Kathōs*. . . does not describe the degree or intensity of the *agapān* (Loisy), nor does it depict the way that Jesus took as a way of service; rather it describes the basis of the *agapān*." Cf. also A. Wikenhauser, *Das Evangelium nach Johannes* (Regensburg, 1961[3]), p. 202.

6. Insofar as the gospel is God's word it is evidently performative speech, that is, *verbum efficax.*

7. G. von Rad, *Old Testament Theology,* tr. by D. M. G. Stalker, 1 (New York, 1962), pp. 193–95; N. Lohfink, *Das Siegeslied am Schilfmeer* (Frankfurt, 1964), pp. 151ff.

8. Cf. B. Schüller, *Die Begründung sittlicher Urteile* (Düsseldorf, 1973), pp. 56ff.

9. G. von Rad, *Deuteronomy: A Commentary,* tr. by D. Barton (Philadelphia, 1966), says on this passage that the text "lays the question of obedience in a most intimate manner on the hearer's conscience" (p. 108).

10. The term "love" also occurs in the lists of virtues. Cf. Gal 5:22; 2 Cor. 6:6, 1 Tm 6:11.

11. H. Schürmann, *op. cit.,* p. 18.

12. For this reason, love of enemies, when contrasted with a love given only to friends, can be proposed as the essence of moral goodness. As such, it is fitted to be the point of the comparision between the action of the heavenly Father and the action of his children; cf. Mt. 5:44–45; Lk 6:35.

13. There is an excellent passage of exhortation in 2 S 12:1–15.

14. *Der Formalismus in der Ethik und die materiale Wertethik* (Bern—Munich, 1966[5]), p. 560. The first italics have been added.

15. *De principiis, de virtutibus et praeceptis,* Pars I (Rome, 1948), p. 43; same teaching in F. Suárez, *De legibus* X, 2, nos 5–12; F. A. Göpfert, *Moraltheologie* I (Paderborn, 1902[6]), p. 27 (see also the important footnote there); E. Genicot, *Theologiae Moralis Institutiones* I (Louvain, 1905[5]), p. 125; J. Mausbach, *Katholische Moraltheologie* I (Münster, 1922[24]), p. 64 [A. Vermeersch, *Theologia Moralis* I (Rome, 1947[4]), no. 153; M. Zalba, *Theologiae Moralis Summa* I (Madrid, 1952), no. 368. All these moral theologians make this thesis a self-evident part of the relationship between nature and grace, creation and covenant; they see it as illustrative of the basic principle:

"Grace presupposes and perfects nature." For this reason, K. Martin, *Lehrbuch der katholischen Moral* (Mainz, 1851[2]), p. 42, writes that the "Christian law . . . by its content gives unity and final completion" to the "natural law." There is an almost identical statement in A. Koch, *Lehrbuch der Moraltheologie* (Freiburg i. Br., 1905), p. 58. Cardinal J. H. Newman shared this view; cf. E. Bischofsberger, *Die sittlichen Voraussetzungen des Glaubens: Zur Fundamentalethik John Henry Newmans* (Mainz, 1974), pp. 174ff. Most of the theologians named see the three evangelical counsels as representing something new in comparison with the natural moral law.

In the Anglican Church R. Hooker (1554–1600) seems to maintain the same thesis in his classical work, *Of the Laws of Ecclesiastical Polity* (Everyman's Library 201; London, 1969), pp. 199ff., especially p. 210. Certainly Bishop J. Butler (1692–1752) holds it in his well-known book *The Analogy of Religion* which was first published in 1736; see the edition in the collection "Milestones of Thought" (New York, 1961), p. 183. So too does H. Rashdall, *Christ and Conscience* (London, 1916).

16. "Preaching: Genuine and Secularized," in W. Leibrecht (ed.), *Religion and Culture: Essays in Honor of Paul Tillich* (New York, 1959), p. 238. For other modern evangelical theologians who express the same view cf. B. Schüller, "Zur theologischen Diskussion über die *lex naturalis,*" *Theologie und Philosophie* 41 (1966) 495, n. 22. Cf. also E. Troeltsch, "Grundprobleme der Ethik," in his *Gesammelte Schriften* II (1922[2]; reprinted: Aalen, 1962), pp. 598–99. Regarding the Reformers Troeltsch says: "For them too the natural moral law represents the requirements of reason and is identical with the Decalogue, which is only a short summary, a divinely composed abstract, of the natural law. The natural moral law is the moral law that governed man's original state, and the moral law of Christ who simply confirmed and restated the Decalogue." See also P. Althaus, *Die Ethik Martin Luthers* (Gütersloh, 1965), pp. 32ff.

17. Thus H. Schürmann, *op. cit.,* pp. 17ff.

18. Thus H. Urs von Balthasar, *op. cit.,* p. 71.

19. F. Hürth and P. M. Abellán, *op. cit.,* p. 43.

20. H. Urs von Balthasar, *loc. cit.,* explains that he does not wish to go into these questions.

21. *Theologische Studien,* no. 20 (1946).

22. *Theologische Existenz heute,* N.F. 34 (1952), p. 8.

23. Cf., e.g., the outstanding essays of H. Schlier, "Vom Wesen der apostolischen Mahnung," in his *Die Zeit der Kirche* (Freiburg, 1966[4]), pp. 74–89, and "Die Eigenart der apostolischen Mahnung nach dem Apostel Paulus," in his *Besinnung auf das Neue Testament* (Freiburg, 1964), pp. 340–57, as well as his book, *Nun aber bleiben diese Drei: Grundriss der christlichen Lebensvollzugs* (einsiedeln, 1971). See also E. Neuhäusler, *Anspruch und Antwort Gottes: Zur Lehre von der Weisungen innerhalb der synoptischen Jesusverkündigung* (Düsseldorf, 1962): In the final chapter of his *Die konkreten Einzelgebote in der paulinischen Paränese* (Gütersloh, 1961),

W. Schrage comes as a close to a normative ethics as is possible without making the transition to systematic ethics.

24. K. H. Schelkle, *Theology of the New Testament,* tr. by W. A. Jurgens, 3 (Collegeville, 1973), p. 34.

25. Ratzinger, *op. cit.,* p. 51, footnote.

26. H. Preisker, *Das Ethos des Urchristentums* (Darmstadt, 1968³), p. 11.

27. W. Schrage, *op. cit.,* p. 204.

28. Conversely, many philosophical ethicians regard it as "bad form" to be occupied with theological ethics. It is possible to meet philosophers who really believe that theonomous moral positivism is the dominant system among theologians.

29. On this point cf. Ratzinger, *op. cit.,* p. 61: "Both are to be found at every time: the semblance of reason and the manifestation of truth by way of reason." Of course. But at every time we also find the semblance of faith and the manifestation of God's word by way of faith.

30. On this point cf. Kant, *Kritik der reinen Vernunft* (Akademie-Ausgabe 3), pp. 100–1. J. Habermas, *Zur Logik der Sozialwissenschaften* (Frankfurt, 1970), writes: "After Moore and Husserl, who came at the matter from different angles, had made a strict distinction between the logical and psychological approaches and had thereby revived an old insight of Kant, the Positivists dropped their naturalism. . . . Since that time, questions of genesis may no longer be vaguely confused with questions of validity" (pp. 52–53). These remarks are important inasmuch as the relationship which Habermas has shown to exist between knowledge and interest has, as experience shows, been frequently misunderstood and used to justify a mixing of questions of genesis with questions of validity.

31. Pius IX, Letter *Gravissimas inter* (December 11, 1862), condemning the errors of Jakob Frohschammer, in Denzinger-Schönmetzer [henceforth *DS*], *Enchiridion symbolorum* (32nd ed.; 1963), no. 2853; in older editions [henceforth *D*], no. 1670.

32. *DS* 3875 (*D* 2305).

33. *DS* 3005 (*D* 1786).

34. Ratzinger, *op. cit.,* p. 64.

35. E.g., J. Butler, *op. cit.,* p. 183: Christ "published anew the law of nature, which men had corrupted; and the very knowledge of which, to some degree, was lost among them. . . . To which is to be added that he set us a perfect example, that we should follow his steps."

Questioning the Specificity
of Christian Morality

Ph. Delhaye

I
THE STATE OF THE PROBLEM
ACCORDING TO A RECENT STUDY

Down through the centuries theologians have set the law of Christ over against natural law and the Mosaic law alike. But, of late, the problem has taken on a new meaning and a new name while, at the same time, attracting increased attention. It is becoming quite a task to keep count of the articles and books treating of the specificity of Christian morality.[1] Fr. J. Fuchs, a professor at the Pontifical Gregorian University has, in his turn, posed the question, "Does a Christian morality exist?", in a book[2] which by reason of its wide circulation,[3] its moderation and also by reason of its author's authority can rightfully be retained as the starting point of an inquiry.

It is Fr. Fuch's merit to have clearly perceived that the problem of Christian morality cannot be resolved if several levels in the Christian command and commitment are not properly distinguished. Accordingly, he considers "transcendental" morality and "categorical" morality separately. What does this mean?

1. Christian Transcendental Morality

"Transcendental morality considers the fact that in a moral act the self-commitment that is activated involves the person as a whole" (p. 12, footnote 1). "There are transcendental attitudes and norms which, as such, penetrate and transcend the different moral categories. These are the virtuous types of conduct such as faith, love, assent to redemption, life as sacrament, the imitation of Christ, etc. Obviously such transcendental attitudes and norms affect not only conduct in this or that particular sphere of life (justice, fidelity, chastity) but they also affect man as a totality, as a person who dedicates himself to faith and to love, to the imitation of Christ, to the will to die and to rise again with Christ" (pp. 11–12). The "transcendental" therefore involves two elements: values and general norms which are difficult to classify thematically with great precision[5] and, on the other hand, the life of grace revealing itself outwardly in theological morality. Fr. Fuchs (pp. 136–137) rightly recalls that in St. Augustine and in St. Thomas the "new law" simultaneously comprises the life in the spirit and exigencies (pp. 136–137). And, quite appropriately, he cites the text of Galatians 5, 22: "But the fruit of the Spirit is love, joy, peace, patience, kindness, goodness, faithfulness, gentleness, self-control; against such things there is no law." It is indeed a question of graces given by the Spirit to the Christian who must correspond to them through his personal commitment and effort: "And those who belong to Christ Jesus have crucified the flesh with its passions and desires. If we live by the Spirit, let us also walk by the Spirit" (24–25).

Obviously, and without hesitation, Fr. Fuchs recognizes that the divine adoption situates itself at the level of grace and that the morality deriving therefrom is proper to the Christian. "Scripture unambiguously and most abundantly expresses itself on Christian and transcendental attitudes and clearly reveals that it is a question of specifically Christian attitudes" (p. 12). The role of moral theology, in keeping with its renewal as recommended by Vatican Council II (p. 134),[6] is to highlight, before all else, precisely this aspect of Christian praxis: ". . . Moral theology must transmit and translate the doctrine elaborated by exegesis and dogmatic theology on the relation that exists between man and the God of his salvation so that it may become a doctrine of Christian life and action in this world" (p. 113). Indeed Fr. Fuchs strongly lays stress on this essential element of transcendental Christian morality throughout Ch. IV (*Moral and dogmatic theology,* pp. 93–115). Regrettably he did not expend a similar effort on behalf of biblical morality: the scriptural dimension likewise is most often absent in his book, not only as regards the exposition of the transcendental aspect but also as regards the categorical level. A greater attention to the New Testament texts might have enabled him to avoid taking radical positions in connection with categorical morality by way of exceptions and corrections verging on contradiction.

2. Human Categorical Morality

A Christian *categorical* morality indeed appears to be excluded by statements such as the following: "The proper and specifically Christian element of Christian morality is not to be sought forthwith in the particularities of the categorical values, virtues and norms of the different spheres of life" (p. 12). "Categorical morality considers the commitment of the person in the performance of a moral act belonging to a precise moral category (truthfulness, chastity, justice") (p. 12, footnote 1) which, in itself, has naught of a Christian character, being purely and simply human in its materiality. Or: "If we disregard the decisive and essential element of Christian morality, of Christian intentionality (as transcendental aspect), Christian morality can be said to be fundamentally and essentially human in its categorical determination and its materiality. Hence it is a morality of authentic humaneness. This means that truthfulness, honesty and fidelity, if considered materially, are not specifically Christian values. Rather, they are universally human values; we are against falsehood and adultery not only because we are Christians but simply because we are human beings" (pp. 14–15). Starting out from here, Fr. Fuchs proceeds to explain that the *humanum* and its imperatives are exactly the same independently of whether one is Christian or not. "Hence it is in man," he writes further, "that we must find the conduct that befits him as a being bounded to the absolute, aligned in a fellowship of being-with-others and who, furthermore, must assume responsibility for the human-mundane reality in such a way that all his action conforms to the essence and, above all, to the personal dignity of being-man" (p. 16).

The severity of these statements is further reinforced by the arguments brought to bear. After asserting that Christ excluded "the world" in the sense of the "world of egoistic inhumanity and, in consequence, the world of sin," he adds: "Christ therefore enjoins us, in a purely material manner, to practice the morality of authentic and upright humaneness" (p. 17). The Pauline texts are submitted to the same secularizing re-reading: "Objectively, according to St. Paul, the same material norm of behavior is applicable to Christians and non-Christians, to Jews and pagans alike (see Rom 2, 1 and 5), hence an authentically human morality" (p. 17). Further we are told: "It belongs to the Christian tradition that Christianity does not bring any new moral code in its wake but a new man who inwardly accepts and respects the moral code of authentic humaneness" (pp. 140–141).[7]

After these declarations of principle Fr. Fuchs clearly sensed, nevertheless, that some attentuations were called for. Indeed the initial statements are modified by so many exceptions and fine shadings that one may legitimately ask whether they were faultlessly formulated from the start.[8]

3. The Christian Impact on Categorical Morality

If "transcendental" and "categorical" seem to be wide apart inasmuch as one is specifically Christian and the other purely human, the former has contacts with the latter and exercises influence on it.

(a) First of all Christianity "motivates more profoundly and gives rise to a humane type of conduct" (p. 22). "The believer is conscious of his self-realization as a person before Jesus Christ and the Father of his salvation" (p. 14). On the other hand, "Christian intentionality is an element that penetrates and pervades the particular categorical comportment" (p. 14).

(b) After frequent and emphatic assertions that there is no categorical Christian ethic, Fr. Fuchs, nevertheless, willingly acknowledges that Christianity "determines also the content of our types of conduct" (p. 23). He explains immediately: "The person who really lives as a believer in the community of believers and in the church guided by the hierarchy, in his life style will not remain uninfluenced by the ethos of the community and of the church; at bottom it will be an ethos of *humanum christianum*" (p. 22). Fr. Fuchs cites three examples: "the significance of renunciation and of the Cross," "the meaning of Christian virginity," "the personal hearkening to the Spirit" (p. 27).

(c) We must not forget to mention an entire sector of the "categorical" which covers an extremely broad expanse even though it can be described in a few words: "Thirdly," continues Fr. Fuchs (p. 22), "we must bear in mind that the religious and cultic relation of man to God is, at the same time, a moral type of conduct. But it hardly needs to be emphasized that this type of conduct is largely determined in its Christian concretization by the *christianum* of the Christian man."[9]

(d) At the level of life, the acts that appertain solely to transcendental morality are relatively rare, but the values at this level of Christian commitment are constantly translated into concrete acts of categorical morality: the discharge of one's professional duties, interpersonal relations. "Through his moral behavior in the sphere of different moral categories, the human person consequently actuates himself in his Christian relation to the Father. He actuates himself in a concrete moral type of conduct as a believer, loving, following Christ, as a person who offers himself in Christian freedom. Hence he actuates his theological life in the acts of categorical morality" (p. 139). Love of God also involves love of neighbor and this is realized in "categorical" acts: being of service to others, being indulgent, dispensing justice. Fraternal charity mobilizes all the virtues: "love of neighbor needs the acts of other moral virtues in order to express itself" (p. 143). This influence of transcendental Christian love is so patent and so strong that along with Fr. Rahner, Fr. Fuchs, in the last page of his book, seems ready to recognize the existence of an "explicit categorical love of neighbor" situating itself alongside love on the transcendental level "a more profound, a more original love of neighbor which, in reality, would be the relation of Christian love totally open to the neighbor and which would bear along the former" (p. 144).

The richness of Fr. Fuchs exposition is clear to see. To be sure it is not flawless and we shall have occasion to explain ourselves on this particular point. Nevertheless he must be credited, at least, for having furnished a problematic and a maze of questions. He has permitted us to sense in advance the reasons underlying the statements in regard to the non-specificity of Christian morality. Indeed, Fr. Fuchs constantly tries to reduce the Christian effort to the level of the *humanum,* to justify norms by purely rational arguments. One senses in them the influence of a morality that has forsaken the reading of the holy books and advanced philosophic arguments exclusively. The desire to do justice to human values, to effect a connection with the morality of non-Christians, indeed to make way for secularization have reinforced these tendencies. But Fr. Fuchs is too good a theologian to neglect the contribution of grace, salvation through Christ, in short the conditions of transcendental morality and thus not fail to reintroduce, by way of exceptions and corrections, that which he neglected to do in connection with his beginning statements. If some are astonished over what has been called his want of "restraints" they will see, by comparison with other theses, how Fr. Fuchs has actually saved the main point at issue once his exposition is viewed as a whole.

II
"IDEOLOGIES" MINIMIZING OR DENYING
THE SPECIFICITY OF CHRISTIAN MORALITY

The very statement: "there is no specific Christian morality" can be understood in different senses, almost contradictory, according to the ideology in which it is situated.

1. The Imperialism of a Certain Conception of Natural Law

If I begin this inquiry on the ideological background of the controversy by the study of this tendency, it is because such elements are to be found in Fr. Fuch's synthesis. It goes without saying that the theologians whom I shall be discussing here never ever thought of adopting the positions being proposed at the present time. Nevertheless, by practically identifying natural law and the law of Christ, they paved the way for the negations of those who reverse the data of the problem by denying the divine character of natural law and the direct authority of the magisterium over the latter.

In any case one will find declarations of a quite curious character in the *Institutiones Theologiae Moralis* of Genicot-Salsmans in connection with the relation between natural law and divine law: *"Praecepta moralia nulla Christus addidit eis quae iure naturali omnes astringebant. Verum quidem est praecepta virtutum theologalium se extendere ad quaedam obiecta nova ex. gr. ad credendum explicite Incarnationis mysterium, ad sperandam remissionem peccatorum explicite per Christum. Sed ista extensio, supposita horum obiectorum propositione a Christo facta, ex ipsa lege naturali sequitur. Proposuit insuper divinus Legislator altiorem prorsus perfectionem, sed per modum consilii, non praecepti."*[10] It will be noted that there is no allusion whatsoever to charity. The theological virtues themselves, which Fr. Fuchs and others, today will say appertain to the typically Christian transcendental morality, are led back to natural law.[11] The evangelical counsels themselves would constitute the sole originality of Christianity in the domain of morality.[12] Fr. Noldin's manual[13] is slightly less radical but, at least, it acknowledges a certain specificity to the theological virtues. But the moral precepts are unqualifiedly treated as identical with the natural law which, moreover, includes the decalogue:[14] "Moralia (praecepta) decalogo continentur: Christus eim legem naturalem non abrogavit, sed explicite renovavit, confirmavit eique maiorem perfectionem addidit."

The program of instruction on the subject of morality that has prevailed in some schools and against which Vatican II registered its protest (*Optatam totius,* no. 16), is included in this perspective. The theological virtues were very often reserved for the course in dogmatics and in every way attention was focused on the purely doctrinal aspects of questions to the detriment of moral problems.

The treatise on faith examined the thorny problem posed by the judgment of credibility but was silent on the place of faith in life. The *De Spe,* against Luther and Fenelon, demonstrates the legitimacy of an interested love of God. The *De Caritate* examined some pages of St. Thomas on the friendship between God and man but quite carefully avoided discussing the influence of charity on the virtues or the commandments. In moral theology there were practically no evangelical elements for the reason that in this course freedom was studied according to Aristotle and law according to the notion of rights. In the treatise on justice, juridical questions were all-pervasive. Professors and pupils spent long hours studying matrimonial and inheritance laws, but no reference whatsoever was made to the boundless teaching of the Bible on interpersonal relations. The encroachment of positive law was such that the recourse to natural law seemed, in fine, to be a horizon-broadening liberation.

I must apologize for making further references to personal reminiscences, but I believe that the testimony of one who has personally experienced the inadequacy of this method of teaching moral theology, makes this remembrance of things past worthwhile. As for me, I became aware of the invasion of moral theology by philosophy in connection with the treatise *De Virtutibus*. I was teaching a course in the history of ancient philosophy at the *Facultés Catholiques* of Lille and I had taken the problem of virtue as treated by the philosophers of antiquity as the theme for my lectures. The professor of moral theology had fallen ill and I had to substitute for him after a rapid review of Noldin's *De Virtutibus*. In this work I once more came upon everything that I had read in the philosophers. Virtue was defined according to Aristotle and Cicero. The oneness of virtue was expounded along the lines of Stoicism. The classification of the virtues owed everything to Platonists and to Aristotelians. The acquisition of virtues was explained as the consequence of knowledge and effort according to Plato and Aristotle. From time to time, of course, there was mention of the theological virtues, but only in order to point out that they constituted an exception to the principle that had just been propounded. It was to facts of this kind to which the deniers of Christian specificity in the moral domain forthwith had referred. When this proposition began to spread around 1968, during discussion periods students constantly posed the question: "How do you expect us to take as being Christian these moral teachings that you have pilfered from everywhere?"

This type of ostracism, moreover, is reinforced by the prejudices of certain historians of ethics. Indeed in one of the rare syntheses devoted to this genre of investigations, as yet so little developed, we can find some declarations of principle that speak volumes for it. In the preface to his "*History of Ethics*," Vernon J. Bourke[15] writes: "religious moralities with no reflective or theoretical base are not included in this history, unless they have had some important influence on ethical thinking." Not a single page here is devoted to the ethics of the New Testament. In this book (which presents itself not only as a history of moral philosophy but of morality pure and simple), a place is allotted to Christian moral teaching only "provided it makes some effort to relate its views to recognized positions in moral philosophy. We do find such 'theological approbative theories' of this kind in the writings of Christians before the thirteenth century and feel that they have a place in a historical survey of ethics."[16]

2. Marxism and Sartrean Existentialism

A wholly different type of denial of the specificity of Christian morality is found in Marxism and in Sartrean existentialism. Not only can an ethics be constructed without God in these systems, but also it can not be considered as authentic if it is not grounded on a base other than that of society and of man.

Marx[17] was to connect his critique of all religious morality to Hegel and to Feuerbach. Along with Hegel, he sees in the relation between Abraham and God the archtype of the slave-master relation. From Feuerbach he borrowed the idea that religion prevents man from achieving full maturity; it gives him the faith to hope for a divine reward and thereby prevents him from revolting against his servitudes. In order to liberate man from the illusion of religious alienation he must be rid of the conditions that create the need for illusion. Man must achieve his maturity in work and in praxis. Then he becomes self-possession (*Selbstaendigkeit*) and self-creation (*Selbsterzeugung*). The relation with the cosmos that is to be humanized and with other men creates the true personality of man who is essentially "an ensemble of social relations" (*das Ensemble der gesellschaftlichen Verhaeltnisse*). Thought no longer is connected to an ontological base, to an objective truth but to social relations: the true is that which is efficacious and liberative. Authentic thought is action, hence correct action is that which rejects any reference to the transcendental norms of an ideology favorable to the ruling class in order to take its criteria in the effectual construction of society and the humanization of the cosmos, according to the interests of the proletarian consciousness.

Leftist intellectuals have found in Marxism the means to propound a purely autonomous morality. In Sartre's[18] view the denial of

God is all the more necessary; for if God exists, I am not free, and, if I am free God cannot exist. The "other," moreover, does not withstand objections any better, for man finds himself caught in a dilemma: in order to remain a subject he must take the other as object and therefore destroy him as interlocutor, or he must accept the other as subject and himself become the other's object. Only the group can permit the harmony of freedoms because the latter are not destroyed in it but, rather, together they construct a will that is common to the group.

These systems of thought, obviously, are hermetically closed, they represent life styles in which it would be futile to try to find a place for God, even less for Christ as a condition of morality. Obviously few Christians are going to refer to such systems of thought when they assert that there is no Christian morality as such. Nevertheless, a certain infiltration, notably of Marxist theses, is evident in many spheres, particularly in that of ethics. Moreover the desire to "meet" Marxism, "to let oneself be heard by it," "to accept what in it is valid," can conduce to the adoption of certain points of view of the system as a condition of the dialogue and, by degrees, become a concession, particularly if doctrinal positions are shifting on the theological level itself.

3. Certain Protestant Positions: Bultmann, Bonhoeffer, Tillich

Obviously it is not the "fundamentalism" of Karl Barth that is going to entertain the thought of making the least concession to Marx. The author of *Church Dogmatics*[20] views the Christian life style as totally original, no overture is made to some natural law in accordance with what is a constant tradition among Protestant theologians. On the other hand, Bultmann, with the utmost ease, was to integrate the existentialist teaching[21] on being-with-others and translate it into the Christian language of charity. Revelation is not the transcendental word of God addressed to men by the prophets and lastly by Christ (Heb 1, 1–2) but it is "this disclosure" *(Erschliessung)* of the hidden which is simply necessary and decisive for man if he wants to attain his salvation, that is to say if he wants to attain his true self *(Eigentlichkeit).*[22] There is nothing typically Christian about the commandment to love others as one's own self. It is merely the awareness of the human situation in the world. The individual cannot retire within himself without denying that he is a being-with-others.[23] This precept can appropriate all the particular commandments that one might wish to include, whether it be a question of the moral precepts of the Old Testament or the Hellenistic catalogues of virtues and vices.[24] Thus Christian morality is only a syncretist patchwork: "Quite early on the christian churches adopted a system of morality, with its pattern of catechetical instruction derived in equal proportions from the Old Testament Jewish traditions and from the ethics of popular philosophical pedagogy, shortly to be enriched by the moral ideals of the Hellenistic bourgeoisie."[25] Thus, if we may again resort to Fr. Fuch's vocabulary, it is not only the Christian "categorical" in ethics that has disappeared here but also the Christian "transcendental." The only original perspective that differentiates the Christian writers from the others is the fact that they preach life-with-others as a "radical obedience" to God.[26] In the first century, this obedience was concretized in the moral ideal of the times; today it will include other attitudes that are inspired by present-day situations.[27]

These ideas have been spread among the general public by J. A. T. Robinson in works such as *Honest to God* and *Christian Freedom in a Permissive Society.*[28] Nevertheless a difference of viewpoint is to be noted: Robinson persistently demonstrates that the morality which he presents must be accepted by today's Christians who defend "the ancient morality" and therefore he tries to connect his teaching to Christianity. Bultmann does not at all concern himself with this apologetic perspective.

Bonhoeffer's secularized Christianity, for its part, continues on the path pioneered by Bultmann. All the less does he give any thought to the idea of claiming an original ethics for Christianity which he invites to merge with human history, with the world, in imitation of the kenosis of Christ. The crucified Lord is the center of Bonhoeffer's theology in the last stages of its development.[29] In Christ we behold the authentic God as absolute poverty and total self-giving, that is to say as a being suffering as a being-for-others. The Christian is duty-bound to be a man like others. If there is a difference between him and non-Christians it is owing only to the fact that the Christian, through faith, knows that he participates in the messianic suffering and in the powerlessness of God in the world. The Christian is the one who fully lives the life of the world and of secularity, he works for the humanization of history. To make one a Christian (if it is still necessary) is to make him feel that secular life also has the sense of a participation in Christ. Christian pedagogy tends only to a consciousness-raising in regard to that which is already in every human being, without any transcendence, without any heterogeneity.

In that perspective Bonhoeffer's thought is very close to that of Tillich.[30] The method of moral theology is the same for these two theologians. It is no longer a question of proceeding from the word of God in order to judge human life. Secular facts and realties are taken as a base, their signification is deepened through the social sciences. Finally they pose the question: in what direction must Christians apply to them the few great instructions of the Gospel: liberation, fraternity? For the possible opposition between the world and God taught in the New Testament, Tillich substitutes the idea of a correlation: man must be given the "courage to live," that is to say, to be himself by interpreting as well as possible the call of circumstances and the voice of the times. To reconcile God and the world would be impossible, but to mark a correlation between the world and a God who has opened himself to history and to contingency in Christ, is precisely the work carved out for the Christian. Easter is not the proclamation of the fact of the resurrection but a summons to be a better human being, just as the cult of the secularized Christian is merely a special period of time set aside so that cognizance can be taken of God's immanence in our service-to-the-world. The Christian should rediscover in this cult of a new style, and in a more distinct, more urgent and more provocative form, the commitment that is proper to him.

The conjunction between the Marxist point of view on a purely human praxis and a Protestant theology that puts in parenthesis the historical revealed datum is effected by E. Bloch[31] and, in an attenuated form, by J. Moltmann.[32] Ernst Bloch makes no secret of his intention to formulate Christian theology in the perspective of Marx. It is no longer a question of making a connection with the past, even less with the message of a revelation already terminated; rather it is one of making history and of preparing the eschatological Christ with great cosmic and human tendencies as the point of departure. If God is eternal, it is not in being immutable, but in a fidelity that ever asserts itself by guiding humankind toward the Christ of eschatology. Accordingly the model of action is not taken from ancient utterances or principles but from the great aspirations that find concrete expression in the venture of humanism, that is to say, the struggle against all alienations, the revolt against all oppressions. To act morally is already to render present the kingdom of heaven. The political commitment of Christians has often been deficient; therefore it was presented as a condition and a part of the moral life since all action has a social and communitarian aspect. But it is necessary to go even further and make morality coincide with the active struggle against social and political alienations with a will to set oneself up as a critic of any established order, the new idol that demands the sacrifice of some human beings. The upshot is that the quest for human salvation supplants the quest for Christian salvation. Humanization takes the place of divinization, however open the latter may have managed to be to human values.

4. *The New Tendencies as Espoused by*
Some Catholic Theologians: Metz, Valsecchi, Blank

J. B. Metz, on the one hand, leans on the "theology of hope" even though he is more distinct in upholding the importance of the *memoria Christi.*[33] On the practical level, however, the instructions of "political theology" are very close to the "theology of hope." For the Church it is a matter of living as a witness to the permanence of a subversive force of freedom against all human alienations, principally against those of public or political life. Thus one will turn his back on a morality of privatization centered on personal conversion and salvation. A *memoria* reduced to a few great instructions can hardly give itself the authority to uphold the proposition that Christianity has a specificity and content peculiar to it. "In Metz's view," writes M. Xhaufflaire,[34] "one of the untouchable particularities of the secularized society consists in the presence of pluralisms of world views, of life styles and of social roles. It follows that if she does not want to impose herself in a totalitarian fashion, the Church must renounce celebrating a particular social order normatively. Here, too, the Church must take note of the eschatological reservation in regard to that which concerns her. The church cannot be faithful to the universal character of her message unless it is mediated through the agency of criticism. *What is demanded here of the church is not a systematic social doctrine, but a social critique.*"[35]

Metz's theology perhaps has only a secondary importance as regards Catholic positions on the non-specificity of Christian morality. It is greatly carried away by the arguments borrowed from sociology and from structuralism, as can be seen in the work of A. Valsecchi.[36]

The *Nuove vie dell'etica sessuale,* written by this former professor at the Pontifical Lateran University who today is experiencing life as a worker-priest, is characterized by the sincerity with which he poses the problem of the hermaneutic and of the specificity of Christian moral teaching. As Msgr. Gotti notes in his preface to this work, Valsecchi "mistrusts explicit calls to the biblical word."[37] But this is not because he argues for a recourse to human nature; he rejects recourse to this from the start.[38] Neither the Bible nor philosophy can teach anything definitive on man and his manner of living. Just as Moltmann and Metz saw in Revelation only one or two liberative directives, Valsecchi is of the opinion that the main point of the Christian message is summarized in a call to responsibility in a life inspired not by egoism but by love.[39] It is this injunction that must be lived in the domain of sexuality; but it would be quite a futile enterprise for one to refer to the numerous norms that scripture has laid down on marriage, adultery, fornication etc., because each of these norms contains the mixture of the divine call to a generous responsibility and changing cultural conditions. "One may wonder," writes Valsecchi,[40] "whether the relation between the different moral propositions and the call to faith-charity is a necessary relation and affirmed each time as such by Revelation or whether it is not a more contingent relation in the sense that the different propositions are the fruit of a convergent human experience at a time and in a place, assumed by the revealed word as the concrete translation of the immutable moral values of salvation, that is to say, faith and charity." The history of culture is thus a place in which God speaks: "The history of humankind, scrutinized with humility and seriousness, does not contradict "the will of God; it discovers it,"[41] Hence, in our time, Christian sexual morality is essentially based on the culture and the anthropology that have compelled recognition by replacing ancient attitudes. In this sense it is common to non-Christians and Christians; the latter nevertheless constantly criticize the culture in the name of the requirement of the responsibiliity inspired by love and by the rejection of all egoism. Here cultural changes are not only an opportunity to arrive at a better understanding of the divine message on man and sexuality; they are an integrating part of a message that God communicates to human beings in a history that evolves without pause.

All this leads Valsecchi to embrace the opinion that rejects the specificity of Christian morality. After citing some studies on this subject, he writes: "These studies bring to light the material identity between Christian ethics and purely human ethics. Faith has the sole task of giving a sense and a salvific intentionality to conduct. The works cited demand from a dynamic anthropological reflection that it individualize the ethical significance of any choice and of the content of the norms corresponding to it."[42]

The positions proposed by J. Blank are less distinct and less negative and they enjoy a wider circulation for this very reason. On some points they link up with Valsecchi's sociologism since in the last instance it is the social sciences that decide what Christian behavior ought to be. But, on the other hand, Blank attaches greater importance to hermaneutic.[43] In his view, the New Testament has not proposed any moral norm in the sense of a code, of a precise law promulgated by an authority external to the conscience, imposed in an absolute and definitive manner. Obviously one can ask oneself whether the dilemma between the norm and the "ideal" or "value" is convincingly established in such a way. Catholic moral theology certainly has not confused canon law with evangelical law . . . if only for the reason that it concerned itself very little with the New Testament. The Fathers and the medieval commentators accorded it more attention, but they knew how to mark the difference between the literal sense, the moral sense and the allegorical sense. They knew very well that the invitation extended to Christians to imitate the Lord washing the feet of his disciples could give birth to an annual liturgical ceremony and to a more general norm of life that was applicable daily: the norm of the humility of service and of the gift of charity. At all events it must be noted that J. Blank's critique has had its effect: some believe that they need take no account of the moral teachings of the New Testament on the grounds that Christ did not promulgate a code.

This is even more the case with those who follow the second part of J. Blank's thesis. In his view the primitive community allegedly formed a certain number of ethical models that blend Christian inspiration with a critical judgment on life seen from the point of view of cultural and historical experience. If Blank seems to grant a privileged status to the interpretation of the first Christian community, Auer[44] opines that from the normative point of view this interpretation is hardly worth more than the Aristotelian or Stoic adaptation that appeared in the course of subsequent history.

III
CRITICAL REFLECTIONS

We have largely given the floor, so to speak, to authors who to different degrees and for extremely varied reasons, deny *in toto* or in part, the specificity of Christian morality. I would now like to compare these positions with the professions of faith and those of classical theology, more precisely with the teachings of Vatican II which I have chosen as an authoritative and easily discernible point of reference.

1. What Is the Specific Difference in Morality?

First of all I would like to state precisely what is meant when we speak of the specificity of a morality. After reading the many authors who discuss this problem the impression that forces itself upon us is that the formula is less distinct than it may seem. *Littré's* dictionary opportunely reminds us that the term "specific" is applied to a species included in a genus. We are very nearly being sent back to scholastic logic and to its definitions *per species et genera*. If we apply the maze of genera and species, we must perforce conclude that the Christian morality recognized as non-specific is not a species proper within the moral genus. In that case the problem that arises is to know what attributes make a morality constitute a species, and why it is recognized as original.

This question does not take the professors of ethics unawares because an exposition of the different moralities is found in all the manuals of philosophy. Jacques Leclercq, in his *Grandes lignes de la philosophie morale*,[45] reviews the principal solutions that have been proposed in regard to the problem of the good. A first principle of classification is the negation or the acceptance of moral rules. He cites skepticism, relativism, sociological positivism among the types of negative solution. If one gets as far as positive solutions, two principal classes present themselves. Some moral codes are empirical and have utilitarianism, altruism or spontaneity as a base. Other moral codes or ethics are rational. Here Leclercq cites: Kant, monism, stoicism, neo-Platonism, Christian morality.[46] A manual preparing students for the *baccalaureat* of the French *lycées*[47] gives a different classification but of the same type. It lists the moralities centered on interest (Bentham, Freud), feeling (Guyau, Bergson), duty (Kant), metaphysics (Plato, Aristotle, Spinoza), experience (Scheler, Rauh).

Setting out from these different specifically "fundamental" or "general" moralities, among which the writers obviously make their choice, expositions are developed that are strikingly similar when it is a question of preaching respect for human life, property, reputation, marriage etc. Noting this agreement of "special moralities" in the enumeration of rights and duties, Jacques Leclercq humorously remarked that it really was not worth the effort to choose a fundamental morality with such care since one would find oneself in agreement with one's adversaries when the matter came around to expounding a special morality. Certainly there is an extensive concordance between the different religions and philosophies in this connection, to the point that a recent study undertook to establish a concordance between the Judaic decalogue (or at least the second part thereof) and the different charters of the rights of man. Alongside this material concordance, there nevertheless remains a radical difference of inspiration, the one religious in the frame of the Covenant, the other philosophical if not political.[48]

The divergencies will not be apparent (at least not in this time of change[49] unless a comparison is made between what some call "ancient morality" and "new morality," for example in connection with abortion, pre-marital relations, fidelity in marriage, revolution etc. If we refer to the chart of specificities in morality drawn up by Leclercq, we will see that these positions of the "new morality" situate themselves on the level of the rejection of pre-determined, fixed and objective moral rules. Recourse to Leclercq, who wrote 25 years ago, automatically removes any suspicion of tendentious judgments on recent attitudes. At all events there are very perceptible convergences between the positions of Marcuse or the *Petit livre rouge des lycéens*[50] and what J. Leclercq describes under the name of moral relativism. On both sides, it is asserted that "only relations exist" in place of "principles of action applicable to everybody", "that there is no single morality but only moralities."[51]

In these perspectives we can see the opportuneness of the distinction between transcendental morality and categorical morality, especially underlined by Fr. Fuchs. But it would be necessary to go further and recognize that the comparison between human moralities, to which ordinarily little thought is given, ends up with the same conclusion: the specificity of the ethics of Aristotle and of Kant also situates itself on the transcendental level much more than on the categorical level. Even if we assume (which I must straightway say I do not believe) that there are no divergencies between the Christian categorical and the philosophical categorical, the specific situation of the ethics of Christianity would not be a situation of so rare a character.

On the other hand, more attention than is ordinarily the case would have to be given to the meaning of the categorical contradictions between the "new" and the "classic" moralities. These contradictions are clear only if they are grasped in the arguments that claim to establish them, that is to say, at the level of the transcendental. But in that case, and this must be noted, the difference does not necessarily lie in the word pairing evangelic-philosophic; it can also be opposed to purely rational moralities. In all the concrete problems of the new morality, it is evident that, at bottom, what makes the difference is an option for the "lived experience" against principles (inspired by faith or reason), for a demand of total freedom against the idea of duty (based on the life of Christ or on human dignity), for the absolute creation of values against their transcendental objectivity, for cultural models determined by the historical state of each society, indeed by its economic condition, against a moral "project" based on a God who transcends time and on a human structure a certain fundamental permanence of which is recognized.

2. What Relation Must Be Established between Christian Morality and Revelation?

Study of the arguments against the existence of a specific Christian morality shows that quite often the negation of the latter is based in part on the rejection of the classic theology of revelation. If one shares the view of Bultmann and others that revelation is not the manifestation of the mystery of the will of God (cf. Eph 1,9) thanks to which men, through Christ, the Word become flesh, have access to the Father in the Holy Spirit and are made participants of the divine nature" (cf. Eph 2,18; 2 Pet 1,4)[52], but simply an historical awareness of what is necessary to become a better human being, it is hard to see how one can speak of Christian morality. On the other hand, in the traditional perspective it is normal to say with Vatican II (*Dei Verbum*, no. 21) that the whole life of the church has its "support" and its "energy" in revelation and that the latter is "the soul of sacred theology" (*Dei Verbum*, no. 24 and *Optatam totius*, no. 16). And as concerns moral theology, the Council states precisely that it must be "thoroughly nourished by scriptural teaching" (*Optatam totius*, no. 16).

Consequently we understand—despite the importance of charity—why Christian morality is traditionally presented as the "morality of the faith." Already, in the Letter to the Romans (3,27) St. Paul speaks of the "law by this faith" (*nomos pisteos*) which he sets over against the Mosaic law of works (*nomos ton ergon*). St. Augustine took up this theme again in *De Spiritu et Littera*[53] and from there it passed on to the scholastics, for example, to St. Thomas who emphasizes the grace aspect of this law to the point of writing: "Et ideo principaliter lex nova est ipsa gratia Spiritus Sancti quae datur Christi fidelibus."

If the classic formula already links "faith and morals," Vatican II, in *Lumen Gentium* (no. 25), has even more exactly noted the incidence of faith on life in its reference to the authorized preaching of the kerygma and of the Pastoral authority of the pope and of the bishops. They are: "the preachers of the faith who lead new disciples to Christ. They are authentic teachers, that is, teachers endowed with the authority of Christ, who preach to the people committed to them the faith they must believe and put into practice (*fidem credendam et moribus applicandam*). By the light of the Holy Spirit, they make that faith clear . . ."[55]

This bond between morality and Revelation accepted in the faith was recalled by Pope Paul VI[56] in an address delivered at the audience he gave on July 26, 1972. Indeed the pope addressed himself to the doubts that had been expressed about that time in regard to the existence of a Christian morality. "Does a Christian morality exist? That is to say, does there exist an original manner of living that can be called Christian? What is Christian morality?" Paul VI thereupon undertook to describe Christian morality on the level of action and precisely to state its perspectives as the essential conditions for its realization, declaring: "It is a manner of living according to the faith, that is to say, in the light of the truth and of the examples of Christ such as they are related to us in the gospel and in the first echo of Christ given by the apostles in the New Testament." The horizons and the finalities of this morality are specific because it is lived "in the perspective of a further coming of Christ and of a new form of our existence, which is called the Parousia." Finally, this morality receives "a two-fold aid: the interior and inexpressible aid of the Holy Spirit, and the exterior aid, historical and social but justified and authorized, of the magisterium of the Church."

In this perspective we can more exactly see the responses that can be made to certain objections or, at least, the paths along which we might be able to seek them. The doctrine of Vatican I and Vatican II makes a distinction between the revelation of mysteries properly so-called which transcend human intelligence and the revelation of natural verities.[57] This distinction is perhaps more utilized in the study of dogma than in that of morality. Nevertheless Revelation is not only orientated towards the knowledge of mysteries but also toward the insertion of the latter in the life of human beings. Vatican I declares that the Revelation of mysteries is absolutely necessary *"quia Deus, ex infinita bonitate sua, ordinavit homines ad finem supernaturalem, ad participanda scilicet bona divina"* (Denz-Schoenm., 3005). Vatican II (*Dei Verbum,* no. 6) centers Revelation on the idea of salvation.

Is it necessary to recall that salvation is not given and lived without an acceptance and a collaboration on the part of man? For the New Testament it is a question of a newness, that is to say, of a reality that exists nowhere else. The life of the Christian is new (Gal 6,15;[58] 2 Cor 5,17; Eph 4,24;[59] Col 3,10). In the Letter to the Romans the renewal of the Christian is effected in faith, hope, charity (Chapter 5), through baptism: "So you also must consider yourselves dead to sin and alive to God in Christ Jesus" (Rom 6,11). We could as well recall the new life in the Spirit (Gal 5,19–25) as Fr. Fuchs does in order to mark the specificity of transcendental Christian morality. Nevertheless, it occasions surprise that Fuchs has given so little place to the Johannine teaching on the new[60] character of the commandment of love and to its practical consequences: "A new commandment I give to you, that you love one another; even as I have loved you, that you also love one another. By this all men will know that you are my disciples, if you have love for one another" (Jn 13, 34–35). Wherein lies the newness? In nothing, according to most of the writers that we have reviewed here: love would be the most banal and common of laws so much so that one wonders how John could, after the Lord, see in it a sign of Christian specificity. Nevertheless, is there not in this commandment a new extension inasmuch as nobody can be excluded, a new sense inasmuch as Christian love is connected to that of Christ who gives his life for his friends (Jn 15,13) as well as for his enemies (Rom 5,8)? Regardless of the attenuations that philologists can bring to the opposition that Nygren has pointed up between eros and agape, the fact remains that human love is before all else a desire for reciprocity whereas Christian love is essentially a gift offered even to those who, as enemies, have no value in our eyes (Mt 5,43–48). It is not only at the level of transcendental morality that charity introduces the specificity but it does likewise in the sphere of the categorical. We cannot love radically without observing the commandments (Jn 14,15; 1 Jn 5,3)[61] anymore than we can be possessed by charity without adopting precise rules of conduct. In 1 Corinthians 13,4–13, St. Paul clearly shows that charity commands "virtues" and excludes "vices" that are precisely defined: be patient, render service, be not envious, boastful or arrogant, do nothing that is ugly, seek not your interest, be not irritable or resentful, rejoice not at wrong, but rejoice in the right, forgive all things, believe all things, hope in all things and endure all things. When St. Augustine and St. Thomas, among others, structured the theology of charity queen of virtues, starting out from these and similar texts, they clearly noted the change that revelation had brought to categorical morality.

Can it be claimed then that these practical attitudes or, at all events, some among them, can be discovered by reason? This is quite obvious but it does not prevent taking cognizance of the fact that revelation has integrated them so that all persons can have access to them with greater facility and greater sureness. Vatican II (*Dei verbum*, no. 6) recalls the doctrine of Vatican I on this subject: that earlier Council, it asserts, teaches that we must attribute to revelation the fact that "those religious truths which are by their nature accessible to human reason can be known to all men with ease, with solid certainty, and with no trace of error, even in the present state of the human race." In dogmatic theology there is frequent mention of this revelation of the natural verities but it is forgotten that this revelation also applies to morality. St. Thomas, who expounded this teaching at great length in the beginning of the *Summa Contra Gentiles*,[62] applies it precisely to the text of Ephesians 4, 17 which demands a greater moral vigor from the converts: "Iam non ambuletis sicut et gentes ambulant in vanitate sensus sui, tenebris obscuratum habentes intellectum." Fr. Fuchs tells us that the philosophical arguments and the human perspectives are "presupposed" (p. 21), for example in connection with the castigation of falsehood (Eph 4.25) and of fornication (1 Cor 6, 16–20). That these arguments and perspectives are not to be denied is all too clear. I would agree that we ought to and that we can utilize these philosophical arguments in the teaching of Christian morality. But I should like others to "return the courtesy" and not to forget the Christian considerations advanced by the apostle: "Let everyone speak the truth with his neighbor, for we are members one of another." I should also like them not to forget the context that immediately precedes this injunction, in which Christ's teaching on the putting off of the old nature, on the renewal of the spirit, on the new nature "created after the likeness of God in true righteousness and holiness (21–24), is precisely recalled. The desire to emphasize human authenticity all the same must not end up with a loss of Christian identity.

Other problems could be cited here in connection with the use of revealed texts in moral theology. Improvements in this direction moreover would have to be made in order to make up for the retarded growth of moral theology to its colonization by natural law and canon law. It would be necessary for example to be more precise in the matter of how the New Testament must be read and interpreted in order to derive rules of life[63] from it, to establish a hermeneutic of the texts of the magisterium similar to that of the *De locis theologicis* used in dogmatics, and to provide a greater space for Christian experience. That we are still wide of the mark we must in all candor admit. But matters will not be advanced by denying the very principle of a Christian morality!

3. Is "Humanization" Threatened by "Divinization"?

In the writings that contest the existence or even the possibility of a Christian morality, we constantly come upon the fear, at times it appears as almost an obsession, that the "Christian project of life" constitutes a threat to human authenticity. To be sure all the writers do not go as far as Marx or Sartre in their observations on the subject of alienation. But many of them revert ceaselessly to the idea that man must realize his full potentialities by himself alone, that he must construct himself and construct the world by his own powers. The theology of secularization obviously tends toward the same goal. Paul VI, in his aforementioned address of July 26, 1972, summarized this tendency as follows: "Some persons, frequently enough also those in the Christian world, would like behavior, especially in its public and exterior manifestation, to be secularized in an exclusive and absolute fashion. There are trends of thought and of action that propose to detach morality from theology: morality should concern itself exclusively with interpersonal relations and with the personal conscience of the individual; there should be no need for any religious dogma in the sphere of morality. Because it is legitimate to say that many expressions of human thought and of human action are ruled by criteria peculiar to them (the sciences, for example) and that a sound and reasonable secularity presides in the organization of the State, some people would like religion not only no longer to appear in public, but also no longer to exercise any influence for the purpose of inspiring or orienting civil legislation and practical conduct."[64]

The "value of man," of which these writers speak and for which consequently they demand recognition in moral theology, can designate quite a number of things: a protest against a moral theology that would deny the legitimate development of man,[65] a concern to go beyond desirable and even necessary forms of cooperation with those who are not Christians, the will also to a total autonomy that excludes any recourse to God.[66] For a clear view of what is at issue here, we must go back to what revelation and the magisterium say on the vocation of man since they connect Christian morality to this vocation. The demand for a Christian morality is meaningless without this dogmatic background.

A first dimension of the Christian person is his/her divinization, whose existence and exigence in the moral life is recalled in *Lumen Gentium* (no. 40): "The followers of Christ are called by God, not according to their accomplishments, but according to his own purpose and grace. They are justified in the Lord Jesus, and through baptism sought in faith they truly become sons of God and sharers in the divine nature. In this way they are really made holy. Then, too, by God's gifts they must hold on to and complete in their lives this holiness which they have received. They are warned by the apostle to live 'as becomes saints' (Eph 5,3) and to put on 'as God's chosen ones, holy and beloved, a heart of mercy, kindness, humility, meekness, patience' (Col 3,12), and to possess the fruits of the Spirit unto holiness (cf Gal 5,22; Rom 6,22)." Does this incorporation in Christ destroy the *humanum?* No, replies *Gaudium et Spes* (no. 22) because ". . . Christ, the final Adam, by the revelation of the mystery of the Father and his love, fully reveals man to man himself and makes his supreme calling clear." Is it for this reason that Christianity ostracises pagans? No again, because grace acts unseen in the heart of all men of good will.[67]

Catholic teaching and moral theology in no wise excludes from this unique divine vocation, as we have just read, all that which belongs to the secular and natural dimension of man. They recognize a consistence proper to it. We are paying very dearly today for the *contemptus mundi* of past ages because it has created the conviction that in order to be man, it is necessary to disengage oneself from the divine. This dualism and this opposition, however, are not the stand of contemporary catholicism. *Lumen Gentium* (no 34) shows how the faithful in ". . . all their work, prayers, and apostolic endeavors, their ordinary married and family life, their daily labor, their mental and physical relaxation, if carried out in the Spirit . . . become spiritual sacrifices acceptable to God through Jesus Christ." *Apostolicam Actuositatem* (no. 7) underlines how "all the many elements that make up the temporal order, namely, the good things of life and the prosperity of the family, culture, economic affairs . . . not only aid in the attainment of man's goal but also possess their intrinsic value. This value has been implanted in them by God." Even more, "this natural goodness of theirs takes on a special dignity as a result of their relation to the human person, for whose service they were created."

Is man to be divided between the divine aspect and the human aspect of his vocation? No, for if the church which groups into a society those who are fastened to Christ (*Gaudium et Spes,* no. 40, par. 2) pursues the saving purpose proper to her and thereby communicates divine life, she "in some way casts the reflected light of that life over the entire earth. This she does most of all by her healing and elementary impact on the dignity of the person, by the way in which she strengthens the seams of human society and imbues the everyday activity of men with a deeper meaning and importance" (*Gaudium et Spes,* no. 40, par. 3).[68]

The synthesis is effected at an even higher level: in Christ. "Last of all, it has pleased God to unite all things, both natural and supernatural, in Christ Jesus that in everything he might be pre-eminent" (Col 1, 18). This destination, however, not only does not deprive the temporal order of its independence, its proper goals, laws, resources and significance for human welfare but rather perfects the temporal order in its own intrinsic strength and excellence and raises it to the level of man's total vocation on earth" (*Apostolicam Actuositatem,* no. 7).

On the existential level, in different ways,[69] the grace of God meets man's need to extricate himself from his radical alienations, to transcend himself. Does not the analysis of the existing situation argue in the same sense? We are doubtlessly very proud of what humanity has been able to create as regards science and technology but we are just as much aware (even outside Christian teaching) that our civilization, on the moral plane of the utilization and the distribution of the created goods, is a failure and that it must seek a social, political and ethical "better-being." Obviously we could dwell on this point of view, as has been done at other times, in order to depreciate man and his secular activities. But we can also, along with Christian existentialism and personalism, take cognizance of a call to God that makes man more clear to himself, more efficacious, more courageous in his action. *Gaudium* et *Spes* (no. 25, par. 3) points out: "the disturbances which so frequently occur in the social order result in part from the natural tensions of economic, political and social forms. But at a deeper level they flow from man's pride and selfishness, which contaminate even the social sphere. When the structure of affairs is flawed by the consequences of sin, man, already born with a bent toward evil, finds there new inducements to sin, which cannot be overcome without strenuous efforts and the assistance of grace." A little further on the Pastoral Constitution (*Gaudium et Spes,* no. 30, par. 2) declares that it will not be possible to go beyond an individualist ethics "unless individual men and their associations cultivate in themselves the moral and social virtues, and promote them in society. Thus, with the needed help of divine grace, men who are truly new and artesans of a new humanity can be forthcoming."[70]

From this point of view, it is regrettable that Fr. Fuchs has not considered the incidence of divine life on human life through grace, on the categorical level as he has done on the transcendental level.[71] One cannot understand the sense and the specificity of Christian morality outside the frame that Christian life and grace give to them. The imperatives of the life of man divinized in Christ are the very consequence of the presence of the Spirit. This is precisely why "the fruit of the Spirit" (Gal 5,22), faith, hope, charity (Rom 5,5) are before all else the action of God in us. All the categorical injunctions that flow from it, and not only in some exceptional cases as Fr. Fuchs thinks, all the most trivial sectors of life, all the action of a Christian ordained to effectuate the humanization of his person, of others, of the cosmos, are always under the prompting of the grace of Christ.

Is this not the reason through which Christian morality, throughout the whole course of history, has transformed the categorical morality that it took over from the different civilizations and more especially from the heritage of Greece and Rome? That this mutation has not always been sufficiently catalogued thematically on the level of principles has been sufficiently stressed here. But if one situates oneself on the level of Christian preaching, of spirituality, of the life of the faithful, one realizes that the non-Christian formulas and definitions, even wrongly preserved, have ended up masking new realities.

Among the pagans prudence is a purely intellectual virtue that is equal to knowledge. Christians have made of it a practical virtue that judges the conformity of an action with the demands of the gospel. Among the pagans relations with others depended on justice or friendship. Christianity completely changed the conditions of intersubjectivity by placing in the foreground love as the bestowal of a gratuitous gift. The change was of such a character that a Proudhon was to reproach Christianity for forgetting the objectivity of justice to the advantage of the subjectivity of charity. To be sure, he had put his finger on a transient deformation but the fact remains that the social justice of the Christian is encompassed by and saturated with charity. The virtue of religion, in Cicero, has the ceremony of the cult as its object. In many Christian authors, such as St. Augustine and St. Bonaventure, it is faith, hope, charity.[72] Magnanimity, in Aristotle's view, was the sense of honor and of dignity. The Christians preserved these formulas but thenceforth they were to designate the strength to live and, if need be, to die as a martyr. The patience of the Stoic was submission to an implacable fate; for the Christian it has become the courageous awaiting of the hour of God in communion with the passion of Christ. Humility was a little known value or, at all events, one that was little prized. It has become one of the most characteristic Christian attitudes. Let us listen to what M. Lot-Borodine[73] says in this connection in his comments on the teaching of St. John Climacus: . . . "It is to humility moreover that he applies what, for his followers, was the loftiest epithet, namely *the exterminatrix of all the passions.*" And, indeed, it is through humility that the greatest and most terrible passion, stamped on the entire soul which it irremediably taints, namely pride, is brought down. Truth to tell, it would be more just to place this beauty, at once mistress and servant, at the root of all the pragmatic virtues, alongside faith, following from it and nourished by it. For humility alone is Christian in the native state, purely and uniquely Christian, alien and irreducible to the pagan mind which never prostrates itself to pray. Together with the scandal of the Cross, humility was to remain the enigma impatiently endured by the Gentiles. Is it not the purest pearl of the Gospels?" We shall terminate this rapid examination of the Christian categorical, born of the grace of God, with a brief reference to the Christian attitude toward sexuality. The case is more clear-cut than are the critiques of certain writers who identify Christian morality in this sphere. Neither Hellenism nor Judaism were able to inspire the Christian morality of marriage which demands a total self-giving of the spouses to the point of excluding divorce. Upon hearing the words of Christ on this subject the disciples protested, saying "if such is the case . . . it is not expedient to marry." But all they obtain from the Lord is a call to celibacy for the sake of the kingdom of heaven (Mt 19, 10–12). The gospel, moreover, does not seem to make of celibacy a purely human value since the grace of God is necessary for it to be grasped: "Not all men can receive this precept, but only those to whom it is given." Marriage obviously remains a human structure but for Christians it is assumed by divinization in different ways that *Gaudium et Spes* has succinctly recalled: conjugal love has been judged by the Lord as "worthy of special gifts, healing, perfecting and exalting gifts of grace and of charity" (no. 49 par. 1); for Christian spouses it is "a special sacrament by which they are fortified and receive a kind of consecration." And, finally, it is "caught up into divine love and is governed and enriched by Christ's redeeming power and the saving activity of the church" (no. 48,par. 2).

Conclusion

It is quite useless, I think, to recapitulate all the speculations that have been expounded here. It suffices merely to state that the different approaches to the problem prove the specificity of Christian morality. On the level of history, the objections raised against this assertion most often stem from a truncated view of the facts. On the doctrinal level, the existence of a Christian morality is linked to revelation and to the doctrine of grace. The objections advanced can be overcome if they are placed in the perspectives of the coordination between faith and reason, grace and nature. Christian morality does not destroy man, it magnifies him and permits him to surpass himself. But for this very reason, it shows that it bestows upon him something of a specific character.

Notes

1. A copious bibliography (pp. 172–178), up to the end of 1971, is found in the work of R. P. Francesco Compagnoni, *La specificità della morale cristiana,* Bologna, Edizioni Dehoniane, 1972, 182 pp. This thesis was presented to the St. Thomas University of Rome in April 1972. G. Pianna and C. Caffara contribute an excellent documentation and study in *Principi di Morale Religiosa,* 1972.

2. Joseph Fuchs, S.J., *Existe-t-il une morale chrétienne?* (Coll. *Recherches et Syntheses-Morale,* 9) Gamloux, Ducolot, 146 pp. Although composed of a series of articles and lectures, this work is well centered on the subject announced in the title. The chapter headings are as follows: 1. *Existe-t-il une morale spécifiquement chrétienne?* 2. *Pour une théologie du progrès humain.* 3. *Le caractère absolu des normes morales de l'action.* 4. *Théologie morale et dogmatique.* 5. *Liberté fondamentale et morale.* 6. *Vie théologale et théologie moral.*

3. Several chapters of this work were first published in reviews, in German, Italian or Latin. The first chapter consists of a lecture delivered at the *Katholisches Akademikerhaus* in Zurich (December 1968), which appeared in *Stimmen der Zeit,* vol. 95 (1970), pp. 99–112. A first collection was published in Italian: *Esiste una morale cristiana?* Rome, Herder-Brescia, Ed. Morcellana, 1970, 180 pp. The French edition, besides new footnotes, includes as an addition the lengthy Chapter III, pp. 52–92.

4. From some reviews in the press one gains the impression that their authors failed to perceive Fr. Fuch's scrupulous distinctions and reservations, and that he made Christian morality identical with human morality. Thus Fr. Fuchs states that, to a large measure, "categorical" morality (the moral virtues, for example) of Christians is based on the exigencies of human nature. For this reason he adopts the theses of the "natural law" school which we shall be discussing shortly. But, in other respects, he acknowledges that concretely the *humanum* of which the Christian speaks has become the

humanum christianum and that the context of Christian life, based on revelation and led in the church, is different: "Certainly, in arriving at the
knowledge of a human morality, the Christian receives a not-negligible aid
from the context of revelation and from its transmission in the Christian and
ecclesial community" (p. 24). Some commentators have taken no account of
these reservations.

5. In recent discussions on the subject of moral theology the term
"framework-laws" has often been employed to designate these primordial
demands. Fr. Fuchs notes that this transcendental aspect of Christian morality has been very little studied. Indeed, he writes: "The immediate relation,
that is to say theological, of the Christian to the God of his salvation in faith,
hope, charity, is not dealt with in moral theology in the specific presentation
of the theological virtues, faith, hope, charity" (pp. 113–134). If we recall
this fact, over which some today would like to throw Noah's garment, we do
so because it is the point of origin of several of the positions that have been
taken against the specificity of Christian morality. "What exactly was Christian in the moral theology that we were taught?" is a question asked by some
today.

6. J. Fuchs, *Le renouveau de la théologie morale selon Vatican II,* Paris, Desclée, 1968; *L'enseignement de la morale,* special issue of *Seminarium*
1971, by different authors under the editorship of Card. Garrone. The excellent re-statement of the question by Msgr. G. B. Guzzetti, *C'e' una morale
cristiana?,* pp. 536–553, merits special mention here.

7. This matter will be discussed later, but I should like to make some
observations here and now. If Fr. Fuchs means to say that categorical Christian morality encompasses the authentically human, no one today would
think of contradicting him. But can one really transform the rules of conduct
and the considerations on which they are based, in the gospels and in the
Corpus Paulinum, into a call to the human? Neither the "Quaerite ergo pri-
mum regnum Dei et iustitiam eius et haec omnia adjicientur vobis" nor the
opposition between the "law of reciprocity" of the pagans and the open and
gratuitous love of the Christians following the example of the Father (Mt 5,
43–48) support this assertion. Even the "natural law school" recognizes that
the Beatitudes transcend the human. St. Paul in Romans 2 does not treat the
moral norms of the Jew and of the pagan as identical: this is proved by his
struggle to prevent converted pagans from being subjected to the Jewish law.
He merely says that Jews and pagans are equally sinners. And he sets over
against this situation a new morality, that of the law of faith (Rom 3,27). Finally, the appeal to the "Christian tradition" strikes me as "astonishing," to
say the least. It irreverently disregards the whole patristic tradition, notably
Augustinian, and of its distrust of the "natural virtues." It also forgets the
transformations to which the Christian spirit submitted the "pagan virtues"
when it, in part, resumed their classification.

8. This impression is heightened when we read Fr. Fuch's summations
of his theses (p. 23). For example, the following: "We were of the opinion

that Christian conduct, in its concrete realization and manifestation, was in substance authentically human in that which concerns the categorical aspect of concrete comportment. Nevertheless we have established that the *christianum* of the Christian person would also be able to influence the latter's concrete (categorical) conduct first of all through a Christian motivation which not only supports philanthrophy but also the Christian love of neighbor, and fosters progress in religious and cultic life as well."

9. Fr. Fuchs discusses this subject further on pp. 141–142, in footnote 4.

10. E. Genicot, *Institutiones Theologiae moralis* quas in Collegio Lovanienski Societatis Iesu, tradebat E. Genicot, S.J. Editio duodecima quam recognovit I. Salsmans, vol. 1, Louvain 1931, no. 90, p. 74.

11. A reasoning of this kind could lead dogmatic theology back to metaphysics because Christian mysteries transcend reason while expressing themselves rationally with the aid of a metaphysics.

12. In a similar conception, the practice of the counsels is not presented as a practical expression of charity in which the only Christian moral perfection resides. *Lumen Gentium* (no. 39) has re-established the traditional doctrine on this subject. In this connection see the valuable commentaries of the late Msgr. G. Philips, *L'Église et son mystère au duexième Concile du Vatican*, vol. 2 (Paris, Desclée, 1968) pp. 75–79 and his admonition against a two-stage morality (precepts without charity-counsels) that has held sway for so long.

13. Noldin-Schmitt, *Summa theologiae moralis*, vol. 1, *De praeceptis*, 23rd ed., Innsbruck, 1935, no. 20.

14. This identification is not rare among modern authors unlike the Fathers and the scholastics. Cf. Ph. Delhaye, *Le décalogue et sa place dans la morale chrétienne*, Brussels, *La pensée catholique*, 1963, p. 43ff. (*L'intégration doctrinale du décalogue dans la morale chrétienne. L'apport des Pères*). p. 87ff. (*Le décalogue se situe-t-il au plan de la loi naturelle . . .?*), La charité, *"premier commandement" chrétien chez S. Bonaventure*, scheduled for publication in vol. 2 of *S. Bonaventure, Volumen commemorativum anni septies centenarii a morte S. Bonaventurae* . . . cura et studio Commissionis Internationalis Bonaventurianae, Grottaferrata, 1973.

15. Vernon J. Bourke, *History of Ethics*, Doubleday & Co. New York, 1968, p. 8.

16. Vernon J. Bourke, *History of Ethics*, p. 48.

17. Re Marx see above all Karl Marx, *Critique of Hegel's "Philosophy of Right,"* Trsl. from the German by Annette Jolin and Joseph O'Malley, Cambridge (England) University Press, and Karl Marx, *Economic and philosophic manuscripts of 1849*. Trsl. from the German by Martin Milligan, introduction by Dirk J. Struik. (International Publishers, New York, 1964).

18. J. P. Sartre, *Being and Nothingness* Trsl. by Hazel Barnes, p. 615: "But the idea of God is contradictory . . ."

19. R. Coste, *Les chrétiens et l'analyse marxiste*, in *Revue theologique de Louvain*, vol 4 (1973), pp. 20–38.

20. Karl Barth, *Church Dogmatics,* authorized translation by G.T. Thomason, and T. Clark, Edinburgh, 1936–1969, especially Vol. II, 2 and Vol. III, 4.

21. Professor R. Vancourt has ably demonstrated Heidegger's influence on Bultmann in connection with "existential" morality: *Faut-il changer le langage théologique? A propos du concept d'existential,* in *Esprit et Vie,* 1971, pp. 417–423. Cf. also W. Schmithals, *Die Theologie Rudolf Bultmann,* Tubingen, 2nd ed., 1967 (especially Chap. 12) and Ch. Kiesling, "Bultmann's Moral Theology," in *Theological Studies,* vol. 30 (1969), pp. 224–248.

22. R. Bultmann, *Glauben und Verstehen,* III, Munich, 1951, p. 2.

23. R. Bultmann, *Glauben und Verstehen,* I Munich 1951, p. 231.

24. R. Bultmann, *Das Problem der Ethik bei Paulus,* in ZNW, vol. 23 (1924) p. 138.

25. R. Bultmann, *Primitive Christianity in its Contemporary Setting,* Trsl. by R. H. Fuller. New American Library. New York 1974. p. 177.

26. R. Bultmann, *Das Problem der Ethik. . . .* p. 138.

27. R. Bultmann, *Glauben und Verstehen . . .* I, p. 234.

28. J. A. T. Robinson, *Christian Freedom in a Permissive Society,* SCM Press, London, 1970. The form critics of the New Testament (*Formgeschichte*), states the former Anglican bishop of Woolwich, show that the teaching of Christ, unknowable in itself, comes to us through the cultural net of the earliest Christian communities which obviously do not correspond to our own although "the embodiment of the divine command in one generation can be its distortion in the next" (pp. 16–17). Revelation is not fixed, it is a quest and a presence that situates itself on the level of existing facts. "The Christian goes on trusting that God is always in the situation before him and that if and as he genuinely gives himself in love he will find God— for God is love" (p. 35).

29. As is known Bonhoeffer's moral theology has gone through three principal stages. In the first stage, the theologian dwells before else on the community that re-considers the Christian message. In the second (that of the struggle of the confessing church struggling against nazism and the "German Christians" who collaborated with it), Bonhoeffer stresses above all the example of Christ who let himself be crucified (Philippians 2) and asks Christians to do likewise. In a third period, moral theology and the church are separated from any religion. The only duty of the Christian is to be with others, to disappear like leaven so that a new world can be born. Cf. *Dietrich Bonhoffer* by Eberhard Bethge, Collins, London 1970.

30. P. Tillich, *Systematic Theology,* combined volume, Herts, 1968; *The Courage to Be,* New York, 1964; *Morality and Beyond,* New York, 1959; *Gesammelte Werke,* Stuttgart, Evangelisches Verlagswerk, 1967; G. Tavard, *Initiation à Paul Tillich, une théologie moderne,* Paris, Centurion, 1968.

31. *Bloch on Karl Marx,* Trsl. by Joseph Maxwell, Herder & Herder, New York 1972. This book contains selections from Bloch's *Prinzip Hoffnung,* Suhrkamp, 1959. The appendix to the work of Moltmann cited in the following footnote reproduces a discussion between Moltmann and Bloch.

32. J. Moltmann, *Theologie der Hoffnung, Untersuchungen zur Begründing und zu den Konsequenzen einer christlichen Eschatologie,* Munich, Kaiser Verlag, 1954. The eighth edition, revised in 1969, was translated into French under the title *Théologie de l'Espérance,* Paris, Le Cerf, 1970. A second volume, J. Moltmann, Wolf-Dieter and others, recapitulates the critiques to which the book gave rise and the replies of the author under the title: *Théologie de l'Espérance,* vol. II, Paris, Le Cerf-Mame, 1973. Several articles by Moltmann have been collected and translated by J. P. Thevenaz, under the title *L'Espérance en action, traduction historique et politique de l'Évangile,* Paris, Le Seuil, 1973.

33. J. B. Metz, *Zur Theologie der Welt,* Mayence, 1968; French translation, *Pour une théologie du monde,* Paris, 1971; *Zur Präsenz der Kirche in der Gesellschaft,* in Concilium no. 60 (Congress of Brussels). Cf. also B. Mondin, *I teologi della Speranza,* Turin, 1970, pp. 87–95 and M. Xhaufflaire, *La "théologie politique,"* Paris, 1972 (contains a list of Metz's writings on p. 8).

34. M. Xhaufflaire, *La "théologie politique,"* p. 55.

35. This last sentence is taken from the French translation of *Zur Theologie der Welt,* p. 144. Metz's opposition to the magisterium is expressed even more clearly on p. 143.

36. A. Valsecchi, *Nuove vie del l'etica sessuale. Discorso ai Christiani* (*Coll.* Giornale di Teologia 62) Brescia, ed. Queriniana, 1972.

37. A. Valsecchi, *Nuove vie . . .,* Editoriale di Tullio Goffi, p. 12.

38. A. Valsecchi, *Nuove vie . . .,* Chapter I, *Le necessarie premesse di metodo, L'analasi della natura umana,* pp. 25–28.

39. A. Valsecchi, *Nuove vie . . .* p. 30 "This free decision for love is, *ex parte hominis,* the central and decisive event of the 'history of salvation'." (In Italian)

40. A. Valsecchi, *Nuove vie . . .* p. 31.

41. A. Valsecchi, *Nuove vie . . .* p. 41.

42. A. Valsecchi, *Nuove vie . . .* p. 90, footnote 1.

43. J. Blank, *Réflexions sur le problème des normes ethiques du Nouveau Testament,* in *Concilium,* no. 25, pp. 23–28; *Was Jesus heute will. Überlegung zur Ethik Jesu,* in *Theologische Quartalschrift,* 1961, pp. 300–320.

44. A. Auer, *Nach dem Erscheinen der Enzyklika "Humanae Vitae". Zehen Thesen über die Findung sittlicher Weisungen,* in *Theologische Quartalschrift,* 1969, pp. 78–85.

45. J. Leclercq, *Les grandes lignes de la philosophie morale,* Louvain, 1946, p. 51ff.

46. J. Leclercq, *Les grandes lignes . . .* pp. 203–206. In his *Essais de morale chrétienne* and *L'enseignement de la morale chrétienne,* J. Leclercq has ceaseless protested against the method of teaching moral science in the seminaries which, in his view, places too little emphasis on a Christian approach and understanding.

47. A. Vergez and D. Huisman, *La philosophie en 60 chapitres et en 300 questions,* Paris, Nathan, 1965.

48. I am referring to the special number of the review *Missi* of Lyons, October 1972: *Commandements de Dieu—Droits de L'homme.*

49. In this connection see J. Gründel, *Peut-on changer la morale?* Paris, Cerf-Desclée, 1973.

50. The reader is referred to two reviews of this work, written by the author, which appeared in RTL, vol. 3 (1971), pp. 367–368 and in *La Foi et le Temps* (Liége), vol. 1 (1971), pp. 574–578.

51. J. Leclercq, *Les grandes lignes* ..., p. 57. Leclercq further asserts that for both skepticism and relativism alike "the perfection of moral science does not lie in arriving at a system exactly proportioned to human nature and applicable to the totality of human beings, while permitting individual differences to make way for themselves. Rather, the perfection of moral science is found in the growing differentiation of moral codes up to an ideal limit which would be tantamount to having as many moralities as there are human beings. The teaching of ethics therefore should consist in opening minds to this quest for a personal morality *peculiar* to each one. Historical moral codes are simply examples of the adaptation of ethics to the different aspirations of minds."

52. *Dei Verbum*, no. 1. Cf. R. Latourelle, *Théologie de la Révélation*, Montreal-Paris, 1969.

53. St. Augustine, *De Spiritu et Littera*, chapt. 24; PL, vol. 44, col. 225.

54. St. Thomas, *Summa theologiae*, 1ª, 2ac, q. 106, art. 1, concl.

55. In this connection Msgr. G. Philips points up the importance of the documents of the magisterium and gives some principles of hermaneutics in: *L'Église et son mystère au deuxième concile du Vatican*, vol. 1, Paris, pp. 322–324.

56. Paul VI, *La morale chrétienne: une manière de vivre selon la foi*, in Documentation Catholique, 1972, p. 752. In this connection the Pope further on cites the article by M. A. Feuillet, *Les fondements de la morale chrétienne d'après l'Epitre aux Romains*, in *Revue Thomiste*, July–September 1970, pp. 357–386.

57. Vat. I, *De fide catholica*, chapt. 2. *de Revelatione* (Denz-Schönm., 3004–6); Vat. II, *Dei Verbum*, no. 6.

58. Gal 6,15: "For neither circumcision counts for anything, but a new creation."

59. Eph 4,24: ". . . and put on the new nature, created after the likeness of God in true righteousness and holiness."

60. It is not rare to read in present-day literature treating of this question that the commandment is not new but an old one. In this connection 1 John 2,7 is cited: "Beloved, I am writing you no new commandment, but an old commandment which you had from the beginning . . ." A footnote in the ecumenical Bible makes short shrift of this interpretation, stating: "The commandment of love is not a recent innovation as are the revelations of the false doctors but it goes back to the beginning (3, 11; 2 Jn 5–6), to the first announcement of the gospel. John insistently recommends fidelity to the tradition (1,1; 2,13,14,24)."

61. 1 John 5,2: "By this we know that we love the children of God, when we love God and obey his commandments."

62. St. Thomas, *Summa Contra Gentiles, lib.* I, *cap.* 4; cf. Ph. Delhaye, *Rencontre de Dieu et de l'homme. Les vertus théologales en général,* Paris, p. 44ff.

63. We draw the reader's attention to the Study Week of the Italian Bible Association held in Rome from September 25th to the 30th in 1972. Cf. also the special number of the *Rassegna di Teologia* January 1973, devoted to the problems of biblical morality. Worthy of special mention here is the article by Fr. Luigi Di Pinto, *Fondamenti biblici della teologia morale. Ricerche recenti, bilancio e prospective,* pp. 32–61. It is a valuable research tool.

64. Paul VI, *La morale chrétienne...*, in *Documentation Catholique,* 1972, p. 752.

65. Fr. Fuchs believes that some ethicians "who wrote since the years 1920–30" have fallen into this error. "The sermon on the mount was viewed as contrary to what is human," he writes, p. 15.

66. On page 16, Fr. Fuchs protests against a radical immanentism and explains what he means by the will of God.

67. *Gaudium et Spes,* no. 22. After discussing the association of the Christian with the paschal mystery, the text (par. 5, adds: "All this holds true not only for Christians, but for all men of good will in whose hearts grace works in unseen ways. For, since Christ died for all men, and since the ultimate vocation of man is in fact one, and divine, we ought to believe that the Holy Spirit in a manner known only to God offers to every man the possibility of being associated with this paschal mystery."

68. In the same sense, see *Gaudium et Spes,* nos. 57 and 58.

69. Need it be recalled that at the level of the necessity of grace for a Christian life, one finds the same distinction that obtains with respect to revelation? There will be an absolute necessity as regards the divine adoption and justification as well as regards knowledge of the mysteries, and a relative necessity as regards secular action on the moral plane.

70. We cannot disregard here the constant teaching of the Church on the necessity of grace in order to live morally. Mention must be made, at least, of the VIth Session of the Council of Trent which speaks of grace for the observance of the commandments (chapters 11 and 16, Denz-Schonm. no. 1536ff with the canons 19 and 20, nos. 1569–70). We see that already at that time it was a question of leading all moral theology back to a central orientation without concerning oneself with particular precepts.

71. After stating (p. 18) that he would not examine the problem of knowing whether humankind would have understood the requirements of love of neighbor without Christ with these words: "There would be much to say on this subject but it does not concern our problem," Fr. Fuchs adds: "The same thing applies when it is a question of knowing whether the above-mentioned exigencies can be fulfilled without the interior grace that comes from Christ."

72. Ph. Delhaye, *La vertu de religion dans l'enseignement de S. Bona-venture* in *Culture,* vol. 26 (1965), pp. 387–393.

73. M. Loi-Borodine, *La déification de l'homme selon le doctrine des Pères Grecs,* Paris, Cerf, 1970, p. 118. Pages 114–126 on the purification of human virtues in Christianity are must reading. Few writings on this theme exhibit such richness.

The Grounding for the Moral Norm in Contemporary Theological Reflection

Enrico Chiavacci

At the start of our study I must define precisely what I mean by "norm" and "grounding for the norm." I am making this the focus of the first part of this article in order to dispel any ambiguities concerning the significance of these terms. At the same time I hope that this exploration will urge Italian Catholic moral theology to reflect critically on its own "groundings" or "bases." Such reflection is present in a remarkable way in the writings of St. Thomas and generally in the early great Scholastics. On the other hand, it is absent—for reasons now quite well known—in the moral manuals written between the seventeenth and twentieth centuries. Our task is an urgent one owing to the crises and tensions inherent in the postconciliar renewal of moral theology. In this endeavor we can be greatly aided by a school of thought that—in spite of historical difficulties—has always kept alive the Thomistic and Scotist regard for the fundamental concepts of moral theology and especially in focusing a critical reflection on them. It is clear now that I am obviously referring to the English ethical tradition and in particular to analytical ethics. I believe that one of the most serious handicaps in Catholic moral theology—up to this point—has been an almost complete unawareness of or disregard for this school of thought. Significant studies have been done by some moralists (notably by the Germans and the Polish), but very little attention has been given them in Italy. Although it is not my intention to describe and evaluate the conclusions of these studies, I do hope to make significant references to them—allowing, however, for my own human limitations of time and space.

I

THE CONCEPT OF THE MORAL NORM

Norm as Prescription
and as a System of Prescriptions

(1:1) The term "norm" or "rule" generally suggests the idea of a comparison between a datum which is to be evaluated and with a datum that is evaluative. The evaluative datum (norm) corresponds to essentially three diverse evaluatory criteria:

1. The statistical datum: which speaks of an event as statistically normative. An event, therefore, can be normal (the usual situation) or abnormal (an exception to it).

2. The instrumental datum: norm here is the path that must be followed for a certain goal to be attained; an event is thus correct or erroneous as it relates to the goal sought.

3. The moral datum: the significance of this kind of norm is that it indicates a path for one to follow in order to live sensibly, or meaningfully. One chooses to give life a certain meaning or to give an absolute significance to a certain idea of the good. Thus a particular behavior can be considered good or bad in an absolute sense.

To live meaningfully—however one wishes to specify this expression—can be identified with living in a morally good way. But this is a senseless expression unless it can be related to each and every significant action which is deliberately caused by an agent with his or her relatively free decision-making ability, as he or she chooses among alternative possibilities.[1] We call the moral norm that way which is to be followed: that way to which every single free action—chosen from among alternative possibilities of behaviors—must conform. Norm, therefore, is the absolute measure of free behavior and, consequently, the model of behavior for whoever is getting ready to act.

Life, however, imposes on us a rather complex series of choices that are materially different, and yet must still be consonant with the unique significance that is attached to our existence. The individual norms that monitor various actions must, therefore, all be in agreement with a unique and central term of comparison. They, therefore, also must be able to work with, or at least be compatible with, one another. This is what we mean in saying each norm has a meaning within a system of norms. There inevitably follow certain levels of abstraction mediating between the individual norm and the ultimate meaning which finds its expression and its partial realization in the individual norm. Therefore, in the expression "grounding for the norm" two senses of the word "norm" are to be understood. They are a single prescription and a system of prescriptions (usually termed "the moral law"). Both meanings must be "grounded" in some way.

I am dealing here with the single prescription rather than with a system of prescriptions. The study of the latter insofar as it is a system calls for a cultural-anthropological exploration that goes beyond the margins of my article.

The Abstract Theoretical Prescription
and the Concrete Situational Prescription

(1:2) At this point of our study, a serious problem must be confronted. For every norm, whether it be a prescription or a guideline, ought to be able to describe the particular action it intends to prescribe or prohibit. Yet the description is never able to portray exactly the reality that is to be evaluated; that is a concrete free action performed by a particular person considered at a specific moment in his or her interior development and exterior context or situation. Who is able to portray or describe this reality other than the person who is facing it? Therefore, normative ethics, in its study and in its formulation of norms must—by the nature of things—stop at a certain level in specifying and describing an action and, hence, in the formulation of a norm. The norm so formulated possesses a universal character of its own. Insofar as life has meaning at all, the norm then will be valid for all people who find themselves in those conditions which the norm specifies and describes. It is not a question of how many people find themselves in this precise situation. Only that those who do find that they are in the precise situation that the norm describes and specifies must be governed by it.

Consequently, when the individual person comes to evaluate his or her own behavior, that person may find that he or she is facing the precise conditions described by the norms. Yet there is always something more to be considered. For there is one condition that is always in principle, new or diverse in each situation; that is the very person of the agent acting in a specific moment of his or her life. In practice, however, many other conditions come into play in addition to those already described. For instance, Catholic moral theology has treated the concept of circumstance equivocally. It has been defined as an accidental element in its relationship to the object. It has, therefore, been concluded that since "circumstance" is accidental it can be there or not be there. The point, however, is this: "accidental" does not mean, in this case, that certain circumstances which are capable of modifying the object *can be present or not present,* but only that such circumstances *can vary* and in the concrete situation are never completely the same. There is never any such thing as an object without circumstances, but the circumstances can never be included in the theoretical definitions of the object. Or, better, they are what *indeed* have been left out of the theoretical definition of the object. I suspect that the distinction between object and circumstance is arbitrary. At the very least, the circumstances "who," "when" and perhaps even "where" are always diverse, unique, and unrepeatable for an individual agent in a particular situation.

Thus, the norm as a product of ethics is never sufficiently descriptive. The grey area between object and circumstances is inevitable. For the ethical norm itself is limited in its capacity to specify everything that is present in all situations. Only the agent himself in the specific situation in which he is called to act can formulate that norm which can be followed passively and with complete obedience. When we are speaking of moral norm, then, we are referring to two distinct prescriptions which, although they do not coincide in principle, may coincide in fact.

Norm as Prescription Functioning in the
Creation of Concrete Norms (Norms of the Second Level)

(1:3) It is true, however, that a system of the first type of ethical norms can contain norms of the second type. These refer to norms which govern the manner in which abstract norms become concrete ones. The principle "voluntary in cause" and that of the double effect are examples of this; so are the principles which govern cases of conflict (*minus malum, pars tutior*). In these cases, the system seeks to render obedience to the abstract norm more accessible to a passive observance, that is, executed more confidently and more easily. The system then helps in creating norms from the evaluating criteria of the concrete variables. The problem of grounding these metanorms is different from the problem of grounding prescriptions for behavior, even if the creation of the concrete norm already involves an action susceptible to being normed. We cannot delve farther into this question here; we merely point it out as a yet unexplained problem in Catholic theology.

A Proposed Terminological Distinction

(1:4,1) It seems to me that in order to be precise, we must make a distinction between these two types of norms: the abstract ethical norm (which we might term inadequate) and the concrete ethical norm (which we might term adequate). Here the two adjectives—adequate and inadequate—do not have an evaluative significance, but rather a connotative one. We will immediately see the importance of the inadequate norm. This first norm always comes to the agent from outside himself or herself or at least from outside the situation. Its creation is what gives purpose to the science of normative ethics in a strict sense (whether it be philosophical or theological—no matter what may be the meaning assumed as the absolute principle). The "inadequate" norm, therefore, always comes, in principle, from outside a concrete situation. (Here we must take note of another problem; the person of the scholar or producer of ethical norms is always in a concrete, conditioned psychological and intellectual situation.) I propose, therefore, what I have done in my *Teo-*

logia Morale: to call such a prescription a "precept"—a command which comes from outside. Such a prescription is not properly a norm except in a remote sense. For it is not a rule to be followed passively. The possibility remains that at times the precept may be transformed, by the weight of things, into a norm. This, however, does not occur as a matter of principle.

The second norm, on the other hand, is adequately descriptive and, hence, adequately prescriptive. This means that it must be followed passively. It is the real rule, the definitive and only truly objective measure of the behavior considered by the agent. Its production or creation is the work of the agent; it cannot be, as we have already stated, the work of other people. This is the norm in its most basic sense; so I, propose therefore, to reserve the term "norm" for it—and for it alone.

Because of the title that has been assigned to my article, I will continue to speak generally of "norm" in both senses of the word. In some cases, however, the term "precept" will appear meaning simply a theoretical norm. This distinction is completely in keeping with traditional Christian moral thinking which recognizes the distinction between the remote norm as the content of moral law and the proximate norm as the content of conscience. Everyone, of course, must act *"ad rectam conscientiae suae normam."*[2]

The Relationship Between Precept and Norm

(1:4,2) Precept and norm are not to be considered antithetical mental realities; rather, there is no norm without a precept. In fact, it is impossible to have an interior moral process in which the norm is created without some point of reference that is external to both the agent and the situation. This point of reference must be encountered in the moral process. The measure of a concrete situation cannot arise from within the situation itself. It may already be in the agent but only in the form of some universal sentiment in which the agent recognizes that what is present to him or her has the qualities of absoluteness and obligation. Furthermore, we must exclude the possibility of a norm which exists without data and which is prior to the situation, unless we wish to renounce speaking of normative ethics completely and even more generally, of the very legitimacy of the moral experience.[3] This is what occurs in some forms of existentialist decision making.[4] Finally, I would like to propose referring to the *complex of data from which the agent in a situation moves to find the norm* by the all inclusive term "moral law" no matter how it is found or in what form it is assumed; whether it be precept, recommendation, or example.[5]

THE QUESTION OF GROUNDING

Grounding as the Ultimate Meaning (Value) and as a Process of Creating the Norm

(2:1) Prescinding, for now, from the distinction described above between precept and norm, we may ask ourselves what is meant by the grounding of a moral norm in general. We can start from an assumption already enunciated above: that life has a meaning—no matter how that is determined—and that individual actions must realize, or be expressive of this meaning. (Such is the basis for moral duty.) We maintain that without this assumption, it is senseless to speak of moral duty and of ethics in general. We have made this point elsewhere.[6] Therefore, the remote grounding of the norm is primarily and inevitably the search for what this meaning is and the rendering of an account for the meaning that is assumed. This task, however, is not that of normative ethics but of metaethics.

But once an ultimate meaning has been assumed—no matter what it may be—a problem still remains; that centers around the movement from the ultimate meaning, which is unique and unifies all the individual actions and, therefore, all the precepts which tend to regulate them, to precisely these norms. The specific problem of the grounding of a normative ethics then involves criteria and their legitimization. This then forms the process by which norms, whether they be precepts or secondary precepts, are established.

First we will consider the latter problem and then return to the former which is properly the domain of metaethics. Once a meaning has been assigned to life—or, if one prefers, once a general definition of "good" has been assumed—a very important preliminary question has been posed. That question specifically involves this: the relationship between my action and this meaning, which from now on we can term value, or values in the plural when it is capable of being subdivided into various elements.[7] The problem can be stated in this way: in what sense can I say that value gives meaning to my actions? Two acceptable possibilities are open. Distinguishing between them may present problems, but it is useful as a clarification to the question just posed.

The Deontological and Teleological Process of Establishing Norms

(2:2) First I must state that every action of mine has meaning insofar as it is a new event. In modifies both me and the cosmos (Umwelt), and at the same time it qualifies me to myself and to others. Are we to follow the rule which, in every type of situation (precept) or in every concrete situation (norm), produces the modifications that are closest to the meaning so indicated? Or is it the one which is rigorously deducible from the value, as a qualification of myself in a concrete action? Thus, we can have the possibility either of a finalist, teleological grounding for the norm, or of a deductive, deontological, grounding for the norm. In the first case, we would have norms of this type: "bring about the greatest good possible" (however we may define good). In the second case, we would have norms of this type: "do good, regardless of what the consequences are for you and for your *Umwelt*." It should be noted that deontological grounding does not exclude the fact that one must let the greatest amount of good come about. It simply does not assume that this criterion is ultimate and unique.

In the abstract, we have two ways of grounding the norm. Take the supposition that human life, mine and others, is to be defended and promoted and that the defense and promotion of life constitute part of the value. A teleological ethics can have no doubts here about prescribing abortion, not as merely licit, but as a duty when faced with the classical problem of the pregnant woman's certainty of death and of the death of the fetus if an abortion is not procured. A deontological ethics, on the other hand, can arrive at the precept "do not kill," regarding the taking of a life as an action against value. In such a case, the precept holds good absolutely, come what may. Of primary importance is that I do not kill, not that both die. The same twofold reasoning can take place for certain cases of suicide out of a motive of love.

The Uncertainty of the Distinction

This classification lends itself to many uncertainties, which we cannot discuss here.[8] In passing, however, we will note a few points for reflection.

Normally, utilitarianism is equated with teleological ethics. But it is rightly noted that utilitarianism and hedonism are not identical; the latter is only one possible species of the former. Utilitarianism takes the idea of doing the greatest good possible as the ethical criterion which grounds every norm. Even utilitarianism can know an absolute norm like "do not kill."[9] It can reason as follows. Even if killing can produce the greater good here and now, once the possibility of violating the norm under certain conditions is admitted, such a possibility weakens the perception of the value of life for the spirit of a group (or for humanity). Thus in the long run it produces more evil than good. Even this type of reasoning is clearly teleological. Hence, there can be an "intrinsice illicitum"—an obligation that always exists, come what may, both in a deontological ethics and in a teleological ethics, although their reasonings have different grounding.

However, the teleological *intrinsice illicitum,* within the framework of some Rule-Utilitarianism can appear—as it does to me—to entail the renunciation of utilitarianism itself. For whoever acts or is acted upon, the greatest good possible—in the short or long run—means all the material and psychological repercussions which the actions will have in some remote future. The knowledge and prophetic capacity that is asked for here is not found in human beings. Few scientists or scholars are in a position to provide teleological precepts with a proof that is acceptable or nearly complete. Even if by lying I can do a good or avoid a present evil, "do not lie" can be a teleological precept since both falsehood in social relationships and the habit of lying in the individual's psyche can ruin the possibility of a human common life. But in that case, to establish the principle that it is *always* better not to lie than to lie is equivalent to establishing a fixed principle from which individual actions are deduced in the here and now, come what may.[10]

The Question of Exceptions

Conversely, every deontological ethics must know at least a few precepts which do not admit of exception regardless of circumstances. But do such precepts really exist? This is doubtful. We have already recognized that a precept is never adequately descriptive of the real situation. To state that a precept does not admit of exception is equivalent to admitting that every descriptive element beyond those already contained in the precept is, in principle, always irrelevant. The classic example, at least for the great majority of Catholic authors, is the precept not to lie. Nature, which is the expression of the Creator's will, and, hence, of the meaning of existence, gives us the capacity to speak, to express what is in our minds. Every deviant usage of the faculty of speaking, then, is contrary to the meaning of human existence. But in the same Christian and Catholic tradition, numerous authors have taken "exceptions" into consideration. These are, for example, the evil use which another can make of the thought communicated, the right of the accused not to have to "betray himself," and the grave harm which can come to others from knowledge of the truth.[11]

De facto, all of us lie with tranquil consciences countless times. This opens up two possibilities for a deontological ethics.

1. *One may attempt to make the exceptions typical*, including them in the precept as an integral part of the description: "Do not lie, except for the case, or cases in which . . ." This then would be the real precept without exceptions. But who will assure us that our very experience, both of fact and of moral sensibility, will not in the future force us to include within the precept other descriptive and more restrictive hypotheses from the contexts in which the precepts are to be applied? The precept is thus valid absolutely—whatever happens—in the present state of conceivability of the diverse concrete situation in which it is to be applied. The precept, however, cannot be considered

valid absolutely if there are even only theoretical possibilities of later modifications which in principle cannot be excluded.

2. *One may accept the fact that there will be certain exceptions* which are to be evaluated case by case, and which cannot be made to fit into a more accurate description of the precept. At this point one admits that there must be an evaluative instance which is superior to the precept itself. One must conclude then that the criterion grounding the precept does not necessarily lead to the formulation of the precept.[12] At times, our historical experience reveals to us that the further specification of the precept, either through description or through an evaluatory assumption, responds to a teleological necessity.

Another problem to be considered is how St. Thomas and St. Augustine viewed the relationship between the deontological and teleological grounding of the precept. Let us grant a typically deontological distinction between positive divine law and the natural law as the manifestation of the very will or reason of God. Here we see that *in God Himself* the teleological element prevails over the deontological. The precept of not killing oneself, for example, was violated by Samson as a result of a divine command in order to attain certain historical purposes. The same precept was violated by some virgin martyrs as a result of a divine command. So, too, Augustine does not exclude it. Only the pursuit of a goal can justify a command contrary to a deontological precept. This goal must be attained ordinarily according to a precept; yet in individual cases which cannot be generalized, the goal can be reached by violating the precept.

It seems to us that in every case, every precept must be radically teleological. In this sense: that it must represent an action which better realizes (compromises less) a certain unfolding of the interior history of the individual and/or the history of humanity and the cosmos.

This follows directly from assuming a unique "meaning" for the existence of the individual and of humanity. From such a meaning—regardless of circumstances—precepts which are always valid can be deduced. This meaning can also constitute a constant goal to be pursued by means of individual acts and in individual situations. And this will give rise to precepts which are changeable from situation to situation or to standard precepts considered—over the long haul—

always fruitful in attaining the goal. *But in every case,* the precept is oriented toward meaning. By his or her choices, the individual must actualize something in the cosmos and in history. To act without a goal unifying the individual actions does not constitute moral activity or at least it is not codifiable in ethical norms. It leaves no room for normative ethics.

The difference between a deductive process and a prudential one in the production of norms certainly depends on the type of "meaning" that is assumed. This will be seen better in the case of Christian ethics (see no. 4). But it seems to me that the deductive-deontological process is not really one which disregards consequences, but one which either establishes once and for all the priority of certain consequences, or establishes *generatim* and *in pluribus* that an action produces the consequences more desirable with a view to a certain goal without excluding in individual cases non-codifiable exceptions (with or without the intervention of God), or through the refinement of the precept. The process of grounding the ethical norm is, therefore, always a rational process which realizes a unique meaning in an infinite series of differing situations that are more or less typical or univocal. Whether it be teleological or deontological, the process of grounding the norm must always be rational. *Rationality in the realization* of meaning is the general rule in the establishing of the ethical norm. To reject this is equivalent to refuting the legitimacy of the demand that the norm be justified in the process of its creation.

The Question of Meaning and the Metaethical Problem

(2:3) A different form of discourse is called for, however, when we move from the justification of the norm's formulation to the justification of the ultimate meaning which the norm must express. Until the last century in Western culture, no doubts existed that even the supreme meaning (or value or series of values) was rationally deducible from a philosophical (metaphysical) and empirical (anthropological—scientific) or theological system. These various systems of the formation of meaning are called, after Moore, naturalism or descriptivism. The ancient maxim, *"operari sequitur esse"* implied that the passage from "is" to "ought" was legitimate. Today, however, the legitimacy of this passage is fiercely contested—and in my opinion, with good reason. No matter which description of "is" we wish to assume, the passage to "ought" entails a logically unacceptable jump. For eudaemonism in all its forms (moral egoism not in a derogatory but solely in a descriptive sense), there remains forever open the question: "Why must I seek happiness?" (or pleausre, or well being, or my fulfillment, etc.). If we transfer eudaemonism from the private to the social level (Rule—Utilitarianism), the following question is left open: "Why must I concern myself with others?" And if our answer is: Because this is the condition for surviving in some form of community life, then we return to eudaemonism's question: "Why should I survive or live well?" Eudaemonism then is not really a suitable grounding for morality, but only of living well. Thus the description of what is necessary for "living (being) well" cannot be translated into "must live well" without the assumption of a prescriptive proposition which is not rationally deducible; namely, "I must live well." The Christianity of the first few centuries assumed the Greek moral experience—typically eudaemonist—of grounding the duty of living well on the creaturely status of the individual, and on the divine origin of the law of nature, which prohibits the disturbance of the order willed by God. But then "the open question" is transformed into this: "Why must I obey God?" (Here we are prescinding from the other urgent question which is whether the capacity for the progressive elaboration of data from experience, which God has given to the person, is not also to be included in the order willed by God.)

If the response is: "Because God wills only good, he alone knows my true good (that which is rational)," then the open question of eudaemonism is proposed again. If the response is that God is my Lord and Master—along the Ockhamist model—the response begs the question. It's like saying: "I must obey God because God must be obeyed."

Although apparently naturalistic, St. Thomas had seen the problem. The problem *bonum est faciendum* is for him analytical, self-evident. As we shall see shortly, this could make us conceive a grounding of "ought" that is absolutely non-naturalistic but one rather that is intuitional. Obedience to the laws of nature (the spontaneous tendencies in the individual) and obedience to God are obligations which are not deduced but intuited. They are not known in a rationalistic-discursive form. What is deduced is the content of the good, of the obedience to God the Creator of nature and the person, but not the fact that good *must* be done. We must note here the grave error of those who in explaining St. Thomas in the light of Aristotle make him into a kind of eudaemonist.

An intuitionalistic solution is a conceivable alternative to a grounding for meaning that is naturalistic (or descriptive or definitionistic—which deduces ought from being). This has many advantages yet here it is not a question of intuiting individual norms, but of intuiting the meaning on which the norms will be rationally based. This thesis grounds every ethics of values whether in Scheler, in Hartman, or in Moore. The serious difficulty which this thesis encounters is that of demonstrability. It finds it impossible to demonstrate that everyone can construct his or her moral life starting from a unique and common value (or series of values). This demonstration is the condition for which meaning can be universal and non-illusory. It is, in other words, the condition for its acceptability as the foundation of a normative ethics. Nowadays, this thesis is rather discredited within the circle of the analytical school itself. But its alternative is either the return to naturalism or to the acceptance of a decisionism which is really the renunciation of morality as we will see directly.

As far as I'm concerned, all attempts to return by other ways to naturalism and deducibility of "ought" from "is" are vitiated by a common defect. All of them (Rawls, Searle, Frankena, etc.) are founded on the mediation of the social.[13] Do not lie, keep your promises, be impartial in judgment ("justice as fairness" of Rawls) are norms which can indeed be deduced from existence, but from existence in society.[14] Thus, they refer to a (non-descriptive) ethical proposition, neither demonstrated nor demonstrable. The following are examples: "I must live in society", or "I must treat every one of my neighbors as myself", that is according to the golden rule defined in an egoistic or in a non-egoistic sense. The deduction of duty from being is thus possible only after having made a choice between egoism and non-egoism. This invalidates the reasoning because such a deduction is possible only after having established a fundamental obligation. This is significant, but even more significant is the fact that all the logical efforts in this direction are centered around the golden rule. We will return to this point in the third part of the article.

The difficulty inherent in intuitionism has been raised largely by the anthropological sciences, but nowadays it appears on the way to resolution. If it is true that diverse cultures have diverse moral codes then we must say that it does not seem to depend so much on the assumption of diverse values as it does depend on the diverse rational deductions from which the diverse structural framework in which those very values must be actualized.

The other alternative to intuitionism is constituted by a series of non-cognitive theories, which can be catalogued under the general term of decisionism. In these theories, meaning is not already given—that is known by deduction or intuition. Every choice then becomes an existential risk. This may seem beautiful and even noble, but in reality it is highly equivocal. Indeed, with it we find ourselves amid two possibilities.

The first possibility. The agent is faced with alternative and reciprocally irreducible values. He or she, then, must take a risk in choosing one over the other. This is not the technical understanding of decisionism but it is a widespread understanding. And here there are again two possibilities. Either the agent chooses without any reason, as if drawing by lot. In this case, the consequent norm is as valid as its contradictory which results from the opposite choice. Thus, the idea of moral evil vanishes and with it the meaning of life, since one choice has no more meaning than any other. Or the agent chooses because he foresees or intuits without the possibility of demonstrating that one value has preeminence over another. In this case, the person lapses into an intuitionism while positing a meaning to life.

The second possibility. The agent has no value present to him, but creates it by his own choice. This really is noncognitivism, but it is also non-morality since every morality as obedience to an obligation has vanished.

In this essay I will not examine the metaethical discourse which is still open and which abounds with still contested solutions. But I would simply like to point out that there is a profound significance in the return of many thinkers from an intuitionism to a naturalism by way of the social fact. I believe that their obligatory return is the result of the incontrovertible fact that the normative concretization for a moral experience exists only within a group. But in a more profound way, the relation with the other (or with others as a group) is the root place for moral experience to originate. Here the other constitutes itself as a call, as a value. The golden rule in such a hypothesis would then be none other than that traditional and felicitious expression which is anterior to the gospel and exists on its own. This experience is not deducible from being. In a context such as this the choice exists either to accept the other as a meaning or to reject the other by automatically accepting myself as a meaning for myself. This is certainly a rational but definitely a moral choice, one which can improperly be represented as decisionism, but one which is in reality an example of intuitionism.

All that has been said up to this point does not pertain to what is properly the theological sphere of moral reflection. It does, however, constitute the framework in which rational possibilities for a theological grounding for the norm exist. If in every case, theology is a rational reflection on revealed datum, then moral theology will not be able to reflect on the datum revealed unless it be by a rational process. It must, therefore, take account of the reasoning process which is typical of moral reflection.

III
THE CHRISTIAN GROUNDING OF THE
FRAME OF REFERENCE (OF MEANING)

We have already studied the twofold problem of the grounding of the norm.

a. the problem of the ethical theories which focus on the process of grounding the norm.

b. the problem of the metaethical theories which focus on the meaning that grounds the norm.

While we have seen that every norm must be rationally grounded, we have also observed the extreme difficulty which is involved in seeking to ground the ultimate meaning of the norm rationally. This also points up the difficulty regarding the frame of reference from which the norms in the deontological or teleological process draw significance. In moral theology, the following two problems must be maintained as distinct: firstly, the problem of normative ethics (justification of the norm): secondly, the problem of metaethics (justification of the meaning). This distinction, although not completely unknown, is not quite usual in the moral theology which we have inherited. St. Thomas knew of it (perhaps in other terms); Ockham did also, but we were not introduced to it in the manuals we studied. I will now seek to explore the distinction further in order to clear up the profound and somewhat mysterious relationship between faith and morality. This is none other than the supreme task of moral theology.

"*I am the Lord.*"

(3:1) Both in the Old Testament and in the New, the Lord presents himself as the supreme value, that is the ultimate meaning of life. Just as the grounding of all Old Testament ethics is certainly "I am the Lord," so is the grounding for New Testament ethics, the following of Christ. At this point, I do not intend to discuss these biblical assertions. I believe that they can be shared by all believers in a substantial way. Here I would rather like to focus on a stimulating expression of Von Balthasar: "Christ is the concrete categorical imperative."[16] Christ does not refer to anything else. Even before his own discourses, Christ is the law. What meaning can such an affirmation have since it is so frequently found in a variety of formulations and possibly even worn out by use?

Christ is the Concrete Categorical Imperative

Christ is certainly the revelation, indeed the self-revelation, of God: the "translation" of the absolute into gestures, words, and human customs. As such, he presents himself as the lived meaning, the uniquely significant life—one in which event and value coincide perfectly. Theology proceeds from this assumption and begins the reasoning process after having accepted this truly paschal faith. For the believer, the problem of meaning no longer exists; it is dissipated, resolved in the gesture of faith.

Manifestation and Acceptance of the Absolute in Christ

In this light, St. Paul's expression "for me to live is Christ" is not a generic but a very precise one. But faith as an intellectual assent to the twofold proposition "God exists" and "Jesus Christ is the Son of God" is not in itself a moral choice. It is the fruit of the reasoning process involved in theodicy or apologetics and certainly even of a cultural conditioning. The moral moment of faith is the moment in which the intellectual *placet* is embraced freely as the ultimate (unique) meaning of existence. The passage from the intellectual *placet* (whether deduced or intuited is of little importance) to total adherence is not part of a logical choice but an a-logical choice. The opponents of a theonomic moral are right when they say that the proposition "I must obey God" is not deducible from anything. Faith is the ultimate meaning, the frame of reference, the solution to the metaethical problem *if we make it such,* that is, only if the *fides quae* becomes in us the *fides qua.*

Conscience as the Link Between Orthodoxy and Orthopraxis

(3:2) The following statement indicates the complex interior reality of every Christian (we will see that is also such for every human being): the acceptance (or the refusal) of a proposal of meaning, the active moment of faith. This is the reflex reception of the gift of God, of the infused virtue—and that in biblical terms can be defined as conscience. Conversion is conversion of the heart; obedience is obedience to the conviction of faith. Faith and conscience play the same role in Romans 14 and 1 Corinthians 10.[17] It is, therefore, true that orthopraxis follows upon orthodoxy. Without orthodoxy, orthopraxis would be a sheer decisionism about individual acts, and, therefore, should not be considered *orthopraxis,* but only praxis.

Truth as an Absolute Moral Call

But if this is true on the level of normative ethics, it is not true on the level of metaethics. Orthopraxis is an act of acceptance; it is a gift of self which does not follow orthodoxy but is identical with it.[18] Truth and the absolute moral call coincide. And conscience is the point where recognition and acceptance of the God who calls are one single thing. Faith in the sense of *fides qua,* of *totum se committere Deo*—is knowledge of the ultimate truth—really the unique mode of such knowledge. *Verum et bonum convertuntur* does not mean once the *verum* is known then the *bonum* is necessarily known and willed. But what it does mean is that the ultimate *verum* is also the *bonum.* This, however, should be termed intuitionism not naturalism.

On the other hand, the effects of our Greek cultural conditioning still make us believe that *fides qua* and *fides quae* really can be distinguished. This results in serious consequences and equivocations which we will take note of shortly. The Christian faith is not a simple commitment to the God of Theodicy. This erroneous conviction gives rise to a moral system whose contents cannot be already determined in the very act of faith. Faith in this view is disponability and openness to a total obedience, but it remains on the formal plane. What God is asking of us must be determined in each individual action with the help of normative ethics. This can come about through reason with a deduction from our creaturely status or by way of a precept which equates the good with God's will. In neither case can I give a content to this basic meaning, which is that conceptual criterion that unifies the plurality and variety of choices. This may be the path which the moral theology of the manuals pursued; it is certainly not the path indicated by the gospels.

For the Christian to believe in God is to believe in the God of our Lord Jesus Christ. It is to have understood that Christ, perfect image of the Father is already law and not only lawgiver. He is already the categorical imperative and not just the font of ulterior and detailed imperatives. To have understood this, in my opinion, is what constitutes the decisive and qualitative leap of contemporary moral theology. It requires the assumption of charity (the total giving of oneself) as the unique supreme value, the unique "meaning".[19] To believe in Jesus Christ, Son of God is identical with believing that God—the absolute, the meaning—is total gift of self. Faith in God for the Christian is not, therefore, the foundation of a heteronomous—theonomic moral which must laboriously know all the required precepts and observances. Rather it is the acceptance of a well defined meaning—or a content of something signified, not necessarily of norms—and this meaning does not refer beyond to further justifications. The active moment of faith takes place in the recognition that meaning is to give oneself, spend oneself, and live for others. *Fides qua* and *fides quae* coincide concretely: I do not commit myself to a God whom I only know as a lawgiver and whose laws I have yet to discover: rather I commit myself to a God who is charity as gift of self.

I find it reasonable to note that this modification of mentality on a biblical and dogmatic level—a modification now consolidated— also entails a radical change of mentality on the moral level. If faith founded on theodicy leads to an ethics of precepts, each of which, in one way or another, must be able to lead back to the will of a law-giving God and thereby receive a deontologic—theonomic justification, faith which is grounded on the paschal acceptance of Christ leads to an ethics which is the affirmation of a value that judges everything and can be judged by nothing. It is a value to be realized in the more complete giving of self in the concrete and historical moment of one's personal life. The norm, then, will be teleological in its ultimate justification.

The Ambiguity of Such a Grounding in Faith

(3:3) On this path, we discover an ambiguity that is dangerous and that gives rise to countless unresolvable debates. This concerns the affirmation that the meaning, the metaethical grounding of Christian moral and of each of its norms is faith itself. That affirmation in itself is perfect. To say Jesus Christ is the concrete categorical imperative or our law, or anything else is certainly most just. It is also undisputed except for a few moralists and ecclesiastics who regard calling charity, the ultimate principle of morality, dangerous, if not erroneous. These people still cling to the preparatory scheme *"de ordine morali"* which the Fathers of Vatican II refused to consider even as a basis for discussion. Regardless, even the acceptance of von Balthasar's expression is not a univocal one. After we have made the preceding precise distinctions, we are now in a position to confront the grave problem of Christian specificity. I presently propose to show how such an expression receives its ambiguity precisely from the assumption of faith as a metaethical foundation.

Grounding as the Autonomous Font of the Deducibility of Norms

(3:3,1) If I say that the Christian faith is the true grounding of morality, I thereby mean that faith—and it alone—makes possible the justification of some (or all) norms. Hence, someone without faith cannot possess a complete and a true ethics. To affirm that in morality there is a Christian specificity, that is, a series of norms which are proper and exclusive to Christianity, is to affirm that there are norms which can be justified solely by basing oneself on the direct revelation of the will of God. Therefore, in principle, they cannot receive any other adequate justification. In this sense, Christian specificity means Christian *exclusivity.* Human reason can certainly discover many norms but it can't discover them *all.* It is curious to observe how such a thesis is foreign to even the recent tradition of the manuals, not to mention St. Thomas. It is flowering today in a very strange manner and for a variety of reasons. They are in part political, in part apologetical toward the magisterium with an absolute lack of logical, theological and traditional groundings. This disconcerts or should disconcert even the most traditional of moralists.[20]

Grounding as the Guaranty and Verification of Christian Morality

(3:3,2) I call your attention again to what I have said above. In the first place, Christian faith offers a meaning. And it imposes a very simple radical alternative; that is, either to live for oneself or to live in openness to others. As far as I'm concerned, this alternative is typically metaethical. It is specifically Christian, but not exclusively so. We have seen above that it is precisely here in the egotistic or altruistic sense of the golden rule that the great game is being played out on the philosophical level. The recognition of self in Christ is specifically Christian. This already supposes, however, an interior choice of "good will." This is a typically Johannine theme, concerned as it is with both the rejection of the light, and of the prior disposition necessary for recognizing and accepting Christ as Son of God.

Grounding as the Formal Obligation of Discernment

All those who rejected Christ during his earthly life believed in God and carried out the observances that were prescribed for them.

But they had not understood—they had not willed to understand by a moral choice—that God is justice, mercy, and fidelity to a plan of love.[21] If we admit that there is an originating moral experience which is linked to a realtionship with the other, regardless of who the person is, then the positive response to this experience is already in its essence charity. Recognition of *self* in Christ (which is already a gift of God, a capacity that is denied to no one) is the discovery that in him exists the objective guaranty of an interior experience which otherwise could be illusory, fallacious and falsified by others in the vanity of their doctrines.

Meaning as a Grounding for an Originating Experience

(3:4) The faith which is given to us as an infused virtue can find an active response only in one who is capable of loving and wills to love. I am taking a position here on an important question which, however, is rarely viewed with lucidity. It concerns the meaning which presents itself to conscience as the value that grounds every normative ethics, every obedience to a norm. The question can be posed in this way: Does that meaning—which is charity—present itself as deduced from faith (theonomic theories), as found by reason (naturalistic theories), or as a grounding and originating experience (intuitionistic theories)? My answer, at the present state of my reflection is decisively the third.

"Love One Another As I Have Loved You"

(3:4,1) In this light we can point to a later development in the problem of Christian specificity. This development was suggested to me by the recent work of Schüller.[22] In the New Testament, the unique obligation of charity, which is the giving of self to God who is seen in one's neighbor, is grounded on the unique fact that God is charity. This was already true in the Old Testament *ethos:* "You too were a stranger in the land of Egypt and I delivered you: *therefore* . . ." (Dt. 15. 12–15) Similarly in the New Testament: "Walk in love *as* Christ has loved us and given himself" (Eph 5:2).[23] "*Therefore,* I exhort you, brethren, through the mercy of God to offer yourselves

..." (Rom 12:1). The fact that God—in his manifestation as philanthropy—is love, does not refer to further justification; it is the ultimate fact. The obligation to love is based only on God's love for us. Thus, the theory which sees faith as the exclusive grounding could be interpreted as biblically obligatory. But in doing so, a great deal of biblical reflection would be disowned. In it we would have to include the Johannine text cited above, as well as the possibility of eternal salvation for those who have no other law but the one written in their heart. I believe that Schüller is right when he assigns a parenetic value rather than a normative value to God's salvific and loving acts. It is true—and I have been repeating it for years—that in the "therefore" of Romans 12:1, we find the entire New Testament ethic. But the call which is voiced by St. Paul would have no meaning for the hearer if the latter were not already aware of himself or herself as capable of love and self-giving.

"Love One Another Because I Have Loved You"

It is true, therefore, that we must love one another because he has first loved us. This justification would make no sense if we were not capable of recognizing in God's action the call to a supreme choice which is already present in us. In this respect, the revelation of God's love is supreme parenesis ("I exhort you therefore"), not supreme precept. In addition, the parenesis relates to an exigency for good that God himself has placed in the heart of every person. The inner logic of the constitution *Gaudiun et spes* is significant in this regard. It moves from the definition of the human person as a creature capable of knowing and loving his creator to the obligation of dialoguing and collaborating with all persons of good will who assume that we are all brothers and sisters. This assumption is conceived as a supreme value in which the human and divine call coincide. The logical move continues with the affirmation that the Spirit of God is at work in the heart of each person and that each person—even the unbeliever—can be associated with the paschal mystery.[24]

The recognition of God in anyone who deprives and humbles him or herself out of love is also the recognition of oneself. It is, in addition, the discovery of the strength and the dimension of a call which is already operating in ourselves. To love because God has loved us in Christ and to love as God has loved us in Christ are not, therefore, two propositions which can be adequately distinguished.

Christian Grounding and Theistic Grounding for Value

(3:4,2) Hence, if we conceive and justify a Christian grounding for the meaning of a supreme value, which can give rise to norms, we are not to understand this as an exclusive, heteronomous-theonomic grounding for value. Actually, it seems to exclude the fact that there can be problems concerning the justification of the meaning—value for anyone who is not a believing Christian. From the point of view of the believer, we know by faith that everyone has in him or herself a call. (This call is none other than the affirmation of the transcendental structure of the person.) And we know that everyone is capable of responding to the call by the grace that mysteriously works in each person. Not to believe in God—in the sense of regarding as true (false) that God exists—is not a moral fault. Similarly, to believe in God is not necessarily a morally good intellectual act. Neither of these two intellectual attitudes is a moral choice. The moral character of the act is born with the experience of a transcendent call. If we hold that such an experience is inseparable from a conviction (no matter how obtained) that a personal and supreme transcendent being exists, then the grounding of the meaning is impossible for the atheist except in some form of non-cognitivism.[25] It would, thereby, exclude for the atheist a metaethics and, hence, even a normative ethics.

An Atheistic Grounding for Value

On the other hand, if we hold—as I do—that the experience of a transcendent interior call is not necessarily connected with the conviction that a transcendent, supreme and personal being exists, then even the atheist can have a grounding for a normative ethics. This is done by starting with the choice to accept or reject the call to give oneself. Even this, then, in a limited and precise sense, is faith: the assumption of a supreme value not deducible but known, not created by the choice, but judging the choice. In other words, what we call the obedience of faith is possible also for the atheist. We should note that if we reject this thesis, we fall directly under the condemnation of the proposition regarding philosophical sin.[26]

IV
THE CHRISTIAN GROUNDING FOR INDIVIDUAL NORMS

From Value to Norm: The Characteristics
of a Christian Normative Ethics

(4:1) After we establish the substantial grounding for the norms in their frame of reference, we must still discuss the process in which the individual norms are grounded. We have, moreover, assumed the value of charity—the giving of self as the foundation of Christian ethics—so we must now state that we know of no other grounding independent of this, from which the process that goes into the creating of the norm can spring. Neither precepts nor—much less— norms have any force unless they are presented as the historic concretizations of this meaning. I think that Cullman is absolutely correct when he, like Barth, affirms that the "dokimazein" of Romans 12:1 sums up Christian ethics. As a Christian normative-ethical process, the church's discernment is the very reason for the existence of moral theology. It includes, among other things, the task of creating precepts. The task of conscience is also one of discernment. Through it the norm now properly named is formulated. Constituted as such only by and in the church, the Christian will obviously receive the benefit of ecclesial discernment. It will provide the essential element in his or her own discernment, whether it be a question of precept, recommendation, guideline, or an example of life. It is also evident that ecclesial discernment doesn't replace the duty of the individual's discernment. We are saying, therefore, that the eventual precept doesn't automatically become a norm.

With the type of grounding for meaning that we have assumed in the preceding section, and with the consequent obligation of discernment, it seems to me that there is now a substantial theological basis upon which to speak of both precept and norm regarding their process of formation. The unicity of the supreme value (recall, it is identical with God himself) calls for a process of mediation: first between it and the individual precepts, and then between it and the norms. This process seeks to find (discern) the better way to love within a limited series of behavioral possibilities. At the level of precept, there is only a certain degree of specificity in the description of a situation; the individual will always have the obligation to continue the process of description and discernment.

Norm as the Fruit of a Rational Mediation in Either a Deontological or Teleological Orientation

(4:2) The necessity for the historization and categorization of a unique precept or value is clearly opposed to a rigidly deductive process for individual precepts which would be valid regardless of what happens. *It is precisely the peculiarity of the precept of charity which forces us to evaluate how our behavior affects others.* Thus, consequences are never morally irrelevant. *This accounts for the substantial teleological orientation of Christian ethics.* "Love does no harm to one's neighbor" (Rom 13:10) is the clear teleological justification which St. Paul offers for the commandments of the second tablet. Matthew 25 tells us that we will be judged according to what we have made happen—in nonmoral good or evil—to our neighbor. In this light, the problem of the *intrincice illicitum* arises. For a discussion of this point, I refer to another work of mine.[28] Here I will limit myself to an example. The prohibition not to masturbate is justified in general in deontological fashion: It is a prohibiiton that must be observed come what may. Pius XII understood it in this sense. My comments are as follows.

If we hypothesize that masturbation in a mature personality is an expression of narcissism, of an egoistic *habitus*, then we must say it is a moral evil in relation to the supreme value. This is true in both approaches—deontological and teleological.

If we describe a context in which masturbation is a useful or necessary means to establish an effective therapy for a couple's sterility, a deontological ethics must say: let the couple stay sterile. Regardless of the consequences of non-moral (and perhaps even moral) evil, the precept of not masturbating remains. On the other hand, teleological ethics which assumes that charity is the supreme precept must say: charity does not simply make masturbation *licit,* it makes it *obligatory* when it is a question of saving or enriching the life of the couple.

Thus, the necessity for a rational mediation between the unique value which unifies our moral life and the concrete individual norm of behavior always exists. And I maintain that it must be substantially teleological At this point, an infinite number of problems can be posed. First, what is the good that is to be promoted? If the good is that of a particular neighbor who is present to me and also that of some future neighbor (an ecological problem), which of the goods from among the eventually—and *ordinarily*—opposing goods is to be promoted (the problem of legitimate self-defense)? What is the relation between the non-moral good of the agent and that of others? I do not intend to spend time discussing the merit of these questions which call not for what is properly a theological reflection, but for a rational one within a sufficiently well-delineated meaning system. I would only like to point out the following at least from the theological perspective: the conflict over which non-moral value is to be promoted is the normal condition for moral choice, not an exceptional one. From the same perspective, while the existence of a conflict over (non-moral) values is normal, a conflict over obligations cannot subsist in principle. Moral obligation, in fact, results only and univocally from the concrete norm.

Rational Mediation and Faith in the Creation of Norms

(4:3) I want to pose the following question. Can rational mediation in these and similar questions, be replaced in Christian ethics by other mediations of faith in the process in which individual norms are created? This is a difficult question. We are not attempting to see if revelation or the magisterium which interprets it authoritatively can be of help in better finding a norm which *per se* would be grasped by reason. Rather we are attempting to see if the process in the norm's creation, in its substantial rationality, can be modified by elements that are proper and exclusive to Christiantiy, and impenetrable by reason. My response is definitely negative. It must be justified in detail with references to precepts contained in scripture, the authority of the magisterium, and the very idea of natural law as it is used dogmatically in the moral tradition of the manuals, and in certain magisterial documents. Since I have already dealt with these themes elsewhere, I will limit myself to these brief observations.

Scripture and Norms

(4:3,1) At the level of the grounding of value, the expression "Christ is the categorical imperative" can be fruitful; however, at the level of normative ethics it is not. In Christ there appears a unique precept *(entolé)* or value, which is Christ himself who dies, and rises. Hence, St. John speaks of the Lord's commandment, of *entolé* in the singular. Every individual saying or deed of the Lord must be read in the light of this unifying principle. It is the paschal faith which illumines every event in Christ's life. This certainly is the basic perspective of the four gospels. And by now it is time for it to be used in moral theology. It follows that no saying or deed of Jesus if taken in isolation is directly normative in a fundamentalistic sense. That is, it does not automatically ground a precept. The Lord's sayings and deeds, the individual events of his life, are not laws directly but example—not norms but paranesis. Thus, for example, the texts of Matthew 5 on not killing, on not resisting evil, on the law of the talion *(lex talionis)* must be read in conjunction with the text of the adulteress of John 8 and the sword of Matthew 26 in order for one to come up with those precepts regarding captial punishment or of legitimate defense.[29] Yet no one of them singly nor all of them taken together form a code of precepts which can be derived from the precept not to kill. Only someone who accepts Christ in *toto,* as the revelation of a God who is charity can read his actions. In this sense, I believe that the new law can be understood as a law of the Spirit rather than one of observances.

This is even more true regarding the primitive church's experience and its initial attempts at establishing norms. They are not actions to be imitated in a strict sense but rather attempts at investigating what the following of Jesus requires in a determined context. They will be binding when it is a case of particular precepts becoming a norm for a particular action. But they will become such then only generally in an adaptive or analogical manner, requiring discernment. And more particularly, in some cases, they are an indication of and a privileged glimpse at the apostolic reading of the Church's paschal faith. In any case, in their adaptive or analogical character, they are an example and call to one who already has faith and who embraces the supreme value of charity. They cannot, however, function as norms which determine the presence of this unique value in individual cases.

Magisterium and Norms

(4:3,2) The Magisterium is infallible only when it gives a deliberate and definitive explanation of an infallible word: *tantum patet quantum divina revelatio.* It is a true authentic magisterium when it expresses what the church holds as the practical consequence of a faith conviction both to the individual concrete agent and to the agent who happens to be a scholar. Hence, in my view, an acritical reading of the magisterium in moral matters is not even thinkable. It is not evident to me why if a hermeneutics of the even infallible Magisterium is uncontestedly admitted in the dogmatic field, it cannot also be admitted in the moral field with even less contestation. I would say then, that scripture and the magisterium are not and should not be alternative or substitute fonts for reason as to its function in normative ethics. Rather they are and should be exemplary guides for reason, in its indispensable and never to be delegated task of discernment.

Natural Law as the Rational Font of the Norm's Creation

(4:3,3) From about the 16th to the 20th centuries—which is a relatively short period of time—*natural law* has been almost sacralized and has been allowed to function as a substitute font for reason. The naturalist illusion has found its most robust support in the degeneration of the natural-law theory. Natural law—which by its very essence and definition is rational—was presented as an alternative font with respect to reason itself. The analysis of this could pursue two directions.

Nature as the *capacity* for discerning the divine call; nature here is the person's rational capacity.

Nature as the *place* for discerning the divine call; nature here is the person as a psychophysical unity and the cosmos—both, person and cosmos taken in their common creatureliness.

But neither one of these alternative directions with the adjective "natural" added to "moral law" indicates a law that can be substituted for reason. On the contrary, they imply a reason which is not an end in itself but is directed to discovering the call of God. This then is the concrete and prudential historical realization of that value which is God himself. We must recall that nature (existence) never becomes a moral obligation without the logically necessary mediation of a moral experience. This moral experience is the call to live for others. Only by starting from this obligation which is not deducible from nature do both the interpretation of nature and the use of reason in the process of the creation of the norm find their significance.

The Equivocation of the Christian Specificity at the Level of Establishing the Norm

(4:4) It is easy now to shed some light on the equivocation found in the expression "the Christian specificity" regarding the matter of normative ethics which

a. moves from the acceptance of faith in a God who is charity (the God of our Lord Jesus Christ),

b. proceeds by searching for actions which better respond categorically to such a fundamental experience, and

c. in so doing moves within an ecclesial moral experience, in the light of biblical parenesis.

We must note, however, that elements (a) and (b) for reasons which are by now known are not exclusives of Christianity. Although they are specifics of Christianity in the sense that a Christian ethics cannot have any other grounding or process, they are not exclusives in that the calling and operative presence of the Holy Spirit on one side, and the capacity to reason on the other are also not exclusive. Element (c) instead is exclusive of Christianity, but it is not decisive in the normative process. It never automatically justifies the norm, but helps and aids in finding it.

The Christian and the Church in the World, Searching for the Norm in Fidelity to Conscience

(4:5) I would like to conclude this laborious exposition with a consideration which is both ancient and new and which cannot be neglected because of a brief parenthesis in the church's long history. Serious moral problems of every epoch, and particularly of our own can be resolved "in the light of the Gospel and human experience."[31] They are never totally resolved, nor will the laborious and loving work of human discernment ever be able to cease. Moral theology and the moral experience of the people of God can never oppose themselves in principle to the experience and moral reflection of every person of good will—of everyone who accepts living for others as a value.

The ever open dispute concerning the criteria which govern the rational process of the norm's formulation is not specifically Christian.[33] Neither St. Paul, St. Ambrose, St. Augustine, nor St. Thomas willed or was able to do without the awareness of human, rational moral reflection. This did not come about as a result of apologetical concerns. Our very bad habit has been and is still to say: "See, the church is right." Rather such reflection is imposed by the Gospel proclamation itself. Anthropology and biology are not intended to defend the faith, or to demonstrate it, or to prove the unprovable. Instead they are provisional and obligatory tools for discovering what the following of Christ is today.

It is precisely in fidelity to conscience—in fidelity to the choice of giving of oneself which is identical with the call of God to all people that Christians can and must unite with all people of good will. They must unite to study and resolve together the grave moral problems of our time—whether they be individual or social problems.[34] It is unacceptable that eleven years after the Second Vatican Council has clearly indicated this road to renewing moral theology, Catholic moral theologians should still be looking with suspicion on the contributions of non-Catholic or even non-Christian moralists. And, it is unfortunate that non-Catholics or non-believing moralists should look disdainfully upon believing moralists. But is not this later face—lamentable and deplorable though it may be—the direct result of a particular type of moral theology. This theology for a few centuries oscillated between a rigid rationalism that was neither Christian nor human and an a-critical and anti-traditional fideism. In both cases, the obligation for discernment has been neglected. If, as I hope, and as everything indicates—especially outside Italy—this phase is on the way to being abandoned, then new horizons are opening up for Christian moral reflection.

Notes

1. When the human act is free, it is always such in a relative sense. Cf. E. Chiavacci, *Teologia morale. Morale generale* (Cittadella, Assisi, 1977), Chap. 1 and 3.

2. John XXIII, Encyclical *Pacem in terris,* part 1: *AAS,* 55, 1963, 260.

3. This is resolved by W. D. Ross, *Foundation of Ethics* (Oxford, 1939), with the distinction between "prima facie" duty and "actual duty." As W.K. Frankena notes in *Ethics* (Englewood Cliffs, 1973[2]), p. 56, the term "prima facie duty" is "somewhat misleading, because a prima facie duty, as he (Ross) sees it, does have a kind of absoluteness."

4. And also in a few interpretations of autonomous morality, such as the citicism of the sociological view given by B. Stoeckle, *Grenzen der autonomen Moral* (Muenchen, 1974). However, the autonomous morality—for example, for an Auer—does not say precisely what Stoeckle criticizes. Cf. also the collective work *Normen in Konflikt* (Herder, 1977), where the confrontation is better explained.

5. This definition of moral law rejects reducing the law to a summary of rigidly codified precepts. In the Old Testament, laws are the salvific works of God; for us, laws are the convincing examples, the testimony, of life. We should take the proposal of D. Mieth seriously, which is summarized in "What Is Experience?" in *Concilium 113: Revelation and Experience* (New York: The Seabury Press, 1979), pp. 40–53.

6. Cf. E. Chiavacci, "Morale e autocomprensione dell'uomo nel-

mondo contemporaneo" in the collective work, *Problemi e prospettive di teologia morale* (Brescia: Queriniana, 1976).

7. As is evident, I will adopt the term "value" in the singular, with the precise signification of the unique meaning grounding the variety of moral experiences. This holds true even in the hypothesis that such a value can be constituted by more elements which are compatible but irreducible to one another, as occurs, for example, in Frankena, *op. cit.*

8. Cf. B. Schüller, "Tipi di fondazione delle norme morali" in *Concilium 1976/10*, pp. 97–112 (not yet in English). The distinction has a complex history, q.v. in *idem.*, *La fondazione dei guidizi morali* (Assisi, 1975), chap. 9, note 1. The realtionships between the proposed distinction and the metaethical classification are very clear in J. Rawls, *A Theory of Justice* (Oxford, 1972, paperback 1976[2]), pp. 24–40. I will return to this important work later.

9. If we distinguish between "Act Utilitarianism" and "Rule Utilitarianism," as I believe necessary, only the latter can know absolute norms; the former cannot know norms at all. For an excellent preliminary discussion about the various forms of utilitarianism, cf. W.K. Frankena, *Ethics*, pp. 34–43.

10. Conversely, this is what happens in Catholic theology. It establishes that the indissolubility of matrimony is a law of nature, and therefore—regardless of the consequences—it can never be violated. The rational demonstration of such a law of nature, however, is based on the ends of matrimony: the education of offspring and the mutual aid of the spouses; when these ends are not in jeopardy in the concrete case, the argumentation is this: the principles must be safeguarded in order not to induce a divorcist mentality, which would be pernicious for *future* couples. It is quite clear—although not many have paid attention to it—that to safeguard the principles is in reality to safeguard the ends, that is, the norm is proposed with a deontological approach and then it is justified with a teleological approach.

11. Cf. E. Chiavacci, *Principi di morale sociale* (Bologna, 1971), chap. 3.

12. This is the weak point in Ross' theory of "prima facie duty" (see note 3 above).

13. J. R. Searle, "How to Derive 'Ought' from 'Is'" in *Philosophical Review* 73 (1964), pp. 43–50, and the critique of R.M. Hare, "The Promising Game" in *Révue Internationale de Philosophie* 70 (1964), pp. 398–412.

14. This is the reason why the fundamental work of J. Rawls, *A Theology of Justice*, leaves me perplexed, regarding its attempts at vigorously grounding the norm. In any case, it is a very valuable study which cannot be discussed in this article, and on which moreover I must continue to reflect.

15. B. Schüller, communication to the congress of the Societas Ethica, Tutzing 1974, dedicated to "Die Rechtfertigung ethischer Urteile."

16. H.U. von Balthasar, "Neun Sätze zur christlichen Ethik," in J. Ratzinger (ed.), *Prinzipien christlicher Moral,* p. 71. The entire text has been

used by the International Theological Commission and an Italian translation is in "Il Regno-doc" 15/1975, p. 350.

17. On this theme, see further clarification in E. Chiavacci, *Teologia morale*, pp. 101–118.

18. J. Ratzinger ("Kirchliches Lehramt—Glaube—Moral" in idem., *Prinzipien. . . .*, pp. 41ff) perhaps does not take sufficient account of this in his critique of contemporary moral theology.

19. The resistance to this "moral of charity" manifested itself before and during the Second Vatican Council; it is not yet entirely gone. Cf. the splendid study of Ph. Delhaye, "Le recente direttive pontificie sull'insegnamento della teologia morale" in *Rivista del Clero Italiano*, 1977, no. 2, pp. 141ff, especially p. 142 and notes 5 and 7.

20. "Mirabile dictu," comments B. Schüller in "Zur Diskussion über das Proprium einer christlichen Ethik" in *Philosophie und Theologie*, 1976, no. 3, p. 332, after having indicated how completely strange such a tendency is in Catholic tradition and even in recent thought.

21. Literally this is the saying of Jesus in Mt. 23:23.

22. B. Schüler, "Zur Diskussion . . . ," *loc. cit.*, p. 1.

23. Ephesians 4:32–5:2: "kathos" (=as), when it introduces a proposition, has—as it does here—a significance not only of comparison *(Vergleich)* but also of motivation (Bergründung): H. Schlier, *Lettera agli Efesini* (Brescia: Paideia, 1965), p. 280. It is noteworthy that here and elsewhere parenesis (exhortation to love up to the *measure* in which Christ has loved us) and normative ethics (deduction of the obligation to love from the fact that Christ has loved us) can be distinguished in an adequate manner only with difficulty.

24. Respectively, numbers 12, 16, and 92, 3 and 22, 22.

25. On this point, I must disagree with the opinion of Schüller—which is moreover barely mentioned—in "Zur Diskussion . . . ," *loc. cit.*, p. 11, p. 343.

26. Proposition 2 of the Decree of the Holy Office of August 24, 1960, *DS* 2291.

27. Oscar Cullmann, *Christ and Time* (Philadelphia: The Westminister Press, 1960), p. 228.

28. *Teologia morale*, pp. 226ff. For me, an obligatory point of reference for this problem is J. Fuchs, "The Absoluteness of Moral Terms" in *Gregorianum* 52 (1971), pp. 415–457.

29. I have attempted a sketch of this reading in *Morale della vita fisica* (Bologna: EDB, 1976), chap. 10 and 11.

30. I believe that we can substantially accept the text of H. Schürmann, "Die Frage nach der Verbindlichkeit der neutestamentlichen Wertungen und Weisungen" in J. Ratzinger, *Prinzipien . . .*, from whom I have taken the terminology. Schürmann's work is the presentation of a series of texts with a short commentary accepted "in forma generica ut textus Commissionis Theologicae Internationalis."

31. GS 46.

32. GS 16 and 92.

33. This open and heated dispute in analytical ethics, can neither be ignored by Catholic theology nor much less easily resolved based on principles of faith. The importance which it is assuming in these last few years in German and Polish moral theology is symptomatic (see in the Acts the relation of the Compagnoni group).

34. GS 16.

Biographical Notes

Joseph Fuchs, S.J. is Professor of Moral Theology at The Gregorian University, Rome.

Dionigi Tettamanzi is Professor of Moral Theology at the Major Seminary of the Archdiocese of Milan.

Charles E. Curran is Professor of Moral Theology at the Catholic University of America.

James J. Walter is Associate Professor of Moral Theology at the St. Meinrad School of Theology.

Norbert J. Rigali, S.J. is Associate Professor of Moral Theology at the University of San Diego.

John Macquarrie is Lady Margaret Professor of Divinity at Oxford University.

James M. Gustafson is University Professor of Theological Ethics at the University of Chicago Divinity School.

Richard A. McCormick, S.J. is Rose F. Kennedy Professor of Christian Ethics at the Kennedy Institute of Ethics, Georgetown University.

Joseph Ratzinger is Cardinal Archbishop of Munich.

Hans Urs von Balthasar is a Swiss theologian who has published more than fifty books, including *Herrlichkeit.*

Bruno Schüller, S.J. is Professor of Moral Theology at the University of Münster, West Germany.

Philippe Delhaye is Professor of Moral Theology at the University of Louvain.

Enrico Chiavacci is Professor of Moral Theology at the Major Seminary of the Archdiocese of Florence.

also available

READINGS IN **MORAL THEOLOGY NO.1**

Contents

Paulist Press
0-8091-2203-0